W9-DBV-104

The
Outsiders

The
Outsiders

**Economic Reform and
Informal Labour in a
Developing Economy**

SUGATA MARJIT . SAIBAL KAR

OXFORD
UNIVERSITY PRESS

OXFORD
UNIVERSITY PRESS

YMCA Library Building, Jai Singh Road, New Delhi 110 001

Oxford University Press is a department of the University of Oxford.
It furthers the University's objective of excellence in research, scholarship,
and education by publishing worldwide in

Oxford   New York

Auckland   Cape Town   Dar es Salaam   Hong Kong   Karachi
Kuala Lumpur   Madrid   Melbourne   Mexico City   Nairobi
New Delhi   Shanghai   Taipei   Toronto

With offices in
Argentina   Austria   Brazil   Chile   Czech Republic   France   Greece
Guatemala   Hungary   Italy   Japan   Poland   Portugal   Singapore
South Korea   Switzerland   Thailand   Turkey   Ukraine   Vietnam

Oxford is a registered trademark of Oxford University Press
in the UK and in certain other countries

Published in India
by Oxford University Press, New Delhi

© Oxford University Press 2011

ISBN-13: 978-0-19-807149-5
ISBN-10: 0-19-807149-3

Typeset in Adobe Garamond Pro 10.5/12.3
by Eleven Arts, Keshav Puram, Delhi 110 035
Printed in India by Rajshree Photolithographers, Delhi 110 032
Published by Oxford University Press
YMCA Library Building, Jai Singh Road, New Delhi 110 001

Contents

Tables and Figures

FIGURES

Preface

This book brings together our accumulated work over the last decade relating economic reforms and the informal labour market through general equilibrium modelling of segmented labour markets. We have also liberally borrowed from our joint work with others.

Theoretical work on the informal labour market has started making some impact over the last two decades and scattered empirical evidence has been emerging. Frankly speaking, the impetus for this kind of work owes a lot to the rejection of a paper on this subject written by one of the authors of this book by a well-known journal. The editor commented that the paper dealt with a 'narrow' subject—one that discussed welfare implications for almost two-thirds of the labour force in the developing world! The irony is that the said journal is known for entertaining research on the impact of immigrants on workers in California and of car imports from Japan on workers in Detroit, not a very clear vindication of a secular idea of generality. Such a decision, coupled with the fact that in general research problems of the developing world are usually compelled to derive their legitimacy from the recognition of journals hosted in the West, several of our papers and this book eventually materialized as a mark of protest against such academic hypocrisy and discriminatory practices. On the one hand, we had to make the subject a well-accepted domain of engagement in recognized outlets and, on the other, we had to put together an analysis of a missing link in labour and development economics.

In course of our journey towards completing this work we received help, support, and intellectual stimulus from a lot of people.

Acknowledgements

We are indebted to Rajat Acharya, Hamid Beladi, Amit Biswas, Udo Broll, Indraneel Dasgupta, Sudeep Ghosh, Martin Kolmar, Dibyendu Maiti, Sandip Mitra, Vivekananda Mukherjee, and others for collaborative research in related areas. Sugata Marjit is grateful to Ronald Jones, Ravi Kanbur, T.N. Srinivasan, and participants in several conferences, workshops, and seminars at the Indian Statistical Institute, Kolkata and Delhi, Universities of Michigan, Monash, Nottingham, Rochester, and Sydney, Presidency College, Kolkata, Indira Gandhi Institute of Development Research (IGIDR), Mumbai, UNU-WIDER, Helsinki, and the MENA division of the World Bank for insightful comments and suggestions which improved the scope of this book substantially. Sugata Marjit also wishes to thank Cornell University, University of Queensland, the Federal Reserve Bank of St. Louis, University of Texas at San Antonio, and Hong Kong Polytechnic University for various academic visits which supported research related to this work. Saibal Kar thanks Sarbajit Chaudhuri, John Cockburn, Basudeb Guha-Khasnobis, Joop Hartog, and Thomas Straubhaar. Academic visits to the Amsterdam School of Economics, Hamburg Institute of International Economics, Santa Fe Institute, and UNU-WIDER, among others, contributed significantly towards this work. The Poverty and Economic Policy Network, Canada, Humboldt Foundation, Germany, and conference participants in Colombo, Addis Ababa, University of East

Anglia, Jawaharlal Nehru University, National Institute of Public Finance and Policy (NIPFP), Institute of Social Studies, Den Haag, Jadavpur University, Kolkata, and Centre for Studies in Social Sciences, Calcutta (CSSSC) have also influenced this research. We have benefited from discussions with our colleagues Pranab Kumar Das, Jyotsna Jalan, and others. We also thank Riddhita Banerjee, Priyanka Chakraborty, and Sananda Mukherjee for exceptional research assistance. We are extremely grateful to two anonymous referees for providing valuable comments on earlier drafts. We are deeply indebted to our family members for everything else.

1 Introduction

THE INFORMAL ECONOMY

The informal economy has emerged as one of the most dynamic, active, and hotly debated domains in the developing world. Unfortunately, at the same time, it also remains one of the least treated subjects in mainstream economic theory and development economics. No text on international trade or development economics offers a separate chapter on informal activities in spite of the fact that much of the workforce in poor countries is absorbed in this segment. In India, the informal sector provides livelihood to more than 90 per cent of the workforce.

If Arthur Lewis (1954) had rewritten a more contemporary version of his classic article on growth with unlimited supplies of labour, he would have definitely brought this phenomenon to the core of the development analysis. It should be noted that Harris and Todaro (1970) failed to recognize the fact that open unemployment among the poor and relatively unskilled in anticipation of uncertain future employment in the formal sector is not a sustainable proposition. Poor workers cannot survive without jobs and as a result the real search costs for a job can be remarkably high for them. Recent employment data published by the National Sample Survey Organisation (NSSO) in India shows that poorer groups have a smaller rate of unemployment. The point is that the observed unemployment rate among the poor should be quite low and unemployment as such is not the right indicator of their suffering. A rickshaw-puller or a porter cannot afford to remain unemployed for too long. Fields (1975), using a closer approach to Lewis' basic model, did include a third option for migrants in terms of the urban informal sector. However, the choice to remain unemployed was still an open possibility.[1]

Modern analyses of rural–urban migration of labour accommodate both open unemployment and informal employment in Harris-Todaro type models. This ensures that the informal wage does not fall below the rural wage, and in some cases these two are equalized. Urban informal wages are held equal to rural wages owing to the perfect inter-sectoral mobility of labour (Marjit and Beladi 2008). Perhaps, open unemployment among the unskilled and poor is something one should abstract from. Instead, one should focus on the quality of jobs that these people have; a common indicator of their well-being will be the real wages that they earn. Thus, expansion in the size of the informal sector should not necessarily be treated as a curse. This can happen both through an expansion of demand and supply with opposite implications for equilibrium wages. For example, one may observe an increase in wages as well as employment and as a consequence an improvement in the general living standards of informal workers. We refrain from committing to a preconceived idea that a booming informal sector is necessarily bad for informal labour. In fact, growth of informal wages in India has played a pivotal role in reducing the incidence of urban poverty (Kar and Marjit 2009).

The primary purpose of this book is to analyse the deeper impact of reformatory or deregulatory policies on the welfare of informal workers by incorporating the general equilibrium effects of such policies. Various implications of a more open and liberal economic environment for the informal unskilled manufacturing sector as well as agriculture are discussed from the perspective of a labour market, which includes both the formal and informal sectors. The empirical backdrop for these models is provided through stylized facts and empirical implications are highlighted in some cases. However, our work is primarily theoretical and grounded mostly in the neo-classical general equilibrium framework.

The other purpose of this book is to provide some analyses of political economic issues, governance mechanisms, and the general policy environment that sustains or penalizes the dynamism of informal markets. We also reflect on the organizational relationship between the formal and the informal and related micro mechanisms.

At the very outset one should be clear about the definition of the informal sector. There are several definitions and terminologies in related literature. For example, International Labour Organization (ILO 1972) initially referred to these activities as belonging to the 'unorganized' sector (see also Mazumdar 1983). In more recent times, the National Commission for Enterprises in the Unorganized Sector in India (NCEUS 2007) has dealt with the definition of the informal sector in great detail and it seems consistent with the international definition recommended by the ILO, where the terms 'organized/unorganized' are used interchangeably with 'formal/informal'. Therefore, we largely follow the following definition of the unorganized sector (NCEUS 2007: 3): 'the unorganised sector consists of all unincorporated private enterprises owned by individuals or households engaged in the sale and production of goods and services operated on a proprietary or partnership basis and with less than ten total workers.' The Commission considers all agricultural activities undertaken on agricultural holdings, either individually or in partnership, as being in the unorganized sector. In comparison, recent ILO documents (2002: 2, 2007: 4) define informal units as those '... engaged in the production of goods and services with the primary objective of generating employment and incomes to the persons involved'. Such production units share common features: 'typically operate at a low level of organisation; with little or no division between labour and capital as factors of production and on a small scale; labour relations—when they exist—are based mostly on casual employment, kinship or personal/social relations rather than contractual arrangements with formal guarantees'. Moreover, these different groups have been termed 'informal' because they share one important characteristic: they are not recognized or protected under legal and regulatory frameworks. This is not, however, the only defining feature of informality. Informal workers and entrepreneurs are characterized by a high degree of vulnerability. They are not recognized under the law and, therefore, receive little or no legal or social protection and are unable to enforce contracts or have security of property rights (ILO 2002: 2). The global definition of the informal sector is presently in concordance with the manual developed by the ILO and the Delhi Group (2007).

National Sample Survey Organisation has been collecting unit level data on these activities for more than three decades in India. Since our purpose is mainly to address theory and policy matters pertaining to the informal labour market, we consider those workers as informal who are not represented by any trade union and their wages are not determined through the process of collective bargaining. As is well known in labour economics, the insiders in labour markets, in the form of sheltered members of unions and those employed with institutionally recognized benefits, are very different from the outsiders who are necessarily exposed to market fluctuations and cannot claim, for example, the minimum wages. The story of the informal labour market is essentially the story of these outsiders. Their wages and employment are largely market determined. More precisely, we are concerned with a dual labour market where a relatively small number of formal sector workers get the benefit of trade union protection or formalized labour regulations, such as minimum wages and retirement and health benefits. The vast majority of the workforce is absorbed in the rest of the economy, including agriculture, at low market-clearing wages. Thus, the informal labour market emerges as a large residual of the employment process. In this book we use the terms formal (informal) and organized (unorganized) interchangeably. More generally, the *organized sector* comprises of enterprises for which statistics is available regularly from budget documents or reports, annual reports in the case of the public sector and through the Annual Survey of Industries (ASI) in the case of registered manufacturing for India. On the other hand, the *unorganized sector* refers to those enterprises whose activities are not regulated under any legal provisions and/or which do not maintain any regular audited accounts. Consequently, data on such enterprises are also of limited reliability. This definition closely follows that developed by the ILO (1972). For India, the enterprises covered under ASI belong strictly to the organized sector (55th NSS Round, Report No. 456/55/2.0/1: 2).

In general, agriculture in developing countries is largely within informal arrangements. The sector usually exhibits full employment and, more often, disguised unemployment owing to large dependence on land. A huge drop in the land–man ratio may not cause open unemployment, but will devastate the per capita income of agricultural workers. It may be argued that the problem for the very poor and the unskilled has never been lack of jobs, but wage rates or the price at which poor workers are likely to find such employment. In addition, the working conditions have also remained sub-standard in industrial and other sectors. Thus, most of the models we work with are full-employment models with wage differentials. The assumption of full-employment among unskilled workers is justified on the ground that if they are observed to survive in the labour market, they must be engaged in some activity however insignificant and undesirable that might be. It should be clearly noted that studies that deal with minimum wages, open unemployment, wage negotiations, and employment subsidies essentially cover a small percentage of the labour force in poor countries. This leaves out the majority for which wage levels and not employment status is of critical importance for measuring living conditions. On this note, we emphasize that the issue of wage determination and wage movements in the informal sector should have received more attention than they ever did.

Our approach aims to address the general reluctance in literature in pursuing general equilibrium analyses of the features embedded in the interactions between the formal and informal sectors. To the best of our knowledge, none of the prior theoretical and empirical studies on the informal sector have discussed the general equilibrium effects of inter-sectoral mobility of capital and labour. Our structure is similar to one used by Carruth and Oswald (1981). Agenor and Montiel (1996) is an exception in this regard, albeit their model is relevant for a macroeconomic structure unlike the general equilibrium approach that we adopt here. The lack of such attempts might have been caused by the fact that transitions in the informal sector are generally slow and often invisible. It is the result of constriction created by state regulations, social constraints, or risks and uncertainties. At other times, such movements may be quite rapid and in effect substantiate the theory that resources in the long run do have a tendency to move from low to high return sectors. An analytical view in this regard is usually restricted to one single industry, one production unit, or even one particular location. Analysis of general conditions based on partial evidence is at best incomplete. The case of the informal sector in India has not been an exception in this regard. In some of the chapters in this book we point out that if capital is treated as a 'black box' one may also obtain certain outcomes regarding wage-employment movements carrying mis-specification problems.

Thus, one recurrent theme that we discuss deals with how informal wages respond to unemployment among the formal or organized/unionized segment of individual industry types. It has been shown theoretically (Marjit 2003; Marjit and Kar 2004, 2008a, 2008b; Marjit et al. 2007a, 2007b, 2009)[2] that informal wages can move up or down depending on assumptions about capital mobility between formal and informal activities. These studies use simple general equilibrium structures to answer a critical question—how do changes in exogenous policies in the formal sector affect wages and employment conditions in the informal sector? For example, roughly between 1995 and 2003 employment in the organized manufacturing sector and wages in the organized sector in India did not show much improvement, and neither did the capital stock. Productivity growth was also quite limited. Compared to this, data on wage-employment and productivity within the informal sector as available from NSSO for most of the states and union territories in India tell a completely different story. It has been empirically verified that labour productivity, fixed assets, per unit value added and real wages in the informal sector, all improved in comparison with the typical organized sector in India. Without capital accumulation in this sector, the observed upward wage movement or productivity growth would not have been possible. It should also be pointed out, however, that according to the 2005–6 NSSO report on unorganized manufacturing units, real informal wages fell below the high level attained in preceding years. It remains valid nevertheless that the post-reform decade in India has seen an unambiguous improvement in the real wages of informal workers in a majority of the states.

In development discourse, whatever be its ideological or rhetorical origin, 'informal' is a derogatory term. Workers in this sector are sometimes called marginalized, underprivileged, dying to be formalized, located at the receiving end of liberal policies and suffering from undesired pitfalls of free market mechanisms. We do not deny the fact that the conditions of workers in this sector can be quite deplorable and improving their conditions to any acceptable standard is the need of the hour. However, one could still highlight the point that this sector, like many others, may easily get the benefit of a more open and liberal economic environment. This point has been noted in various recent works, such as in Harris-White and Sinha (2007) in the context of India. It is important to realize that the informal sector can be far more dynamic than the organized sector provided the workers in this sector have the right opportunities to flourish. Contrary to general wisdom, the informal sector is not synonymous with an entity that necessarily stagnates in a low-level equilibrium trap. In fact, both informal manufacturing units and self-employed units accumulate fixed assets, invest and prosper, and they may do so even at a time when their formal counterparts show much less dynamism. No doubt, outcomes facing informal units are more likely to be mixed than uniform, but there are situations when markets deliver clear benefits to the workers engaged in this sector. It is, however, contingent not only on the degree of capital mobility as the pre-deployed capital needs to be reallocated from non-viable sectors to those offering higher returns, but also on institutional capabilities to reformulate existing regulations.

A number of issues that necessitate discussion at an early stage have to do with the emergence, sustenance, and characterization of the informal economy. What causes the informal sector to emerge and grow? Is it all economics or a refined political strategy? What are the focal points of analyses that relate informal labour to the broader issue of development? Is formalizing the informal the right solution? What is a good theory of enforcement of labour regulations? Besides addressing these questions, we also try to highlight some work done in the interface of economics and politics, including that on the association of informality with property rights, social welfare, and the general issue of governance.

The following chapters provide a detailed treatment of some of these issues. However, even such comprehensive coverage is far from exhaustive in view of the large number of potential issues that could not be accommodated and shall motivate both the readers and us equally to ponder over in the future. Chapter 2 discusses the political economy aspects of the survival and performance of the informal sector. This, to our understanding, is one of the core issues that demands much more involved research in order to deal with subsequent questions, theoretically, empirically, and in terms of policy propositions. Chapter 3 brings in the flavour which essentially is the germinator of all analyses on the informal sector, namely, the transition from agrarian societies to urban economies. The factors of production trapped in the middle of the process of this transition now constitute the well-known informal sector. Therefore, a legitimate space is offered towards an understanding of this mobility issue; these are re-evaluated in terms of developments either in the agricultural sector or in the advanced urban manufacturing sector. Chapter 4 deals with the case of production organization between the formal and informal sectors. Once it is realized that the political economic environment of the country or the region therein accepts the coexistence of both the sectors, the immediate question is whether production takes place in the former or in the latter. This involves an understanding of complex optimization decisions by different agents—producers, workers, and labour unions, and their interactions with the state.

Chapter 5 is devoted to a comprehensive coverage of the informal sector through the use of general equilibrium models. So far many studies have used general equilibrium structures to understand wage and employment behaviour in the informal sector. We offer a review of the important results and develop a model with capital mobility between the formal and informal sectors to improve upon the present state of analyses. The welfare implications of such wage movements in the informal sector come as a natural follow-up and this is what Chapter 6 discusses in detail. Further, that goods produced within informal regimes may be traded directly or indirectly generates an additional characteristic. Chapter 6 deals with trade in informal commodities and measures the welfare levels under various exogenous shocks. As extensions of the basic model, we relax assumptions on full-employment of labour and allow unemployment to re-evaluate conditions that improve the general welfare of the economy. This chapter also incorporates possibilities that many of the informal commodities and services are of the non-traded variety. This leads to a more comprehensive coverage of the issue of welfare in the informal sectors. Chapter 7 discusses the role of unionization in the economy when a sizeable informal segment exists in the country. The models in this chapter are developed from the extended Heckscher-Ohlin framework, which offers enormous scope to manoeuvre within various combinations of formal–informal interactions. Therefore, Chapters 2 to 7 are designed to accommodate various theoretical contributions on the functioning of the informal sector; these chapters are categorized as Part I of this volume.

Part II is shorter and deals mainly with aggregate empirical evidence for India as well as smaller case studies from different locations to buttress our main findings. Chapter 8, the first chapter in Part II, provides an explanation on how informal real wages increased across most states in India over a period of two decades. We contemplate a number of explanatory variables as responsible for such increase in real wages and figure that capital mobility between the formal and informal sectors may be deemed as one of the most influential sources. However, throughout this part we keep lamenting about the paucity of data that could lend empirical support to our results. In fact, the empirical evidence is not an exact test of the theory developed in Part I. A proxy variable capturing inter-sectoral capital mobility serves to drive some empirical findings in concurrence with our theoretical predictions. However, the subsequent statistical findings are based on data from primary surveys and the issue of production organization between the formal and informal sectors offers a rich basis for further theoretical and empirical investigations on the subject. The aggregate study on informal wages, nonetheless, seems quite powerful in explaining the role it plays in poverty alleviation among a large number of workers engaged in the sector (Chapter 9). In fact, we found that a 1 per cent rise in real informal wages, as influenced by factors discussed in Chapter 8, lowers poverty by 0.229 per cent, or roughly a 23 per cent reduction against doubling of informal wages. This chapter proposes that exogenous shocks might lead to reallocation of resources within the informal sector and that more industry dominance shall replace the menial work that informal labour is often forced to undertake as a sheer survival strategy. The proposition reflects the mobility of resources within informal activities and enriches the scope of empirical investigations in the future. This is followed by an estimate of the productivity effect of informal workers on their wages, and to this end we use the Data Envelope Method (DEM) to disentangle the growth in efficiency as a component of total factor productivity. Chapter 10 offers these results. Chapter 11 discusses two independent case studies from Dharavi in Mumbai and Surat in Gujarat. Dharavi's reputation was partly linked to the production of leather goods that were regularly exported to rest of the world. The boom in real estate and its implications for land prices seems to have outcompeted an otherwise successful informal activity in Dharavi. Once again, these are issues where a lot more attention in needed and, more importantly, these features can raise new and interesting questions in economics. The paper industry in Surat, on the other hand, is a turnaround from formal large company structures to smaller informal firms which find it easier to compete with the growing participation of countries like China and Indonesia in similar trades. Therefore, in terms of theory and statistical evidence culminating into policy propositions, these case studies can be veritable sources of information.

Finally, Chapter 12 summarizes the results of the volume and discusses relevant issues and areas for further research. Since we deal with elements of economic reforms as important instruments for the series of results in this book, a short introduction on the nature of reforms implemented in India is now discussed. Although the specific nature and scope of these elements would differ across major developing economies around the world, the direction of reforms has been quite similar everywhere, especially since the introduction of the World Trade Organization (WTO) and the drive towards multilateralism. This section puts the link between economic reforms and informality in a context that we explore throughout the book.

ELEMENTS OF ECONOMIC REFORMS IN INDIA

The process of economic reforms undertaken in the Indian economy in the early 1990s paved the ground for a unilateral restructuring of trade policies with significant departures from the policy focus of the preceding decades. At the point of formal initiation of the restructuring programme, the then Finance Minister of the Government of India (GoI) highlighted that the post-Independence trade policy in India, mired in a system of administrative controls and licenses, had been largely responsible for a bewildering number and variety of lists, appendices, and licenses. Consequently, the system led to wasteful delays, inefficiencies, and rampant corruption and rent seeking by the bureaucratic coterie. Exercise of discretion and intervention by the authorities responsible for the distribution of licenses or quotas stifled enterprise and spawned arbitrariness. The government, therefore, decided to embark on trade policy reforms, embodied in the EXIM (export–import) policies, to address the tasks of phasing out various impediments to trade. GoI aimed to provide an environment conducive to increased exports and linked up all imports (other than essential commodities like petroleum and related products, fertilizers, and edible oil for which the protection would continue) to exports by enlarging and liberalizing the replenishment license system (Marjit and Raychaudhary 1997 is a relevant reference in this context).

At the same time, the government realized that improvement of India's Balance of Payment (BOP) situation could be achieved not so much by import restrictions as through promotion of exports. The more recent policy measures as part of the continuing liberalization process have, therefore, laid further emphasis on strengthening the impulses of industrial and export growth. Since the unorganized sector or the informal sector in the country consists mostly of units that are also unregistered, there was obviously no direct trade or reform policy aimed at such production and service facilities. It is also quite common that though the minimum wage law has been instituted in places, it suffers from non-compliance. Workers in the informal sector continue to earn less than the minimum wage. Thus, the plausible ways in which informal sector units and workers could gain from an increase in exports or a contraction in imports include: First, registered exporters may sub-contract the informal sector for the production of various intermediate commodities or semi-finished items, and if they grow due to favourable trade policies, the informal sector would grow in turn. Such a linkage is discussed in this volume. The other possible channel is through mobility of capital and labour between the dwindling formal import-competing sector and informal units. As the import-competing sector contracts due to import liberalization, capital and labour often relocate to informal units (theoretical possibilities and some exploratory evidence along this line is available in Marjit 2003 and Marjit and Kar 2007). Studies show that if capital is fully mobile between the formal and informal sectors, retrenchment of workers from the contracting import-competing industries and their relocation to the informal sector could improve real wages of all informal workers. While it is difficult to identify the exact path through which capital relocates to the informal sector, Marjit and Kar (2007) show that in the post-reform period high growth of real fixed assets and gross value added in the informal sector coincides with declining production and real capital stock in the formal sector. Undoubtedly, some part of the capital is relocated in other formal industries, including export sectors. However, a large portion is relocated to the informal sector along with the retrenched labour leading to an increase in activity both in Non-Directory Manufacturing Enterprises (NDMEs) and Own Account Enterprises (OAEs) within the unorganized sector. Cities in India that hosted state-owned large-scale manufacturing enterprises from the planning period show such tendencies, where the newly developed informal sector units cater as ancillary industries to the formal sector. It is argued that at the all-India level this is one of the factors that led to real wage improvements for informal workers in the post-reform period.

Thus, both export promotion policies and import liberalization policies may have indirectly led to the growth in the informal sector with a consequent impact on the poverty levels of the workers. We highlight a few policies that are most likely to have been beneficial for producers belonging to the informal sector in general, including those in the agricultural sector. The GoI announced modifications in the EXIM Policy 1997–2002 on 31 March 1997. These included Export Promotion Schemes (EPCG) and Duty Exemption Scheme (DES) to be extended to agricultural exporters.

Primacy was given to the promotion of agricultural exports and for this purpose agro-economic zones were formed. The policy laid special emphasis on market access initiatives to underpin industry in R&D, market research, specific market and product studies, and retail market infrastructure in select countries. In the EXIM policy for the five-year period 2002–7 as declared on 31 March 2002, emphasis was given to pushing India's exports aggressively by undertaking several measures aimed at augmenting exports of farm goods, the small-scale sectors, textiles, gems and jewellery, and electronic hardware. Apart from these, the policy aimed to reduce transaction costs for trade through a number of measures to bring about procedural simplifications. In addition, the EXIM policy removed Quantitative Restrictions (QR) on exports, except for a few sensitive items. On 1 April 2003, the then commerce minister Mr Arun Jaitley announced the EXIM policy for 2003–4 where he unveiled a package of incentives to boost exports of services and farm products.

In agriculture, the ministry promised a host of incentives to those in the corporate sector willing to invest in 45 agriculture export zones, including development of infrastructure, agriculture extension, processing, packing, storage, and research and development facilities.

In gems and jewellery, the policy allowed exporters dealing in sale and purchase of diamonds and diamond-studded jewellery to open dollar accounts. The policy also allowed import of precious metals like gold, silver, and platinum equivalent to the value of jewellery exported. The policy has avoided offering direct subsidies to encourage exports, as that would go against WTO regulations. However, it has used the method of duty free imports as an incentive for exporters. The new EXIM policy was selective in picking up services and farm products as the major engines of export promotion.

On the import side, it is expected that the following policy reforms have changed the characteristics of informal production and services significantly: On the one hand, survival strategies in the face of competition led to large sub-contracting from the formal to the informal sector and, on the other, the informal service sector expanded to cater to growing consumer requirements. These included a large variety of occupations starting from small automotive servicing units to suppliers of food and related consumer non-durables to a more affluent consumer base.

The list of items imported under the Open General License (OGL) were expanded to facilitate easy access to import of items that are not available within the country. The number of capital goods items permitted under OGL was increased from 1,261 to 1,343. This has been the major thrust of liberalization.

Further, 894 items were added to the free list of imports and an additional 414 items were put on the Special Import License (SIL) route.

Import restrictions on the remaining 715 items were removed among which mutton, butter, fresh grapes, black and green tea, coffee, basmati rice, wine, beer, whisky, woven cotton fabrics, synthetic staple fibre, leather footwear with plastic and synthetic soles, and motorcycles are important. Imports of second-hand or used vehicles, meat and poultry products, primary agricultural products, and textile articles were allowed. Import of farm products, such as wheat, rice, maize, other coarse cereals, copra and coconut, petrol, diesel, aviation turbine fuel, and urea has been permitted only through designated state trading agencies.

This provides a snapshot of the trade policies that may have contributed the most to the growing informalization in the country. It must also be noted that the other important influence might have been reforms in the labour market. Although labour market reforms in India are yet to be institutionally recognized, hiring and other employment practices over the last decade have increasingly bypassed much intervention by labour unions. Waning memberships and a consequent decline in the controlling power of labour unions have increased contractual services in most industries, including the education sector, and may be treated as another form of an informal arrangement within the formal sector.

NOTES

1. Also see Fields (2005), Gupta (1993, 1997), Ranis (2004), and Ranis and Stewart (1999). Initial attempts at modelling the informal sector are available in Rauch (1991).

2. For evidence on other countries, see Goldberg and Pavcnik (2003), for example. Also, for a set of recent contributions see Chaudhuri and Mukhopadhyay (2009). Very recently, Beladi et al. (2010) have discussed the general equilibrium effect of technological progress in segmented labour markets.

I

THE THEORIES OF INFORMALITY

2 The Political Economy of Informality

The definition of informal activities can be both varied and quite specific at the same time. The populist interpretation seems to be in terms of activities that are illegal, or at least extra-legal, often amounting to criminal activities, highlighting tax evasion and/or undocumented production–employment relations. In a broader context, unregistered firms escaping tax payments, labour regulations, and environmental strictures or indulging deliberately in unrecorded activities are treated as the informal sector. For our purpose we concentrate on such activities that are extra-legal, that is, in violation of some officially specified codes of conduct but are not criminal activities per se. Note that the absence of codes of conduct outside the formal sector does not imply that informal activities are beyond legal considerations. On the same note, activities that are unrecorded are not outside legal jurisdiction. For example, the incidence of child labour (also discussed in ILO 2002 as a component of informal activities) is not recorded anywhere, but it is far from legal. In fact, the choice between formal and informal production units is strategically decided by an entrepreneur clearly in view of relevant legal boundaries set by the country. Consequently, the choice is not unconstrained—entrepreneurs factor in penalties for violating minimum wage laws and other strictures applicable for the hiring of labour. On the basis of the definitions offered in Chapter 1, the existence of informal sector units is in violation of the minimum wage law in most cases and therefore both NDMEs and OAEs are illegal or at least extra-legal. In this chapter we develop models where the extent of governance and the existence of the informal sector are discussed in detail.

Pertaining generally to such a set of activities, we focus on one of the segments within the labour market that functions without proper adherence to labour regulations and the officially recognized collective bargaining process. These requirements are satisfied by the unionized high wage sector within the labour market. The inter-relationship between sectors, formal and informal emphasized by factor mobility constitutes the core of our general equilibrium analysis. For analytical simplicity and to avoid unnecessary complications we use the terms informal and unorganized interchangeably. This chapter incorporates an elaborate description of the issues that taxation and governance conjure up for prevalence of informal sector in the economy. The next section discusses the relevant literature in detail. This is followed by a description of the first model where weak governance and consequent proliferation of the informal sector is a conscious choice on the part of the government to avoid political pressure in event of non-performance. The other issue of corruption and sustenance of the informal sector is dealt within the following section. The main conjecture is that external reforms like trade liberalization and internal reforms, such as interest rate restructuring may have conflicting impact on the size of the informal sector. Consequently, political incentives for promoting informality and pure rent-seeking activities must both decline, when better access to the formal credit market drives more firms on to formal spheres. The last section provides a conclusion.

THE ELABORATE VIEW

Before we move on to the analytical domain of models dealing with informal labour, we must offer a discussion on why and how the informal sector has emerged and whether it is a deterrent to the process of development. Is it partly a conscious choice of the state or is it something that is imposed on the state? The borderline between legal and extra-legal can be an endogenous political choice in a democracy, a thesis which has again been somewhat neglected in discussions on the politics and economics of development.

A couple of texts that set the stage for such discussions are by Hernando De Soto (2000) and Avinash Dixit (2004), albeit they are written from two different perspectives. De Soto's book *The Mystery of Capital* brings to the forefront the lack of property rights and legal contracts in the informal segment that locks in a huge amount of capital, blocking development all around. The policy of guaranteeing property rights and enforcement of legal contracts is expected to release capital for investment and growth. Dixit, on the other hand, talks about the lawlessness of economies that necessitates appropriately designed contracts for conducting business. Dixit's book is oriented mainly to varied treatment of the intricacies of contractual arrangements reflecting on the boundaries between legality and extra-legality that are often rather thin. De Soto's contribution draws on some casual empirical work and offers a range of persuasive anecdotes. Nevertheless, in a sense both admit the problems and complications that arise from informal economic activities. However, while De Soto's position seems in favour of legalizing the extra-legal, Dixit provides a workable structure *within* the domain of the extra-legal. Both these approaches indirectly hold the state and the regulatory structures responsible for the emergence of informal arrangements, and formalizing the informal seems to be the first best choice that is somehow not implemented by the state.

Contrary to these, two studies by Marjit et al. (2006) and Dasgupta and Marjit (2006) provide a political rationale on the part of the state to perpetuate informal arrangements. We use the first of these to develop a model in the following section. The essential arguments in Marjit et al. (2007c) complement the analysis from corruption and reform issues that also significantly affect the existence and functioning of the informal sector. Further, Marjit et al. (2006) argues that given the high incidence of poverty and absence of a social welfare system, a democratic state uses the informal sector as a buffer for the poor people. The extra-legal occupations work as substitutes for social security and emerge as an innovative and effective redistributive strategy.

The degree of enforcement of property rights by itself becomes a strategic political variable at this juncture. Typically, in median voter models, tax is the only instrument for redistributing income from the rich to the poor. However, there can be alternative instruments as well, which are somewhat under-explored in the related domain. In the developing world, a majority of the workforce is employed in the informal sector in activities that are illegal or extra-legal. Studies by Choi and Thum (2004), Marcouiller and Young (1995), and Marjit (2003) deal with cases where government policies determine and interact with the size of informal or shadow activities. Allowing extra-legal activities to flourish, which amounts to a thriving informal sector, may be a conscious strategy on the part of the government in a poor country since it helps in tackling the problem of unemployment and poverty. Sarcastically, one might coin it as the policy of 'development through the backdoor'. It often delivers the desired goals set by the government in power, essentially *being in power* for a long time. This is not unusual when frontal development initiatives turn out to be difficult owing to levels of vested interests within the government. Doubtless, such strategic negligence on the part of the government may be harmful for an environment fostering legitimate income generating processes. For example, allowing street vendors to congest the streets, ignoring illegal electricity connections, allowing people to sleep on the pavements or on railway platforms, and allowing slums to develop in public spaces may all reflect tolerance by the government and civil society alike, not necessarily on humanitarian pretexts.

For developing countries, it seems that the jury is still out on whether the state as an authority can set limits on the use of public space for private consumption, albeit there are well-defined rules one way or the other. In fact, this debate lies at the core of the larger choice between formality and informality, which requires further clarifications in similar contexts. Recently, a few studies, such as those by McKenzie and Sakho (2010), Dabla-Norris et al. (2008), and Fugazza and Jacques (2004) discuss the channels leading to informality among firms. Of these, Dabla-Norris et al. (2008) finds that the quality of the legal framework is crucial for determining the size of the informal sector. If the legal system is functional, then the significance of taxes, regulations, and constraints are of limited importance. Not surprisingly, they also find that the firm size and the degree of informality are negatively correlated, although stringent legal norms, and not credit constraint so much, may still push larger firms to operate in the informal segment.

McKenzie and Sakho (2010) argue that tax registration for firms in Bolivia, where the incidence of informality is the largest in South America, leads to lower profits among smaller and larger firms, while it increases profits for mid-sized firms. They show that very small firms, deemed as own account enterprises, have little to gain from formalization. Conversely, firms which can grow to the extent of hiring six workers, too have little to gain from formalization as they end up paying more taxes without the added benefit of tapping the extra clientele. The ones in the middle, stand as the only group which thrives on aspirations of growing bigger and often realize such profits that come from the ability to show tax receipts as an instrument of reputation and consequently consumer confidence. Further, Straub (2005) argues that compliance with formal registration procedures at a cost allows firms to benefit from key public goods, enforcement of property rights and contracts. This would ultimately enable firms to participate in the formal credit market as well. Access to the formal credit market, according to Straub, is evaluated against the relative costs of existence in either of these regimes and should be considered as a critical determinant of the choice between formality and informality.

It is possible that imposition of a high tax burden on the formal sector may create more informality in the system. The tax burden intended for redistribution and rehabilitation may be so high that those in the formal sector get dissuaded from working. They may choose to become net recipients by switching sides, drying up the tax base in the process. Thus, the problem is not one which lends itself to unmixed solutions. At the same time, it can hardly be denied that some of these extra-legal activities may actually hurt legal income earners by creating negative externalities both in the production process as well as in public life. In this context, once again a few recent attempts deal with the determinants of informality, such as that by Chong and Gradstein (2007). It proposes a simple theoretical model where the extent of informality is positively related to income inequality present in the country and is positively sensitive to the presence of weak institutions. The size of the informal sector is also negatively related to the economy's wealth. The choice of producing in the formal sector vis-à-vis the informal sector is based on the equality of expected utilities from the two decisions. The equality offers a critical income level below which all are poor and produce in the informal sector. As the country becomes richer, this cut-off point is pushed up leading to more informal units in equilibrium. This result must appear counter-intuitive and could lend itself to analytical reasons and empirical evidence for a large number of countries—developed and developing. It is based on the argument that the positive growth effect is countered by the negative effect on the size of informal sectors due to tightened institutional quality that follows economic development. Nevertheless, the study further establishes that both the proxies for tax burden and labour rigidity turn out to be not robust and are mostly not significant except for a limited number of specifications.

On the basis of these arguments, we now discuss two instruments in the hands of the government for redistribution—tax and governance. A relatively weak governance structure allows for extensive informality, which helps the poor but hurts people with tax paying capacity, whereas strong governance protects legal tax payers but increases the possibility of social unrest as the incidence of poverty and inequality increases. The cost of sustaining governance is financed by income tax. All societies considered in various models, with different poverty levels and different extents of income inequality, face identical political support functions, and we do not consider totalitarian regimes. In most cases, as in this model that we discuss briefly, the political regime consists of a two-party democracy. It is well known in the political economy context that policies targeted at satisfying the preference of the median voter help win elections. With the aid of a simplistic model we show that there is a reasonable case for strong governance and high tax for those societies that experience lower incidence of poverty and lower income inequality. Conversely, in societies where the incidence of poverty and income inequality is high, the level of governance is chosen to be weak, and the income tax rate is lower. If the government perceives that the effect of the tightness and rigidity in the level of governance on the informal income is not very strong, then also it might choose a relatively higher level of tax rate and regulatory controls. In this regard, we follow the standard 'political support' approach developed by Stigler (1971) and Peltzman (1976). Interested readers may also refer to Persson and Tabellini (2000) and Hillman (2003) for a textual treatment of issues related to the median voter approach. In addition, we offer a little more elaboration on this in Chapter 4.

The existence of an unorganized sector helps organized firms take advantage of liberal economic policies and in a way use a disadvantage to gain competitive advantages, locally and globally. This is adequately demonstrated in Maiti and Marjit (2008) and Marjit and Maiti (2007). Dasgupta and Marjit (2006) use a framework with unionized labour and informal workers and show that the state will have reasons to undermine the strength of trade unions and stealthily promote the culture of the informal sector, again to push forward liberal policies.

Essentially, therefore, these papers look at possible reasons as to why the state may be reluctant in clearly defining the boundaries of legal institutions and consequently choose an optimal degree of enforcement. In a related paper, Sarkar (2006) writes on the economic policies of the left-ruled state government in West Bengal in India and argues that the ruling coalition has encouraged proliferation of the informal sector as if on a clientele mode, such that they are always in a position to control the economic lives of the poor. This is also in line with the general tenet of the argument that the informal sector becomes a necessary element of a state-sponsored political strategy, especially when the institutions themselves are endogenously designed and their limits are manipulated to obtain highest political returns. It may perhaps be best viewed as the well-known dilemma of rules versus discretion as exemplified in the macroeconomic theory in a different context (Barro and Gordon 1983). Institutional commitment specifies certain rules of the game as relatively sticky and not manipulable. On the other hand, the state sometimes needs flexibility to foster adopted policies and at times to steer political self-interest. The informal sector provides a great opportunity to practise discretion. A great many concerns behind formalizing the informal often miss out this simple motivation prevalent in a democracy. Marcoullier and Young (1995), an elegant piece related to the political issues discussed here, talk about the predatory state that uses informal arrangements to extract revenues.

We devote our attention to this issue in tune with one of the purposes of this book, that is, dwelling on a number of serious contemporary concerns regarding the organization of production in the informal sector for developing countries in general and for India in particular. One could extend the line of argument developed by Marjit et al. (2006) and Sarkar (2006) and analyse how the state actually renders a fairly organized form of political supervision and control of the unorganized sector in India. In fact, there seems to be a tremendous 'organized' intervention if one takes the case of the left-ruled West Bengal. The parallel informal economy employs people, leads to politically recognized and guarded activities, and generates revenues that are redistributed to strengthen political patronage. If markets and policies promote relatively unfettered growth of small private investments, poor people's dependence on politics and politicians will be far less and that undoubtedly poses a threat to the political power structure. Unlike in the developed countries politicians in India hardly have alternative occupations. Fully functional market capitalism, if it delivers, shall go against such entrenched vested interests. Yet, politicians need markets, to the extent that they absorb the poor and help them have an economically meaningful existence. The fear of social unrest and, worse, civil war or revolution powerful enough to shatter the very foundation of political power in a democracy seems to have driven important considerations behind the visibly large patronage of the informal sector acting as a pure substitute for front-door development efforts on the part of governments. It is this kind of trade-off that makes the informal sector a strategic conduit of development. This issue, to our understanding, remains a wide and open research question.

Another important departure from existing literature is the issue of governance. This relates our paper to the economics of corruption and its impact on the informal sector. Interested readers may look at Choi and Thum (2004), Dessey and Pallage (2003), Gupta and Chaudhuri (1997), and Marjit et al. (2006), among others. Use of informal workers is illegal in our set-up since this involves violation of labour laws. We argue that if the producer is monitored and apprehended for operating an 'informal' segment, he faces a penalty, such as losing the license to produce the import-competing product, thereby losing tariff protection. However, he can escape by paying a bribe to the apprehending agent. It is reasonable to argue that the opportunity costs of such actions are increasing in the benefits received due to tariff protection. We develop an explicit Nash-bargaining structure to determine the equilibrium bribe. This outcome is internalized by the firm while deciding on the allocation of production and employment choices between the formal and the informal sectors. Our focus is on reforms related to the external sector involving a decline in the tariff rate and deregulation of the capital account, thereby causing the cost of capital (or the borrowing cost) to fall. This has been a worldwide phenomenon for some time now and real interest rates have drastically come down, especially in the developing world. For example, in India, one of the redeeming consequences of reforms has been a phenomenal increase in foreign exchange reserves and a sharp decline in interest rates.

GOVERNANCE AND INFORMALITY

Drawing on Marjit et al. (2006), we consider a society that consists of two classes of people: the rich and the poor. The classes are homogeneous in themselves. In terms of distribution of workers and earnings in the labour market, we make some simplifying assumptions. The entire rich population is employed in the formal sector while the entire poor population finds employment only in the informal sector of the economy. The earnings in the formal and informal sectors are unequal: the rich earns Y in the formal sector, while the informal income of the poor is given by $y < Y$. The income distribution is highly skewed: the number of poor in society, n, far exceeds the number of rich, m. The poor want the government to adopt policies that raise their per capita income levels. We assume that the society exists in a democracy with two political parties competing in elections.[1] The political competition in this society provokes the incumbent government as well as all the political parties seeking election to support the position of the poor. Therefore, the government adopts a redistributive strategy that maximizes the per capita income of the poor.

We assume further that the government has two instruments at its disposal to operationalize the objective of redistribution. One is the conventional tax-transfer policy. The government taxes the rich through a system of income tax and transfers the proceeds to the poor. The other assumption is somewhat unconventional and quite unique to developing societies in general: the quality of governance is considered as a choice variable and includes issues like security of property rights, legal recognition and enforcement of contracts, controlling social unrest, and maintaining general law and order.

A weak governance structure results in the informalization of the economy. It is quite plausible that the existence of informal units helps to raise the income earning capacity of the poor at the cost of the rich. Thus, it too should be deemed as a mode of redistribution. At the same time, the acceptance of cohabitation between the formal and the informal also implies that the poor in the informal sector cannot be taxed. Therefore, the tax burden, not surprisingly even otherwise, is bestowed on the rich alone. Suppose it is a proportional tax, $t \in (0, 1)$ This implies that if the rich earn an aggregate income Y, they pay a tax revenue,[2] tY. The total tax revenue collected, mtY, is used for financing government expenditure, including the transfer $S > 0$. Everyone in the society across the rich and the poor receives the transfer.[3] The index representing the quality of governance is denoted by g. A lower value of g implies a higher degree of informalization. Both Y and y depend on g, while t affects only Y. The functional relations of Y and y with t and g can be written as:

$$Y(g, t)$$

where $\dfrac{\delta Y}{\delta g} > 0$ and; $\dfrac{\delta Y}{\delta t} < 0$; $y(g)$ where $y'(g) < 0$.

The argument put forth earlier explains the signs $\dfrac{\delta Y}{\delta g}$ and $y'(g)$. On the other hand, the explanation of the sign of $\dfrac{\delta Y}{\delta t}$ is based on the assumption that the substitution effect dominates the income effect in the labour-leisure choice of the rich. Consequently, as the tax rate rises, wage income falls and an individual faces a lower incentive to work. We make the additional assumptions $\dfrac{\delta^2 Y}{\delta t^2} < 0$ and $\dfrac{\delta^2 Y}{\delta g^2} < 0$. We also assume $\dfrac{\delta^2 Y}{\delta t \delta g} = \dfrac{\delta^2 Y}{\delta g \delta t}$. Regarding the redistribution programme, consider that it is not radical enough to lift the poor to the echelon of the rich; it leads only to marginal changes within the classes themselves.

Suppose $z(g)$ represents the cost of governance where $z'(g) > 0$ and $z''(g) > 0$. Formally, the government's problem is the choice of $\{t, g\}$ subject to the budget constraint $mtY(g, t) = z(g) + S$ such that the per capita income of the poor $X = y(g) + \dfrac{S}{m+n}$ is maximized. Substituting $S = mtY(g, t) - z(g)$ from the budget constraint into the objective function, the problem turns to one of unconstrained optimization where the government chooses $\{t, g\}$ to maximize $X = y(g) + \dfrac{[mtY(g,t) - z(g)]}{m+n}$.

Suppose $\{t^* > 0, g^* > 0\}$ represent the solution to the problem. Then, at the optimum, the first-order conditions for maximization are:

$$Y(g^*, t^*) = -t^* \frac{\delta y}{\delta t} \tag{2.1}$$

$$mt^* \frac{\delta Y}{\delta g} + (m+n) y'(g^*) = z'(g^*) \tag{2.2}$$

For the second-order condition to be satisfied at the optimum it must be true that:

$$\left[t \frac{\delta^2 y}{\delta t^2} + 2 \frac{\delta Y}{\delta t} \right] < 0 \text{ and}$$

$$\Delta = \left[\left(t \frac{\delta^2 y}{\delta t^2} + 2 \frac{\delta Y}{\delta t} \right) \left(mt \frac{\delta^2 y}{\delta g^2} - z''(g) + (m+n) y''(g) \right) - m \left(\frac{\delta Y}{\delta g} \right)^2 \right] > 0.$$

In deriving the value of Δ we have used the assumption that $\dfrac{\delta^2 Y}{\delta t \delta g} = \dfrac{\delta^2 Y}{\delta g \delta t} = 0$. The assumptions made previously about the slopes and curvatures of the $Y(g, t)$, $y(g)$ and $z(g)$ functions also ensure that $\left[t \dfrac{\delta^2 y}{\delta t^2} + 2 \dfrac{\delta Y}{\delta t} \right] < 0$. We assume $\Delta > 0$ for convenience. So, the second-order condition is satisfied at the optimum. Given m if n rises, poverty increases at the equilibrium distribution of income as the 'head-count ratio' of the poor increases in society. If we think about the society without any redistribution schemes, then income inequality also rises as n rises. The first proposition of the model states the effect of the rise in poverty in a democratic society on its equilibrium choice of $\{t^*, g^*\}$.

PROPOSITION 2.1.   *A government under democracy but with a high level of poverty chooses lower values of t^* and g^**

Proof.   From equations (2.1) and (2.2) it follows that:

$$\frac{dt}{dn} = y'(g)\frac{\left[\frac{\delta Y}{\delta g} + t\frac{\delta^2 Y}{\delta g \delta t}\right]}{\Delta} \tag{2.3}$$

$$\frac{dg}{dn} = -y'(g)\frac{\left[2\frac{\delta Y}{\delta t} + t\frac{\delta^2 Y}{\delta t^2}\right]}{\Delta} \tag{2.4}$$

Since $\Delta > 0$, from the second-order condition the sign $\frac{dt}{dn}$ is determined by the sign of $y'(g)\left[\frac{\delta Y}{\delta g} + t\frac{\delta^2 Y}{\delta g \delta t}\right]$, whereas the sign $\frac{dg}{dn}$ is determined by that of $-y'(g)\left[2\frac{\delta Y}{\delta t} + t\frac{\delta^2 Y}{\delta t^2}\right]$. From equations (2.3) and (2.4), and using the assumptions of the model $\left[y'(g) < 0, \frac{\delta Y}{\delta g} > 0, \frac{\delta^2 Y}{\delta t \delta g} = 0, \frac{\delta Y}{\delta t} < 0, \text{ and } \frac{\delta^2 Y}{\delta t^2} < 0\right]$ it follows that, $\frac{dt}{dn}$ and $\frac{dg}{dn}$ are both negative. Hence, the statement of the proposition holds.

Notice, that the rather 'unconventional' redistributive instrument, i.e., the quality of governance, plays a crucial role in the proof for Proposition 2.1. The choice of a lower quality of governance creates an income-opportunity for the poor, and this is implied by $y'(g) < 0$. Because of the fact that $y'(g) < 0$, the government with its objective of maximizing per capita income of the poor strikes a balance in its choice between the two instruments t and g. It chooses lower values for both as poverty and income inequality increase in society. In the absence of the instrument g, in a similar situation one would expect the government with such an objective to choose a higher value of t, as the conventional political economy models would predict. Interestingly, inclusion of the additional instrument for redistribution through the choice of the quality of governance changes the result remarkably. This largely explains the empirical findings that stood as exceptions to the predictions of the conventional political economy models, where a higher level of poverty and inequality goes hand in hand with a higher tax rate.

So far, we have not said much about inequality. A simple measure will be the relative average income of the rich vis-à-vis the poor. It can be shown that if n increases, income inequality also goes up, provided the rich have a higher average income initially. However, as g and t respond to a rise in n, there are various cross-effects. A decline in total subsidy and a drop in t strengthen the rising inequality effect, but a rise in y through a fall in g weakens the same. One can show that if the response of y to g is really sharp, the rising inequality effect as an initial condition will be offset to some extent by alterations in g. Thus, societies with very high n can reduce the degree of inequality by altering g. In fact, a very high n to start with means that the effect of the subsidy component will be negligible, that is, alterations in the total value of tax revenue to be used as per capita subsidy will have little impact, and then it is likely that the g effect will dominate. A purpose of this section is, therefore, to show how the income level of a typical poor person is positively affected by a weak governance structure. This is the reason why we abstracted from considering the inequality impact. After all, the poor voter should care much more about individual income than the social measure of inequality.

Of course, the nature of informality is not the same in every society. In some societies a change in the governance level has a significant impact on the income of the informal sector, while in some others it does not have much of an impact. It can be argued that societies where change in the governance level has a negligible impact on the income of the informal sector, choose a higher level of governance and tax rate. Thus:

PROPOSITION 2.2. *Societies where change in the governance level has a negligible impact on incomes in the informal sector choose higher tax rates and higher levels of governance*

Proof. If the change in the governance level has negligible influence on the income of the informal sector, in terms of our model, it implies $y'(g) \approx 0$. We compare the equilibrium choice of t^* and g^* of the two societies with $y'(g) < 0$ and $y'(g) \approx 0$. The equilibrium values of t^* and g^* satisfy equations (2.1) and (2.2) in the situation where $y'(g) < 0$. Given $t=t^*$ if $y'(g) \rightarrow 0$, equation (2.2) changes to:

$$A = mt^* \frac{\delta Y}{\delta g} - z'(g^*) > 0 \qquad (2.5)$$

The previously chosen value of $g=g^*$ cannot be the optimum in such a situation. Suppose, $g = \bar{g}$ defines the new optimum. The value of $\bar{g}$ must be chosen in such a way that $A=0$. Once again, it follows from the assumptions of the model and from equation (2.1) that $\frac{\delta A}{\delta g} < 0$. Therefore, it must be the case that $\bar{g} > g^*$.

As the value of g increases to g^* from equation (2.1) it turns out:

$$B = [Y(\overline{g}, t^*) + t^* \frac{\delta Y}{\delta t}] > 0 \qquad (2.6)$$

The previously chosen value of $t = t^*$ cannot be the optimum in such a situation. Suppose, $t = \overline{t}$ defines the new optimum. The value of $\overline{t}$ must be chosen in such a way that $B = 0$. Observe that the second-order condition for optimization implies $\frac{\delta B}{\delta t} < 0$. Therefore, it must be the case that $\overline{t} > t^*$. This has a feedback effect on equation (2.5), which further boosts the value of g.

This justifies Proposition 2.2, which in other words shows that in its choice of the tax rate and governance level, if the government does not take into account the effect of the former on the incomes earned by workers in the informal sector, then it chooses a higher level of governance and a high tax rate.

However, there are situations when the government is constrained in its choice of tax rate. An example would be the behaviour of the governments under the threat of capital flight. To retain capital within their own jurisdictions, governments often compete with each other by lowering their tax rates. The next comparative static result of the model, therefore, treats the tax rate as exogenous to the government's choice of g and tries to see the effect of lowering the tax rate on its choice.

PROPOSITION 2.3.   *If the government is constrained in its choice of the tax rate, a stricter constraint implies a lower choice of the level of governance*

Proof. Suppose the government is constrained in its choice of the tax rate t such that in its maximization of $X = y(g) + \dfrac{[mtY(g,t) - z(g)]}{m+n}$ with respect to $\{\tilde{t} > 0, \tilde{g} > 0\}$ it is allowed to choose among the values of t satisfying the constraint $t \leq \hat{t}$. Then the Lagrange expression for optimization can be written as:

$$Z = y(g) + \frac{[mtY(g,t) - z(g)]}{m+n} + \lambda(\hat{t} - t) \qquad (2.7)$$

where, $\lambda \geq 0$ stands for the Lagrange multiplier. The Kuhn-Tucker conditions for maximization imply at $\{\tilde{t} > 0, \tilde{g} > 0, \tilde{\lambda} \geq 0\}$ that the following equations must be satisfied:

$$\frac{m}{m+n}\left[Y(\tilde{g}, \tilde{t}) + \tilde{t}\frac{\delta Y}{\delta t}\right] = \tilde{\lambda} \qquad (2.8)$$

and,

$$m\tilde{t}\frac{\delta Y}{\delta g} + (m+n)y'(\tilde{g}) = z'(\tilde{g})$$ (2.9)

If the constraint $t \le \hat{t}$ binds then $\{\tilde{\lambda} > 0\}$, which implies $\{\tilde{t} = \hat{t}\}$. Otherwise, $\{\tilde{\lambda} = 0\}$, which implies, $\{\tilde{t} < \hat{t}\}$. In the case where $\{\tilde{t} < \hat{t}\}$, the choice of $\{\tilde{t} > 0, \tilde{g} > 0\}$ is guided by equations (2.1) and (2.2), already discussed earlier. Suppose, the constraint binds and it is always $\{\tilde{t} = \hat{t}\}$. Then, we have the case of Proposition 2.3. Now equation (2.8) loses its relevance. The choice of $\tilde{g}$ follows equation (2.9) in the way:

$$m\hat{t}\frac{\delta Y}{\delta g} + (m+n)y'(\tilde{g}) = z'(\tilde{g})$$ (2.10)

from (2.10) it follows, $\dfrac{d\tilde{g}}{d\hat{t}} = -\dfrac{m\dfrac{\delta Y}{\delta g} - mt\dfrac{\delta^2 Y}{\delta g \delta t}}{mt\dfrac{\delta^2 Y}{\delta g^2} - z'' + (m+n)y''}$ (2.11)

Since, $[\frac{\delta Y}{\delta g} > 0, \frac{\delta^2 Y}{\delta g \delta t} = 0$ and $\frac{\delta^2 Y}{\delta g^2} < 0, z'' > 0$ and $y'' < 0]$, equation (2.11)

implies $\dfrac{\delta \tilde{g}}{\delta \hat{t}} > 0$. This is what we claim in Proposition 2.3.

The intuition behind Proposition 2.3 is also straightforward. If the government is forced to lower the tax rate, it is left with lower tax revenue for redistribution, which hurts its chance of winning the election. Therefore, it lowers the governance level, which indirectly favours redistribution towards the poor.

INFORMALITY AND CORRUPTION

This part of the chapter deals with a firm's decision to hire formal and informal workers and is based on Marjit et al. (2007c). We start our model in a simplified way where initially there is no capital requirement. Labour is the only input of production that is shared by the formal and informal sectors. The formal–informal distinction is captured through the assumption that the wage level in the former is higher than that in the latter. Such wage determination is beyond the control of a particular firm. Initially, we assume that there is no difference in the productivity of labour between the segments. Therefore, it is quite likely that the entire production should shift to the informal sector. However, this cannot be done since 'informal' production is 'illegal' due to its violation of labour laws and hence calls for punitive measures from the state.

For the producer, the probability of being apprehended while producing in the informal sector will depend upon the size of the informal sector. In our model, the probability of getting caught increases with the visibility of such a sector, that is, due to an increase in employment levels. Clearly, when the product serves as an import-competing good and is protected, the level of employment in each sector depends on the level of protection. If the producer gets caught while producing in the formal sector, he has to pay either a bribe or the punitive cost. He will have to pay the bribe to the monitoring officer, who receives a salary otherwise independent of his monitoring capabilities.

We now analyse the collusive game between the potentially bribing producer and the potentially corrupt monitoring officer. As a firm's profit level is a function of the prevailing tariff rate, and that all monitoring officers are corruptible, the punitive cost is assumed to be severe in that the producer is pushed to his reservation pay-off. Then the interesting part is to obtain the optimal level of bribing through a 'Nash-bargaining' approach. The net profit of the dishonest producer with tariff protection would be the profit at the given tariff rate less the bribe. But if he does not pay a bribe, he is punished and the net profit falls to the reservation pay-off level. On the other hand, if the monitoring officer takes a bribe his total income increases by the amount of the bribe; otherwise it remains at the level of his salary.

The producer will try to rationally allocate the total production into two different sectors in order to maximize his total profit, under the condition that he might get caught with some probability if operating in the informal sector. Using the Nash-bargaining solution regarding the optimal bribe paid, which is increasing in the level of tariff protection, one can show that if tariff protection falls, total production and, hence, total labour requirements will fall. This is a conventional result. But what is more striking is that labour requirements in the informal sector will rise while labour requirements in the formal sector will fall.

Intuitively, as the tariff rate goes down, the equilibrium amount of bribe also goes down. Therefore, the effective marginal cost facing the informal segment also goes down which leads to a change in the composition of production in favour of the informal sector. Declining tariff and the resultant fall in bribes indicates the beneficial effect of reformatory policy. However, this also increases the extent of extra-legal activity, that is, the size of the informal output. Needless to say, this is the natural outcome when labour market reforms are kept on hold while trade reforms are prioritized.

Apart from reforms in the external sector, it is also possible that internal economic readjustments also engender similar shifts in the production organization, with interesting twists as one encounters in the presence of large informal arrangements. For example, consider the plausible consequences of introducing reforms in the capital market, that is, lowering interest rates. We introduce a notion of 'working capital' in the basic model. The notion of working capital has become quite significant in recent discussions of firm-level investments with an imperfect credit market (interested readers may look at Fazzari and Peterson 1993). The firm under consideration needs to pay workers at the beginning of the period and then repays the principal and interest at the end of the production period. This is the standard idea of working capital or credit which affects the profitability of firms in a big way. To prove our point we need not distinguish between formal and informal interest rates. So we keep them the same at r. Once again, maximizing the objective function of the producer where the choice is between labour allocation between the formal and informal segments with the probability of getting apprehended for such activities and the consequent punitive cost/bribe leads to the following outcome: As the rate of interest goes down, total labour employment should increase. However, sectoral reallocations take an interesting turn. We observe that a fall in the rate causes formal employment to expand and informal employment to shrink.

In brief, therefore, if the market interest rate falls given unchanged tariff protection, total labour requirements will rise along with an increase in formal employment and a fall in informal employment. As the per-worker investment is more in the formal sector as workers have to be paid higher wages, a fall in the interest rate lowers the relative cost of hiring formal workers and therefore the formal sector expands. Our earlier assumption suggests that the amount of bribe depends on the tariff rate because in case the entrepreneur has to close down his business, he will lose the protection induced incentive.

In this case, however, as the interest rate goes down, the overall profit of the firm goes up and now the enforcement officials in this sector may ask for more bribes if the informal activities are to continue. This discourages the use of informal workers further. Nevertheless, there is a possibility that albeit the size of the informal sector contracts, the total bribe may actually go up. Our main intention here is to focus on the size of the informal sector. What we have shown so far is that a drop in the tariff rate will increase informal employment while a drop in the interest rate will reduce the same. Therefore, if one is looking at reforms driven by two different instruments, one should expect offsetting effects on the size of the informal segment as we have discussed in Chapter 4.

* * *

This chapter constructed a political support model and an interlinked reforms–bribery model to generally show that the level of 'informality' can, on the one hand, be the outcome of a conscious choice of society and, on the other, may behave unexpectedly in the presence of corruption in the system. In such societies where income levels in the informal sector depend significantly on the level of governance adopted by the state, the government chooses lower levels of governance and tax rates. As poverty increases in these economies, similar choices are manifested by state authorities. Introduction of the informal sector in such models plays a pivotal role in challenging the prediction of conventional political economy models where more poverty and inequality triggers a choice of higher tax rates at the political equilibrium.

The first model discussed in this chapter shows a way to capture more than one policy variable—variables that are independent of each other in political economy models of general interest. It also shows their interdependence in policy formulation and relates closely to empirical observations. In this chapter we also considered the case where the government is constrained in its choice of tax policy. We find that as the constraint on the choice of tax rate becomes more binding, the government reacts by choosing a lower level of governance.

The term 'governance' has been conceptualized essentially as security of a tax payer's right over property and public life. Improvement in the governance level has a positive impact on income levels in the formal sector, while it has a negative impact on income levels in the informal sector. However, incomes in the formal and informal sectors could show complementarities as well if the existence of the informal sector helps the formal production process. In developing economies with widespread informal sectors, empirical evidence on this abounds where the presence of the informal sector reduces the cost of production in the formal sector. In such a situation, a lower governance level benefits incomes in both the formal and informal sectors. Following the logic of the first model, under such circumstances, the government should choose the lowest possible level of governance and the highest possible level of tax rate.

On the other hand, when it comes to a choice between labour allocation to the formal and informal segments, which coexist in many cases for the same product category, this chapter discussed a model with simple intuitive arguments. To begin with, a firm is assumed to take advantage of the wage differential between the formal and informal units, a feature quite common in most developing countries. However, like most other cases where flouting of norms comes at a price, here too, there is either a high punitive measure or a bribe for corrupt officials, non-zero but lower than the punishment allowing the set-up to continue operations. Interestingly, if the same product is in the nature of an import-competing good, and is protected by a tariff, withdrawal of protection lowers the stake for such producers, who can settle for lower bribes and, therefore, reallocate labour favourably to the informal segment. Conversely, a drop in the rate of interest reduces the cost of working capital and with cheaper credit, formal employment goes up. Thus, capital market reforms have a potential to reduce the size of informal output unlike in the previous case.

On the whole, therefore, political and economic choices made by governments and firms can be of significant interest and credence when the issue rotates around the prevalence of the informal sector in a country. An elaborate description of the characteristics and equilibrium conditions was supported by some explicit modelling in this chapter and we are mindful of several other possible directions that this analysis may adopt, including possible modifications of the results through the introduction of other crucial agents like labour unions.

NOTES

1. The assumption of two-party democracy makes the analytical solution easier compared to a multi-party democracy. See Myerson (1999) for further details.

2. We assume truthful reporting of income level. For all practical purposes, the post-tax income is positive.

3. We assume the transfer to take the form of impure public good, like free roads and free health facilities, which are not excludable but rival and that the marginal cost of providing these goods is 1.

3 Informal Wages in the Presence of Agricultural and Manufacturing Sectors

So far we have restricted the analysis of informal activities to those mainly within the industrial sector and sought complementary relationships with their formal counterparts. In this chapter we study the overall welfare implications of changing wage and employment situations in the informal sector by constructing a comprehensive model. The structure involves an agricultural sector and incorporates several allied issues central to the considerably neglected analytical relationship between agriculture and informal activities. While we emphasize that our intellectual debt goes back to the early work by Harris and Todaro, the results obtained under this framework yield unconventional implications. In particular, it is well known that better prospects for agricultural exports and productivity should increase agricultural wages. However, we argue that such an outcome depends on capital movement between the formal and informal manufacturing sectors. The inter-relationship sought between the agricultural and manufacturing sectors offers added value to a general set of results that focus on effects of external shocks to movements in informal wages and employment.

THE LINK BETWEEN AGRICULTURE AND THE INFORMAL SECTOR

Agriculture constitutes the backbone of many developing countries in Asia, Latin America and Africa. This is in spite of the fact that the share of agriculture in GDP has been declining, making way mainly for the service sector. Yet, in large countries, such as India and China, the rural sector absorbs a significant chunk of the workforce. Typically, agricultural workers represent a segment of 'informal' labour. Together with informal workers in manufacturing and services, they occupy a formidable share of the workforce. For example, in India their share is about 90 per cent. That is, less than 10 per cent of the workforce is employed in the organized or formal sectors. Agenor (1996) provides a detailed survey of literature, which estimates the size of the informal labour market in developing countries. The share of the informal workforce is simply overwhelming everywhere.

Given that there is a natural link between informal urban and rural workers, through migration or otherwise, it is commonly perceived that rural and informal wages should be close in magnitude, if not the same. At least, one can safely assume that they will tend to move together. Liberal trade policies and/or land reforms can unleash the productive potential of agriculture and are likely to improve agricultural wages.[1] While such an assertion is fairly instructive, we would put this to test in a framework that explicitly models the link between formal and informal manufacturing, mobility of informal workers between the rural and urban sectors and, most important, mobility of capital within the urban sectors. Given this backdrop, the simple relationship between agricultural productivity and agricultural wages turns out to be more complex and fairly interesting. Our analytical structure is primarily one of simple general equilibrium *a' la* Jones (1965, 1971). The framework for modelling formal–informal labour markets has been drawn from earlier work by Carruth and Oswald (1981) and Agenor and Montiel (1996). Related work also includes Agenor (2006), Fields (1990), Gupta (1997), Kar and Marjit (2001), Marjit (1991, 2003), Marjit and Beladi (2002) and Marjit et al. (2001, 2007b). These contributions, however, have not looked into the relationship between agriculture and informal wages.

The model and the results are discussed in the next section. The section that follows confirms the robust nature of the results under various alterations. The last section provides concluding remarks.

BASIC MODEL AND RESULTS

There are three sectors in our economy—agriculture, formal manufacturing and informal manufacturing. Agriculture uses land and labour. The formal manufacturing sector uses labour, hired at a unionized fixed nominal wage rate and capital. The informal manufacturing sector uses labour with market determined wages and capital. Formal wages are higher than informal wages. Agriculture and informal manufacturing pay the same wages. If workers cannot find jobs in the urban formal sector, they find alternatives in either agriculture or in urban informal sectors. Consistent with the typical assumption about 'informal' labour, both agriculture and informal manufacturing represent the informal segment. It is a small open economy with exogenously given prices. Markets are competitive and technology represents CRS and diminishing marginal productivity.

The following symbols are used to describe the model.

$\bar{w}$	Fixed formal wage
w	Informal-rural flexible wage
r	Return to capital
R	Return to land
X	Agricultural sector output
Y	Formal manufacturing output
Z	Informal manufacturing output
P_i	Price of ith good, $i = X, Y, Z$.
$\bar{L}$	Total workforce
$\bar{K}$	Total supply of capital
$\bar{T}$	Total supply of land
a_{ij}	Input–output coefficients

Competitive equilibrium implies:

$$wa_{LX} + Ra_{TX} = P_X \qquad (3.1)$$

$$\bar{w}a_{LY} + ra_{KY} = P_Y \qquad (3.2)$$

$$wa_{LZ} + ra_{KZ} = P_Z \qquad (3.3)$$

Full-employment conditions:

$$a_{LX}X + a_{LY}Y + a_{LZ}Z = \bar{L} \qquad (3.4)$$

$$a_{KY}Y + a_{KZ}Z = \bar{K} \qquad (3.5)$$

$$a_{TX}X = \bar{T} \qquad (3.6)$$

Two points to be noted here are that capital moves freely between Y and Z and L is fully employed even if there are differential wages, that is, by assumption of $\bar{w} > w$. There is no open unemployment in the model. This is the difference between the present structure and the traditional Harris-Todaro type frameworks.

Given (P_Y, P_Z), from (3.2) we can get r and from (3.3) we can get w. Then from (3.1) given P_X we solve for R. Once factor prices are determined, a_{ij}'s is determined as well. We can solve for X, Y, Z from (3.4) – (3.6). The exercise we are interested in is the impact of a rise in P_X or in the productivity of agriculture on w, the informal wage. We assume that our small open economy exports X and Z and imports Y.

Rise in Price of X

Suppose, due to brightened export prospects, P_X rises. Note that as (P_Y, P_Z) are given, there is no change in w and r. Therefore, a rise in P_X will raise R and not w. In fact, R will rise by a magnified amount.

$$\hat{R} = \frac{\hat{P}_X}{\theta_{TX}} \tag{3.7}$$

'∧' denotes proportional change and θ_{ij} is the share of ith factor in the unit cost of producing good j.

PROPOSITION 3.1. *A rise in P_X does not raise w, the agricultural or informal wage*

Proof. See the discussion above. QED

As P_X goes up, production of X demands more workers. However, workers can only be hired from Z as those working in sector Y for $\bar{w} > w$, would not obviously relocate. This in turn implies that there is a pressure of excess demand for informal workers. Naturally, one should expect w to rise. But such tendency is thwarted by capital leaving Z for Y, since capital can earn the same r in both the places. This helps to keep the capital–labour ratio constant in sector Z even if there is an initial exodus of labour. Thus, perfect mobility of capital between formal and informal manufacturing does not allow a jump in rural wages even if there is a rise in P_X. As capital goes into Y, it employs more labour in the sector as well. A similar result will be obtained if one considers a rise in productivity in sector X.

Now consider the case where capital does not move between Y and Z. Therefore, equations (3.2), (3.3) and (3.5) change in the following way, such that (3.10) and (3.11) now offer elements of a specific factor model:

$$\overline{w}a_{LY} + r_Y a_{KY} = P_Y \tag{3.8}$$

$$wa_{LZ} + r_Z a_{KZ} = P_Z \tag{3.9}$$

$$a_{KY}Y = K_Y \tag{3.10}$$

$$a_{KZ}Z = K_Z \tag{3.11}$$

Now, there is no relationship between r_Y and r_Z and capital is sector-specific. Given P_Y we determine r_Y from (3.8) and (3.10) given K_Y we determine Y. Equations (3.1), (3.9), (3.4), (3.6) and (3.11) give us a typical specific factor model of Jones (1971) with variables w, r_Z, R, X and Z getting determined accordingly.

PROPOSITION 3.2.   *A rise in P_X must raise w when capital is sector-specific*

Proof.   We involve results in the magnification effect in Jones (1971).

$$\hat{R} > \hat{P}_X > \hat{w} > \hat{P}_Z = 0 > \hat{r}_Z$$

A rise in P_X must raise R and w and reduce r_Z. QED

As P_X rises, X rises demanding more labour from Z. Now, capital in Z is sector-specific and therefore cannot relocate. Thus, as labour moves out of Z, $\dfrac{K_Z}{L_Z}$ increases raising w and reducing r_Z. Note that real agricultural or informal wages go down in terms of the agricultural product, independently of the assumption of capital mobility.

VARIATIONS IN THE STRUCTURE

Mobility Costs of Labour

We have assumed that rural and urban informal wages are the same. However, one could assume the following.

$$(1+\mu)w_R = w_U \tag{3.12}$$

where, μ is a premium that has to be attached to w_R, the rural wage, to cover the cost of mobility. Note that as long as w_R and w_U are positively correlated, our results will go through. Therefore, we do not need the assumption of perfect mobility.

Informal Sector and Non-traded Final Good

One may argue that a large chunk of the informal sector in the developing world is engaged in producing non-traded service goods. We now recast our structure to include such a possibility.

Suppose we take the case of perfect mobility of capital and add another informal sector, which produces a non-traded good (N), with capital and labour. Note that (w, r) continue to be determined from (3.2) and (3.3) and therefore P_N, the price of the non-traded good, gets determined in a similar manner. If P_X goes up, we have exactly the same outcome as before except for some added complications. P_N will not change as w and r do not change.

In the case of sector-specific capital, a rise in P_X will raise w and reduce r_Z. P_N can go either way. But again, the wage impact is the same as before.

Informal Sector and Non-traded Intermediate Good for Y

Suppose the non-traded product is an intermediate input used in Y. Since P_N depends on w, r, the direct plus indirect requirements make P_Y a function of $\bar{w}$, w and r. Then given P_Y and P_Z, w and r are determined. A rise in P_X continues to have no impact on w, given P_Y and P_Z.

With immobile capital the structure is a bit complex, as Y will use labour, formal and informal, and two types of capital. In fact, 'capital mobility' does not mean much in the current context, as there is indirect mobility through the use of the non-traded good.

* * *

Agriculture constitutes a major fragment of economic activity in a typical developing economy and maintains a dominant share in the workforce. Does rising agricultural prosperity necessarily improve rural wages? We built a simple model, in line with ongoing work on the informal labour market and argued that reverse migration into the rural sector can be achieved without any increase in the wages if capital can costlessly shift from informal to formal manufacturing. Implications of such inter-sectoral mobility are rarely highlighted in literature. In the very short run, wages may increase because capital is stuck. As time elapses the impact on wages will taper off.

It should be clear by now that perfect mobility and complete immobility yield very different results. One could formulate a model with restricted mobility of capital and then relate the wage outcome to the 'degree' of mobility. If such 'degree' falls below a threshold, one would guarantee wage improvements following a rise in P_X.

NOTES

1. See for example, Banerjee et al. (2002) on land reforms in India.

4   Outsourcing, Informality, and Informal Wages

One of the salient points of this volume is exploring a range of avenues through which exogenous policy changes affect organization, output, factor prices and other critical aspects associated with the functioning of the huge informal sector present in several developing and transition countries. This chapter introduces an issue with substantial contemporary relevance for the entire world, which is of particular significance for rapidly industrializing countries of the South, including India, China, Brazil and South Africa. At the very outset, however, it should be acknowledged that empirical support for most of these countries is hard to come by and the few empirical studies that we know of are discussed in Chapter 8. Presently, we intend to theoretically investigate the connection between production and outsourcing from the formal sector and its implications for economic development within its large informal counterpart. Therefore, we primarily discuss the nature of production organization between the formal and informal sectors operating through vertical linkages and subjected to external shocks.

Thus, we contemplate that deregulation, economic reforms, and increasing global exposure should affect informal activities, wages, and employment in a developing country. It appears that the more productive firms will not necessarily increase their total demand for formal labour if they have an opportunity to access informal labour markets and pay lower wages than those paid to the organized workforce. This is a common characteristic among firms involved with outsourcing of production in different parts of the world. We keep the analysis simple by neglecting direct off-shoring from a formal unit in a developed country to an informal unit in a developing country, although similar instances are quite common among traders engaged in procuring certain commodities that are produced outside mass factory systems. Handcrafted artefacts, garments, utensils, and gems and jewellery are often purchased directly from informal sources in developing countries through intermediaries and traders. This is a feature that creates a strong vertical linkage between formal and informal organizations. We explore such interaction theoretically in this chapter and offer appropriate case studies in Chapter 10.

It should be made clear at the beginning that the route that outsourcing/off-shoring usually takes is somewhat different from the delegation of production from the formal to the informal unit. Despite certain broad similarities between the two phenomena, such as convincing appropriate authorities (labour unions, board of governors, shareholders, and others) that outsourcing is the only possible avenue to help a firm survive, the major distinction lies elsewhere. It is the extra-legal nature of informal activities that often raises a big question mark on whether the act of outsourcing is legitimate or not. In addition, there are glaring issues with regard to quality control, violation of labour laws and standards, and so forth that can jeopardize an otherwise prudent economic decision. In other words, there are both direct as well as countervailing issues in formal-to-informal outsourcing that need to be streamlined before the larger implications are understood. For example, a formal unit can decide to outsource to an extra-legal unit and expose itself to the risk of being apprehended by regulators of labour laws and standards. The important question at this juncture is whether or not to use informal sources at all. A model incorporating such intricacies of decision-making is presented in the next section and the issue circumvents the choice of formal or informal labour as the two categories available to a formal unit. In the section that follows we discuss the issue of employment and political strategy behind enforcement. The last section provides a conclusion.

VERTICAL LINK BETWEEN FORMAL AND INFORMAL UNITS

It is generally observed that units under the informal sector produce more non-traded goods and services than traded commodities. The non-traded goods are sold either to the consumers directly or used as intermediate inputs by producers of final goods in the formal sector. Apparently, if the share of intermediate inputs is quite high, then significant changes in the formal sector should also affect informal producers. For example, if industrial deregulation or withdrawal of protection leads to contraction in the formal segment, informal producers of intermediate inputs cannot escape the burden. A pertinent question is: might this reduce informal wages? Common sense suggests that it would.

However, Marjit (2003) argues that it is far from a foregone conclusion. If, for example, the informal segment consists of two sub-segments, one supplying an input to the formal sector and the other producing a final good, informal wages and employment can still rise despite an adverse supply shock affecting the formal sector. Further, if the sub-segment linked vertically to the formal sector is capital intensive relative to the other sub-segment, there is a convincing case that informal wages and employment must increase. The informal service sector, to which we have briefly alluded earlier, might serve as an appropriate example in this regard. As capital moves out of the sub-sector producing the intermediate good and into the labour intensive service sector offering the final output, informal wages are likely to receive a positive thrust so long as the demand facing the sector is not very inelastic. The exact measure of this elasticity along with other empirical facts about the informal sector in India is discussed in Chapter 8.

Apart from Indian evidence, Goldberg and Pavcnik (2003) argue that trade liberalization has an ambiguous effect on the 'informal' sector, since the evidence from Brazil shows little or no connection between trade policy and informality, while for Colombia liberal trade policies have led to the expansion of the informal sector. Goldberg and Pavcnik (2003) use a 'shirking' model of the labour market to justify their empirical claim. In an earlier attempt, Funkhouser (1994) used household surveys to provide detailed evidence on informal activities in Central American countries. It seems that the inconclusiveness of this relationship warrants a reevaluation of the issue both theoretically and empirically. Presently, we construct a simple model with a formal–informal relationship, and use tariff and interest rates as two policy instruments. Interestingly, a lower tariff is likely to expand informal production, while a lower interest rate generates countervailing implications. In Chapter 8 we revisit these issues empirically and pursue the results offered here.

The Model

Consider a firm in the import-competing sector protected by an import tariff, t, and hiring workers at a wage rate w_1 in the formal sector and w_2 in the informal sector, such that, $w_1 > w_2$. Clearly, production in the informal sector implies non-compliance with labour laws, that is, avoiding the effectively higher cost of production. However, since this may lead to infringement of certain legal procedures, firms should internalize a punishment cost, if apprehended. We postulate that penalty increases in the size of informal production. However, there is another crucial point. By enjoying tariff protection the firm is better off compared to any other activity undertaken. Thus, t also denotes the margin of benefit for being in the protected sector. There is a chance that in case the firm is apprehended and punished, it may lose its license and therefore lose the benefit from protection as well. Note that this is equivalent to a situation when the firm is apprehended but it pays a bribe to escape punishment. It implies that the equilibrium bribe should be increasing in t, since the possible loss facing a firm moves positively with t. The firm maximizes the following:

$$\text{Max } \Pi\,(L_1, L_2) = (1 + t)\,f(L_1 + L_2) - (w_1\,L_1 + w_2\,L_2)\,(1 + r) - z(L_2, t)$$
(4.1)

L_1 is the employment in the formal sector, L_2 in the informal sector and $z(.)$ represents anticipated punishment costs, $z_1 > 0$, $z_{11} > 0$, $z_{12} > 0$, $f' > 0$, $f'' < 0$. We define r as the interest rate on working capital, assumed to be the same for the formal and informal sectors. However, this is not a strong assumption for our results.

Therefore, consider t and r as the two policy instruments. Economic reforms generally imply a decline in both t and r (developing countries have historically maintained a high interest rate and high protection in the manufacturing sector, for attracting foreign capital and protecting the domestic manufacturing sector).

First order conditions from (4.1) yield:

$$(1+t)f' = w_1(1+r) = w_2(1+r) + z_1$$
(4.2)

Second order conditions are satisfied. Figures 4.1 and 4.2 describe the equilibrium.

In Figure 4.1, initially L_o is total employment with L_{10} in the formal and L_{20} in the informal sectors respectively. If t falls, $(1+t)f'$ shifts down, and so does z_1 since $z_{12} > 0$. This shows that total employment declines, but L_{20} increases, and the informal sector expands.

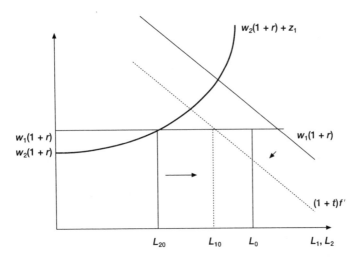

Figure 4.1 Equilibrium in Linked Markets

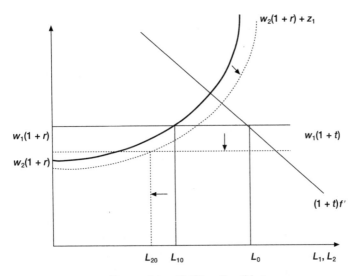

Figure 4.2 Shifting Equilibrium

In other words, a drop in t will reduce aggregate output and employment. At the same time, the anticipated marginal cost of punishment also goes down increasing L_{20}.

On the other hand, a drop in r will shift both $w_1(1 + r)$ and $w_2(1 + r)$ down, although the former drops more than the latter as $w_1 > w_2$. Total employment will increase as we move down the $(1 + t)f'$ line. Therefore,

L_{10} will increase and L_{20} will contract. The theoretical point we intend to convey is that a drop in r reduces the marginal cost in the formal sector more than in the informal sector as $w_1 > w_2$, leading to a fall in L_2.

Note, however, that reduction in t and r generate countervailing effects. The model in this sub-section is motivated by experiences in Brazil and Colombia where trade liberalization had different impacts on the informal sector. Evidence drawn from various issues of the International Financial Statistics provided by the IMF shows that while import tariffs went down both in Brazil and Colombia, the interest rate declined only in Brazil during the same time. It may be the case that for Brazil this interplay of offsetting effects was responsible for little or no change in the size of the informal sector, while for Colombia the tariff effect alone caused expansion in the unorganized sector.

Essentially, therefore, what this brief theoretical construct offers is a characterization of equilibrium and possible changes in it when economic reforms lead to restructuring of both the external sector and the internal economy. The informal sector through its vertical linkage with the formal sector under the circumstances can end up hiring more workers if the changes are instrumented through a tariff reduction. In other words, outsourcing of production from the formal to the informal sector is propagated through a decline in the tariff rate for two prime reasons. One, the negative supply shock provokes formal producers to look for avenues where the cost of production can be lowered in order to stay competitive domestically: the informal sector provides an answer for this. Two, the lower tariff lowers the apprehension and expected loss due to switching to the informal sector from the protected environment that the formal firms enjoyed previously. The two effects together might lead to an increase in employment in the informal sector and raise wage levels as well. This is also the case when the informal sector works independently of formal connections and the effects are facilitated through mobility of capital as we describe in Chapter 5. On the other hand, a drop in the interest rate facing formal industries allows them to invest more, employ more and assuming a near full-employment condition, draw labour away from the informal sector. A lower degree of informality in the system may be particularly beneficial in view of the lower pressure that it imparts on the maintenance of law and order and general governance over factors like land and property rights.

ENFORCEMENT AND THE INFORMAL SECTOR

The simple structure developed in the last section, and the discussion in Chapter 2 have suitably clarified the choice facing a typical firm in delegating production activities to formal and informal workers. The associated figures summarize the basic observation. An interesting consequence of the problem is now discussed.

Suppose firms are heterogeneous in the sense that some have low productivity and some have high productivity. It is straightforward to conceive from Figures 4.1 and 4.2 that firms with too low productivity will hire only informal workers, having a low marginal product of labour. On the other hand, firms with higher productivity will hire both. For the latter group of firms, if minimum wages are enforced, there will be no change in the total employment, only informal employment will be substituted by formal employment. However, for firms which depend only on informal employment, such enforcement will definitely reduce total employment. Now let us ponder over the political consequences of such employment effects in a typical democracy.

Referring to Chapter 2, where we raised several issues in the political economy of the informal sector, it was pointed out that the passive acquiescence of the state plays a significant role in the prevalence of such sectors. In the absence of social security benefits, unemployment benefits and a host of other welfare instruments, which are common in rich countries and either completely absent or paltry in the developing world, non-interference with localized extra-legal activities and infringement of various legal strictures (say, copyright laws, or ill-defined private property rights) has contributed largely to the evolution of this sector. The state treats this as a self-created cushion for poor people in developing countries, despite cognizance of the fact that many of these activities remain unrecorded, unregistered and classify broadly as extra-legal. As hinted earlier, we use this as a motivation to offer a policy dialogue.

In our framework q epresents an index of the monitoring intensity or stringency of the legal structure in place. Higher q implies stringency with which minimum wages are enforced. If the government cares about aggregate employment as well as the importance of the legal institution, one may propose the following objective function of the state:

$$\Omega = \Omega(q, E) - C(q) \qquad (4.3)$$

with, $\Omega_1 > 0$, $\Omega_2 > 0$, $\Omega_{11} < 0$, $\Omega_{22} < 0$, $\Omega_{12} = \Omega_{21} = 0$, $C' > 0, C'' > 0$,

where $C(q)$ denotes cost of preserving law or rules of law and regulatory framework.

Note that the objective of the government is related to the one used in Marjit et al. (2006). However, the explicit role and working of the informal labour market was not introduced in this structure.

Conversely, in Marcoullier and Young (1995) a leviathan state allowed informal activities or corruption to sustain itself for material gains. But ours is drawn from a more welfarist perspective.

As discussed earlier, a higher q will not affect the total employment of the better productive firms, but will reduce employment in the less productive ones. Therefore, the marginal social cost of enforcement, that is, imposing a higher q will be much less in economies where firms are generally more productive.

* * *

This chapter outlined various avenues through which outsourcing from the formal sector affects functioning in the informal sector. It is certainly possible that even without a vertical connection between the two, effects on the formal sector often gets transmitted to the informal sector, as a well-constructed general equilibrium model should be able to justify. While we reserve this fully developed structure for Chapter 5, this chapter analysed firm-level decisions regarding outsourcing to the informal sector.

In brief, therefore, we discussed how the advent of economic reforms— either through tariff reduction or reduction in prevailing interest rate may create a countervailing impact on the wage-employment dynamics within the informal segment. This has essentially been out of a drive to understand why according to previous empirical evidence some countries display little or no impact of economic reforms on the sizeable informal sector vis-à-vis palpable impact in some others. The tariff effect will be very different from the effect of a cut in the cost of capital. Therein, we argued that the vertical linkage that usually exists between the formal and informal segments is considerably important in seeking the right answer.

In case of a tariff reduction, it appears that the informal sector expands at the cost of the previously protected formal industries, draws in labour and intensifies the extent of informal activities even without a conscious choice of reorganization adopted by formal firms. On the other hand, a drop in the borrowing rate often helps to reverse and consolidate waning output and employment situations in the formal sector by drawing in resources from the informal segment. This might balance the opposing effects facing the informal sector and leave it unperturbed.

The follow-up discussion used the earlier model to suggest that the negative employment effect of enforcement may not be so severe for more productive firms as they switch between formal and informal employment.

5   The Informal Sector in General Equilibrium Models

The previous chapters of this book discussed certain characteristics of unorganized/informal sector activities generic to most developing countries. These labour market features and their relationship with production organisation are also not completely alien to developed countries. The political and economic strategies leading to emergence and sustenance of unregulated economic activities have also been discussed in considerable detail. Note that, although we have subsequently analysed the relationship between agriculture and urban informal sector and implications of production outsourcing to the informal sector, a crucial broad-based discussion on the informal sector is still missing. The present chapter offers a general equilibrium model to incorporate complex economic interactions in the presence of large informal sectors in a country.

In this connection it should be emphasized that apart from the development implications of the informal sector following the Harris-Todaro tradition there has been little attempt at situating the informal labour market in the world of general equilibrium. However, there have been a number of studies looking at the connection between aspects, such as trade liberalization, the informal sector, and poverty using computable general equilibrium (CGE) models for specific countries (see, for example, Gibson 2005; Carneiro and Arbache 2003; Harrison et al. 2003 for African and Latin American countries). Notably, a series of papers capturing the general equilibrium implications of trade liberalization on the informal sector in India using CGE structures are also available in Harris-White and Sinha (2007). In contrast, this book and this chapter in particular situate the analytical general equilibrium models dealing with the informal sector on a larger canvas amenable to further theoretical and empirical verifications. We emphasize the roles played by capital and other factor inputs for capturing the diverse nuances that are generally unexplored. This is discussed in relation to exogenous shocks affecting the relatively small formal sector and subsequently its vast informal counterpart in developing countries. In particular, we argue that the mobility of capital between the formal and informal sectors can provide a completely new and unconventional set of results that theoretical and empirical studies entrenched in partial equilibrium models fail to recognize. Therefore, the next section discusses the general perspective, which is followed by a model with emphasis on the role of capital mobility. The last section provides a conclusion along with additional discussion on the subject.

THE SCOPE

While we offer detailed empirical analysis in a subsequent chapter (Chapter 8), this chapter uses the findings to motivate a much-needed theoretical structure for the informal sector in an economy where the transactions between different sectors of the economy is substantial. Even from a rather exploratory angle, it is observable that the wage and employment situations in the informal sector across many countries have been fairly sensitive to exogenous shocks transmitted through international trade, and the waves of globalization per se. In existing literature, labour market and welfare implications of trade reforms, with the informal sector as an important part of the economy, have recently come up for much discussion (Chandra and Khan 1993; Chaudhuri 2003; Chaudhuri and Mukhopadhyay 2002; Kar and Marjit 2001; Marjit 2003; Marjit and Kar 2007; Marjit et al. 2007a; Sinha 1999; Sinha and Adam 2006). Further, a recent volume by Chaudhuri and Mukhopadhyay (2009) accommodates many facets of the informal sector treated under general equilibrium models. A primary reason for such enthusiasm is that leaving out the informal sector fails to capture the actual impact of many policy reforms, given that on an average 70 per cent of the labour force in the least developed countries (LDCs) works under arrangements outside the purview of what is typically known as the formal/organized sector. Data from Southeast Asian, East

European, African, and Latin American countries show varying rates of urban informal sector employment within a range of 15 per cent to 20 per cent in Turkey and Slovakia to 80 per cent in Zambia, or even more, to about 83 per cent in Myanmar. Moreover, considering the state of agricultural and rural activities in these countries, it is quite apparent that the total share of the informal sector in these countries is quite high (ILO 1999). This is also corroborated by some other studies (for example, Turnham 1993), which provide evidence that in low-income countries like Nigeria, Bangladesh, the Ivory Coast, India, and elsewhere, the share of the urban informal sector is at least as high as 51 per cent. Alternatively, seen from the point of view of 'minimum wage' earners, only 11 per cent of Tunisia's labour force, for example, is subject to minimum wages; in Mexico and Morocco, a substantive number earns less than the minimum wage; in Taiwan, the minimum wage received by many is less than half the average wage and so on (Agenor 1996).

There are suggestions that the level of informalization in a country increases as economic reforms are initiated. A more general concern that follows is that such expansion will reduce informal wages with retrenched workers crowding in from the formal sector. Some of the studies mentioned earlier show that despite contraction of the previously protected and often state-run formal sector as a consequence of trade liberalization, and subsequent relocation of relatively unskilled and older workers into the informal segment, informal wages can still rise if capital also relocates to the informal sector.

Analysing the impact of industrial and trade reforms on various activities and on the workers employed should offer critical insights in favour of appropriate policy formulations. It is to be noted that given the considerably large share of employment in these sectors, even small positive gains in real wages can increase the economic attainments of millions in most developing and transition countries.

As briefly referred to earlier, let us re-emphasize the fact that mobility—more specifically, the degree of mobility of capital—is one of the instrumental factors in tracing the connection between either prosperity or ruin in the formal sector to the implications this might have for its informal counterpart. In this connection, it is imperative to discuss the precise mechanism that captures the issue of capital mobility, typically since there is neither a measure nor statistical evidence on how capital takes flight from dwindling industries and relocates into prospering ones. Marjit (2003) and later Marjit and Kar (2007) and Marjit et al. (2007b) have explored this issue in greater detail.

Marjit (2003) shows that even if a part of the informal sector is vertically linked with the formal sector and the formal sector contracts due to trade liberalization, informal wages can still increase. In the other papers capital mobility plays a major role in a two-sector formal–informal framework. Capital immobility reduces informal wages when informal employment expands, whereas allowing for freer capital mobility leads to an exactly opposite outcome.

While there are several other mechanisms that can generate such positive economic impact for the existing group, here the argument behind invoking the issue of capital mobility comes from the observation that several developing countries have been experimenting with policies on trade reforms for quite some time. The critical feature has been the contraction of formal protected industries, either via import liberalization or through state initiatives in withdrawing support from loss-making public enterprises. This implies that a large amount of capital and labour that were earlier part of these industries would now have to relocate to more profitable ventures. In most of these countries, the vacuum left by the vanishing large-scale public industries has been filled not by similar manufacturing units, but by predominantly service-oriented industrial structures, which face less stringent labour laws and industrial regulations. Moreover, the new opportunities that have emerged in the so-called sunshine industries are incapable of accommodating the retrenched capital and labour, a larger share of which has hence been devoted to less formal applications. There may be several explanations for this transition, including the fact that workers in typical import-competing public or private enterprises would not find easy access to the more formal service industries, which recruit high-skilled professionals with advanced technical expertise that the older industries rarely employed. We present a formal model, which captures the exact mechanism whereby capital mobility affects informal wages subject to the downsizing of the formal sector.

THE MODEL

Assume a two-sector small open economy. X is produced in the formal manufacturing sector and Y in the informal manufacturing sector. Both X and Y use labour and capital. Wages in the formal segment are fixed through bargaining. Initially, X is protected either through a tariff or by a state-subsidy, which artificially increases the price of X. Trade reforms or withdrawal of subsidy implies a decline in the tariff/subsidy rate, denoted by t. Workers, who do not find jobs in the formal sector flock to sector

Y where they receive market-determined wage rates. We call this the informal wage. There is no open unemployment in this model. People must find jobs to survive, and wages in the informal sector adjust fully to accommodate workers moving into the sector. Markets are competitive and technology exhibits CRS and diminishing marginal productivity.

The model, similar in spirit to Agenor and Montiel (1996), Carruth and Oswald (1981), Marjit (2003), and Marjit and Beladi (2002), uses the standard textbook treatment of simple general equilibrium models (Caves et al. 1997). Capital and land are fully employed.

The symbols we use are:

$\bar{w}$	Formal unionized wage
w	Informal (flexible) wage
r_i	Return to capital in sector i, $i=X, Y$
X	Output of the formal sector
Y	Output of the informal sector
(P_X, P_Y)	Exogenous commodity prices
$\bar{L}$	Supply of labour
$\bar{K}$	Total supply of capital
K_i	Supply of capital in sector i,
(a_{LX}, a_{LY})	Per unit labour use in X and Y
(a_{KX}, a_{KY})	Per unit capital use in X and Y
t	Import tariff

'$\wedge$' represents percentage changes for particular variables and the symbols used bear the same implications as in Jones (1965).

Competitive price equations that describe the system are given by:

$$\bar{w}a_{LX} + r_X a_{KX} = P_X(1+t) \tag{5.1}$$

$$wa_{LY} + r_Y a_{KY} = P_Y \tag{5.2}$$

Commodity prices are given from the rest of the world. Let us suppose Y is exported and X is imported.

Full employment conditions imply:

$$a_{LX} X + a_{LY} Y = \bar{L} \tag{5.3}$$

$$K_X + K_Y = \bar{K} \tag{5.4}$$

$$a_{KX} X = K_X \tag{5.5}$$

$$a_{KY} Y = K_Y \tag{5.6}$$

Let $\hat{\bar{w}}$ be so determined that:

$$\hat{\bar{w}} = \alpha \hat{P}_X + \beta \hat{P}_Y, \quad 0 < \alpha, \beta < 1 \tag{5.7}$$

Finally, the capital mobility condition:

$$\frac{K_X}{K_Y} = \phi\left(\frac{r_X}{r_Y}\right), \phi' > 0 \tag{5.8}$$

Equation (5.8) suggests the following: At any point of time $\bar{K}$ is allocated between X and Y. But such allocation depends on the return differential. Hence, there is imperfect mobility of capital. If $\left(\frac{r_X}{r_Y}\right)$, increases, $\frac{K_X}{K_Y}$ will also increase. $\frac{K_X}{K_Y}$ describes the relative supply of capital in sector X. The usual way to model this is to assume sector-specific capital for X and Y without any mobility with $\phi' = 0$. Perfect mobility will always imply $r_Y = r_X$ and there is no relevance for a separate sectoral supply function of capital. Relative supply adjusts to demand in each sector and this is the standard Heckscher-Ohlin structure. We shall demonstrate that our comparative static depends on the curvature of $\phi' = 0$.

Given $(P_X + t, P_Y)$, $\bar{w}$, L, and K, we have $w, r_X, r_Y, X, Y, K_X, K_Y$ to solve from (5.1)–(5.6) and (5.8). The determination of general equilibrium proceeds as follows. From (5.1) we can determine r_X. Now using (5.4) and (5.8) we get (5.8)':

$$\frac{\bar{K} - K_Y}{K_Y} = \phi\left(\frac{r_X}{r_Y}\right) \tag{5.8'}$$

As r_Y increases, given r_X and $\phi' > 0, K_Y$ must rise. This defines the relationship MM in figure (5.1). Now using (5.5), (5.6) and (5.3):

$$\frac{a_{LX}}{a_{KX}}(\bar{K} - K_Y) + \frac{a_{LY}}{a_{KY}} K_Y = \bar{L} \tag{5.9}$$

Since r_X is given by CRS, $\frac{a_{LX}}{a_{KX}}$ is given. Now as r_Y increases, from (5.2), $\frac{r_Y}{w}$ must rise and $\frac{a_{LY}}{a_{KY}}$ must rise as well. Hence in equation (5.9) the LHS unambiguously increases. To bring back the balance, K_Y must fall substantially. As long as $\frac{a_{LY}}{a_{KY}} > \frac{a_{LX}}{a_{KX}}$, LHS must decrease with a decline in K_Y. Such an assumption implies that the informal sector is labour-intensive; an assumption by virtue of its being realistic is kept all

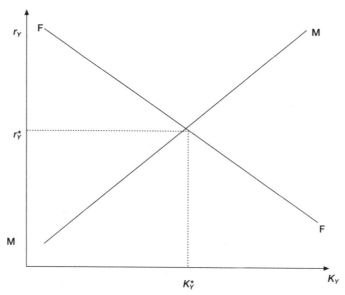

Figure 5.1   Determination of First Equilibrium

through the chapter. Therefore, as r_Y rises, K_Y must fall. This defines FF in Figure (5.1). Once (r_Y, K_Y) are determined from Figure (5.1), the rest of the variables can be determined easily.

The key comparative static exercise we are interested in is a decline in 't'. Figure 5.1 helps us to trace out the consequences of both. A decline in t reduces r_X, given $\bar{w}$ and P_X. Given r_Y, a drop in r_X increases K_Y, as $\phi' > 0$. This will mean a rightward shift of MM to $M'M'$.

At the same time, given r_Y and K_Y, a drop in r_X reduces $\dfrac{a_{LX}}{a_{KX}}$ and therefore LHS in (5.9) declines. The balance is restored through an increase in K_Y at a given r_Y. FF shifts to the right as well. The way Figure 5.2 is drawn suggests that Y must expand. But r_Y may remain unchanged and can in fact go either way. Note that if MM shifts quite a bit relative to FF, r_Y will decline and w will increase. The mobility effect has to be significant for a positive effect on the informal wage. A drop in $\dfrac{a_{LX}}{a_{LY}}$ releases labour to Y sector, which implies that FF shifts up requiring more K_Y to accommodate displaced labour. Additional capital that comes to Y because r_X is lower must outweigh the required amount needed to absorb displaced labour at a given r_Y, hence at a given w to induce an increase in w. With zero mobility MM is vertical and remains unchanged. Hence, r_Y must increase and w must decrease through a shift in *FF*. With perfect mobility *MM* is horizontal at $r_Y = r_X$ and as r_X drops, *MM* shifts down. Notwithstanding the shift in *FF*, r_Y must adjust to the new level of r_X and w must increase. Figure 5.3 describes the effects of such adjustments.

These two cases explicitly demonstrate the partial and general equilibrium results that can be derived from this model. In Figure 5.2, the vertical line *MM* represents perfect immobility of capital between the formal and informal segments. Under the circumstances, formal job losses and crowding in of workers into the informal sector leads to wage cuts in the latter. The situation undergoes a complete reversal if capital is perfectly mobile and is represented by a horizontal line *MM* (Figures 5.2 and 5.3). Retrenchments from the formal sector and additional job creation in the informal sector could even lead to wage gains for informal workers, thus establishing the general equilibrium implications of our model. Finally, the precise condition for $\dfrac{dw}{dt} > 0$ is given by:

$$\hat{w} > 0 \ \textit{iff}, \ \varepsilon > \sigma_X K_X f\left(\frac{\lambda_{LX}}{\lambda_{KX}}\right). \qquad (5.10)^{1,\,2}$$

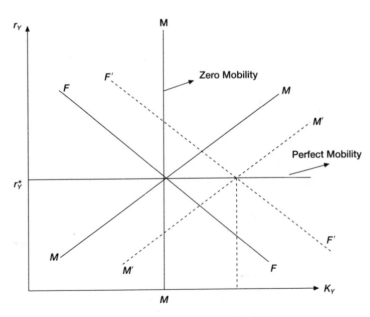

Figure 5.2   Equilibrium Interest Rate under Different Patterns of Capital Mobility

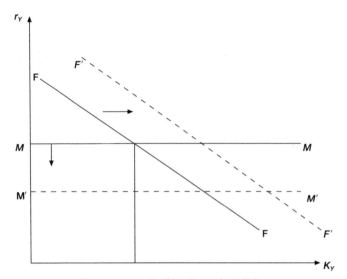

Figure 5.3 Perfect Capital Mobility

* * *

This chapter offers a different approach compared to prior attempts at quantifying and theorizing the activities of the informal sector in dual economy labour markets. By linking the unorganized sector to the organized sector through aspects of capital mobility and labour productivity, we were able to estimate and theorize in more formal ways the effects of reforms on the wages and employment status of workers in the informal sector. The results, as we have discussed, are quite revealing. We established via rigorous general equilibrium models that trade liberalization in the formal sector can, contrary to conventional wisdom, raise both employment and wages in the informal sector if capital is easily mobile between the two sectors. Even if capital is sticky, as we explored in subsequent studies, downsizing of the capital-intensive import-competing sector may lead to increased output in the labour-intensive informal segment and an increase in informal wages. The issue of capital mobility thus takes on an important role in shaping the magnitude and directionality of informal wages subject to exogenous policy changes in the organized sectors of an economy.

Further, the role of labour productivity in both the formal and informal sectors can also impart strong influences on employment and wages in the informal sector. Labour productivity improvement in the unskilled labour-intensive segments of the formal sector can improve informal wages even in the short run under free mobility of capital, and with the formalization of informal labour. As argued in the chapter, these features did not surface until a set of recent papers that opened up the scope and dimension of research in this context.

NOTES

1. See Appendix 5A for detailed algebraic proof.

2. Condition (5.10) offers a directly testable hypothesis. However, it requires matching data on product-specific capital stock in both the formal and informal sectors, and the return such capital fetches in each sector. Annual Survey of Industries in India offers data on formal commodities until 1997 only, and reliable data on the return to capital in the informal sector is unavailable. Thus, we set aside this direct exercise for future work effort and use a proxy measure instead.

APPENDIX 5A

Proof of condition (5.10).

$$\bar{w}a_{LX} + r_X a_{KX} = P_X(1+t) \qquad (5A.1)$$

$$wa_{LY} + r_Y a_{KY} = P_Y \qquad (5A.2)$$

$$\frac{K_X}{K_Y} = \phi\left(\frac{r_X}{r_Y}\right), \phi' > 0$$

$$\frac{\bar{K} - K_Y}{K_Y} = \phi\left(\frac{r_X}{r_Y}\right) \qquad (5A.3)$$

From (5A.1),

$$\hat{r}_X \theta_{KX} = \hat{P}_X - \theta_{LX}\hat{\bar{w}}$$

$$= \hat{P}_X(1 - \theta_{LX}\alpha) \qquad (5A.4)$$

where, $\hat{\bar{w}} = \alpha\hat{P}_X + \beta\hat{P}_X = \alpha\hat{P}_X$, since $\hat{P}_Y = 0$.

From (5A.2), $\hat{w}\theta_{LY} + \hat{r}_Y\theta_{KY} = 0$. This implies, $\hat{w} = -\dfrac{\theta_{KY}}{\theta_{LY}}\hat{r}_y$. (5A.5)

Now using equations (5.3) to (5.6):

$$a_{LX}X + a_{LY}Y = \bar{L}.$$

Reformulating, $\dfrac{a_{LX}}{a_{KX}}(\bar{K} - K_Y) + \dfrac{a_{LY}}{a_{KY}}K_Y = \bar{L}$

Again, $\lambda_{LX}\hat{X} + \lambda_{LY}\hat{Y} + \lambda_{LX}\hat{a}_{LX} + \lambda_{LY}\hat{a}_{LY} = 0$ and

$$\lambda_{LX}\hat{K}_X + \lambda_{LY}\hat{K}_Y + \lambda_{LX}(\hat{a}_{LX} - \hat{a}_{KX}) + \lambda_{LY}(\hat{a}_{LY} - \hat{a}_{KY}) = 0 \quad (5A.6)$$

But, as $K_X = \bar{K} - K_Y$

$$\hat{K}_X = -\hat{K}_Y / \phi, \text{ where } \phi = (K_X / K_Y).$$

Substituting these information in (5A.6),

$$-\frac{1}{\phi}\lambda_{LX}\hat{K}_Y + \lambda_{LY}\hat{K}_Y + \lambda_{LX}\sigma_X\hat{r}_X - \lambda_{LY}\sigma_Y(\hat{w} - \hat{r}_Y) = 0 \quad (5A.7)$$

Rearranging, and using (5A.4), and $\theta_{LY}(\hat{w} - \hat{r}) = -\hat{r}_Y$

$$(\lambda_{LY} - \frac{1}{\phi}\lambda_{LX})\hat{K}_Y + \lambda_{LX}\sigma_X\hat{P}_X\left(\frac{1 - \theta_{LX}\alpha}{\theta_{KX}}\right) + \lambda_{LY}\sigma_Y\frac{\hat{r}_Y}{\theta_{LY}} = 0.$$

Thus,

$$(\lambda_{LY} - \frac{1}{\phi}\lambda_{LX})\hat{K}_Y + \sigma_Y\frac{\lambda_{LY}}{\theta_{LY}}\hat{r}_Y = -\lambda_{LX}\sigma_X\hat{P}_X\left(\frac{1 - \theta_{LX}\alpha}{\theta_{KX}}\right) \quad (5A.8)$$

Now, taking '*ln*' on (5A.3),

$$\ln(\bar{K} - K_Y) - \ln K_Y = \ln \phi \left(\frac{r_X}{r_Y} \right).$$

Taking percentage changes,

$$\hat{K}_X - \hat{K}_Y = \frac{1}{\phi} d\phi = \frac{1}{\phi} \frac{\delta \phi}{\delta \left(\frac{r_X}{r_Y} \right)} \frac{r_Y dr_X - r_X dr_Y}{r_y^2} = \frac{\phi'}{\phi} \frac{r_X}{r_Y} \left(\hat{r}_X - \hat{r}_Y \right)$$

Using (5A.4),

or, $$\hat{K}_X - \hat{K}_Y + \frac{\phi'}{\phi} \frac{r_X}{r_Y} \hat{r}_Y = \frac{\phi'}{\phi} \frac{r_X}{r_Y} \left[\hat{P}_X \left(1 - \theta_{LX}\alpha \right) / \theta_{KX} \right]$$

We define, $\varepsilon = \dfrac{\delta \phi}{\delta \left(r_X / r_Y \right)} \dfrac{r_X / r_Y}{\phi}$, as the elasticity of capital mobility between sectors X and Y.

Thus, $$-\hat{K}_Y \left[1 + \frac{1}{\phi} \right] + \varepsilon.\hat{r}_Y = \varepsilon \hat{P}_X \left(1 - \theta_{LX}\alpha \right)$$

Therefore, $$\hat{r}_Y = \hat{K}_Y \frac{1}{\varepsilon} \left[1 + \frac{1}{\phi} \right] + \hat{P}_X \left(1 - \theta_{LX}\alpha \right) \qquad (5A.9)$$

Rearranging equations (5A.6) and (5A.7),

Define, $$\mu = \left(\lambda_{LY} - \frac{1}{\phi} \lambda_{LX} \right) = \left(\frac{\lambda_{LY}}{\lambda_{KY}} - \frac{\lambda_{LX}}{\lambda_{KX}} \right) K_X = \frac{\lambda_{LX}}{\lambda_{KX}} \frac{K_X}{\left(\frac{\lambda_{LY}}{\lambda_{KY}} - \frac{\lambda_{LX}}{\lambda_{KX}} \right)}$$

$$(5A.10)$$

$$\sigma_Y \frac{\lambda_{LY}}{\theta_{LY}} \hat{r}_Y + \mu \hat{K}_Y = -\lambda_{LX} \sigma_X \hat{P}_X \left(\frac{1 - \theta_{LX}\alpha}{\theta_{KX}} \right) \qquad (5A.11)$$

and

$$\hat{r}_y - \frac{(\phi + 1)}{\phi \varepsilon} \hat{K}_Y = \hat{P}_X \left(1 - \theta_{LX}\alpha \right) \qquad (5A.12)$$

Using Cramer's rule to solve for $\hat{r}_Y$,

$$D = \begin{bmatrix} \left(\sigma_Y \dfrac{\lambda_{LY}}{\theta_{LY}} + \dfrac{\lambda_{LZ}}{\theta_{TZ}} \dfrac{\theta_{KY}}{\theta_{LY}} \sigma_Z \right) & \mu \\[2em] 1 & \dfrac{-(\phi + 1)}{\phi \varepsilon} \end{bmatrix}$$

$$= \begin{bmatrix} -\dfrac{\sigma_Y \dfrac{\lambda_{LY}}{\theta_{LY}} (\phi + 1)}{\phi \varepsilon} - \mu \end{bmatrix} < 0$$

Therefore, $\hat{r}_Y = \dfrac{1}{D}\left[\dfrac{\lambda_{LX}\sigma_X\alpha(\phi+1)}{\phi\varepsilon} - \mu\right].\hat{P}_X(1-\theta_{LX}\alpha)$ (5A.13)

Now, suppose $\hat{P}_X < 0$, then $\hat{r}_Y > 0$ iff, $\dfrac{\lambda_{LX}\sigma_X(\phi+1)}{\phi\varepsilon} > \mu$

Finally, using (5A.5)

$$\hat{w} > 0, \ iff, \ \dfrac{\lambda_{LX}\sigma_X(\phi+1)}{\phi} < \mu\varepsilon \tag{5A.14}$$

or, $\varepsilon > \dfrac{\lambda_{LX}\sigma_X(\phi+1)}{\phi\mu}$

or, $\varepsilon > \dfrac{\lambda_{LX}\sigma_X}{\mu}\dfrac{\phi+1}{\phi} = \dfrac{\lambda_{LX}\sigma_X}{\mu}\dfrac{1+\dfrac{K_X}{K_Y}}{\dfrac{K_X}{K_Y}} = \dfrac{\lambda_{LX}\sigma_X}{\mu}\dfrac{\bar{K}}{K_Y}\dfrac{K_Y}{K_X} = \dfrac{\lambda_{LX}}{\lambda_{KX}}\dfrac{\sigma_X}{\mu}$

Using (5A.8), $\hat{w} > 0$, iff, $\varepsilon > \sigma_X K_X f\left(\dfrac{\lambda_{LX}}{\lambda_{KX}}\right)$

The above derivation provides the proof of condition (5.10).

6 International Trade, the Informal Sector, and Welfare

Theoretical and empirical policy research in international economics addresses crucial questions about structural adjustments, both in the real and in the financial sectors. Among these, theoretical papers on trade deal with the use of trade policies and tariffs or tariff equivalents to improve national welfare, appropriately defined. Here we address how the consideration of informal production units, an area scarcely dealt with in trade theory, works with more generalized applications of some of the basic theories related to trade policy. This chapter is essentially divided into two parts. In the first part, we offer a full-employment model of trade in the vintage of the traditional Hecksher-Ohlin-Samuelson (HOS) framework with full-employment in all the sectors of the economy, but with the standard characterization of a segmented labour market as we have introduced in the beginning of this book. Thus, it is a standard HOS model with fixed-flex wages and full employment of resources.

The second part introduces the possibility of open unemployment. As one might argue quite reasonably that one of the characteristics of developing countries is the existence of open unemployment we extend the basic model with full-employment and capital mobility by grafting it on to a conventional Harris-Todaro type migration framework. The intention is to focus on the inter-linkage between international trade and the impact on the unorganized sector of an economy.

In terms of pure normative implications, a negative impact of trade policy reforms especially on unemployment in the deregulated sectors, can generate considerable disagreements in the public domain. To the extent that the notion of welfare in populist forums dictates policy instruments, particularly in democratic societies, it offers a curious resemblance with the well-known Gresham's Law in monetary theory. While total unemployment will be determined by the relative size of contraction and expansion, models of trade policy and unemployment have to rely on specific conditions that affect aggregate unemployment. The dominant wisdom seems to be that greater trade is more likely to hurt import-competing sectors all over and thus employment should suffer. In an interesting contribution, Sarkar (1989) argued how in a Keynesian model trade definitely leads to more unemployment as the sector suffering from effective demand constraints becomes more efficient through trade. But in the neo-classical paradigm, impact of trade on unemployment has been an open question. This chapter tries to answer some of these questions.

As far as the purpose of this chapter is concerned, a general review of literature reveals that so far considerations of the urban informal sector have been embedded in rural–urban migration models of the traditional Harris-Todaro (henceforth, H-T) type. Gupta (1993), for example, considers a three-sector static model of a small open economy, with wages and employment determined endogenously in the informal sector. The hypothesis that rural migrants expect to get jobs in the urban formal sector with some probability 'λ', holds in these models, although some of the subsidy policies in this structure run counter to those generated by the original model. The problem with these models is that informal employment offers wages that have to be lower than rural wages, because the weighted average of formal and informal wages equals rural wages. We argue that the poor labourers, moving freely between rural and urban centres, cannot afford to remain unemployed while expecting higher earnings only in the future. Instead, they form what is known as the urban informal sector, where they earn less than the urban formal wage rates. However, with free mobility of labour between the urban informal and rural sectors, there is high probability that informal wages are closely related to rural wages. Accordingly, in our model, we consider them equal. We capture these characteristics in a full-employment general equilibrium model. Subsequently, we wish to check the welfare implications of trade policy reforms. With this view, we define a welfare parameter and see how it changes when trade policy reforms are introduced at various levels of the economy.

In the existing literature, welfare implications of trade reforms, with informal sector as an important part of the economy have not come up for much discussion so far despite the overwhelming presence of informal production relations in a large number of developing countries.

The importance of the present theoretical construct is that in earlier literature, the informal sector, urban or rural, was not modelled in a quasi full-employment general equilibrium framework such as this (see Agenor and Montiel 1996). Stark (1982), for example, has also noted that there is a need for some more specifications while modelling the informal sector in the presence of zero inter-sectoral transfer cost, perfect information, and so on. In the typical H-T framework, he considers an extension where the migrant faces a two-period time horizon and undertakes two competing strategies given the probabilities of getting a job in the formal sector in two different periods. In a similar H-T framework, Fields (1975) introduces another variation. Bulow and Summers (1986) also treat Keynesian unemployment in dual labour markets, while Chao and Yu (1995) treat urban unemployment in similar models in the presence of international capital mobility.

According to Chao and Yu (1995), open unemployment might exist in the presence of wage flexibility in the informal sector, when the migrant posits a trade-off between informal sector employment and the search for formal sector jobs. The familiar three-sector models of the kind are often used to address policy questions as under the H-T framework and policy effects differ when various assumptions are made regarding the mobility of labour and capital across sectors (Gupta 1997; also see Grinols 1991). But, as mentioned earlier, the H-T type models must imply an informal wage rate lower than the rural wage rate—a phenomenon hard to justify with significant labour mobility between the two segments.

Although, generally informal sector activities pertain to non-traded items in the economy, from street vendors to domestic help, in many countries they produce exportable and import substitutes with sub-contracts from formal sectors. In such cases, the formal sector adds the capital content (like the brand name) only. In many other cases, small industries that produce garments, leather goods and small tools and machines, export directly without formal regulations and procedures (University Grant Commission 1996). Apart from this, in all developing countries, agriculture is largely outside the formal net and agricultural output and consumer non-durables like fish and meat are largely exported. The domestic production of these is well-protected at varying rates. Adequate consideration of these activities is therefore important with regard to policy changes, given the high share of employment involved in these sectors.

Recent studies in trade theory use production structures that capture complementarity in production. This chapter uses a similar production function. This is actually an application of the Gruen-Corden (1970) structure, laid out extensively in Jones and Marjit (1992) and Marjit and Beladi (1996, 1999). Our treatment of the informal sector exhibits a quasi-full-employment model amenable to interesting general equilibrium results. For macroeconomic applications of related structures, one may look at Agenor and Aizenman (1999) and Agenor and Montiel (1996). In a way, we exploit the notion of informality and complementarity in production to reflect on the welfare implications of liberal trade policies. The idiosyncratic feature of this model is that we consider all the three commodities that a developing country produces to be tradable. It is often the case that commodities and services produced in the so-called unorganized sector are non-traded in nature. However, there are several products manufactured with little or no formal institutional regulations that are traded globally. These include products ranging from leather goods, garments, carpets, gems and jewellery, and wooden furniture to commodities from iron foundries like manhole covers and other utilities. Exporters retain a competitive edge by bypassing formal labour rules and wage structures in addition to already low wages prevailing in the poorer countries. Moreover, substantially high import tariffs usually allowed producers protection from external competition.

We offer a variant of this pattern in a subsequent chapter where much of what the unorganized sector produces is non-traded. However, even with traded informal commodities, modified Harris-Todaro structures have often been used to look at the impact of trade policies on open unemployment and welfare. The second strand of analysis in this chapter relates to a particular genre of H-T literature that deals with the informal sector, with an added feature of inter-sector mobility of capital that facilitates critical understanding of wage-employment dynamics in the informal sector.

The next section presents the basic model, while the section that follows checks the welfare implications of three policy changes pertaining to the first set of assumptions with full-employment. Subsequently, we introduce the case of open unemployment in the economy and a variant of the benchmark model. This is followed by a discussion in favour of structural modifications. The last section provides a conclusion.

THE MODEL WITH FULL-EMPLOYMENT

There are three sectors in a perfectly competitive small open economy. These sectors are defined as Formal (F), Informal (I) and Rural (R). Capital (K), one of the factors of production, flows between F and I only, whereas production in R requires use of a specific factor land (T). Labour is the other factor of production in all the three sectors, except that formal wage rates are administered at $\bar{w}$. Labourers try to find a job in the formal sector where the wage rate is $w < \bar{w}$.

Those who cannot find a job are forced to work in the urban informal sector or in the rural sector. Hence, labour is fully employed in our structure although wage rates vary across sectors. The formal sector produces an import-competing commodity; the informal sector also produces an import substitute, whereas the rural sector produces an exportable. We assume neo-classical technology and X_F is capital intensive relative to X_I, where 'X_j' along with other symbols is defined below.

To build the system of equations, we use the following notations:

$\bar{w}$ Formal negotiated wage

w: Wage in other sectors

r Return to capital

τ: Return to land

X_j Output in the jth sector, $j = X, Y, Z$

P_j^* World price of jth good, $j = X, Y, Z$

t_j Protection in the jth sector

$\bar{L}$ Total labour force

$\bar{K}$ Total stock of capital

$\bar{T}$ Total supply of land

a_{ij} Input coefficients

The system follows standard neo-classical assumptions, such as constant returns to scale and diminishing returns to factor inputs and functions in competitive markets for commodities and factors. The general equilibrium structure is therefore given by a system of six equations comprising the competitive price equations as well as factor endowments and full-employment conditions for each input, in that order.

$$\bar{w}a_{LF} + ra_{KF} = P_F^*(1 + t_F) \qquad (6.1)$$

$$\bar{w}a_{LI} + ra_{KI} = P_I^*(1 + t_1) \tag{6.2}$$

$$wa_{LR} + \tau a_{TR} = P_R^* \tag{6.3}$$

$$a_{LF}X_F + a_{LI}X_I = \bar{L} - a_{LR}X_R \tag{6.4}$$

$$a_{KF}X_F + a_{KI}X_I = \bar{K} \tag{6.5}$$

$$a_{TR}X_R = \bar{T} \tag{6.6}$$

From the competitive price conditions as in equations (6.1) to (6.3) and the full-employment conditions as in equations (6.4) to (6.6), we solve for six unknowns, w, r, τ, X_F, X_I and X_R. Equations (6.1) and (6.2) form the Heckscher-Ohlin sub-system or a 'nugget' (Jones and Marjit 1992). As far as the structure of protection in such an economy is concerned, we consider three different types of protectionary regimes: 't_F', 't_I', are the tariff rates that are exogenous and imposed on import of commodities in these sectors.

Note that albeit $\bar{w} > w$ by assumption, labour does not leave the informal/agricultural sector because given capital constraints, only a certain number of workers can be employed in F. This implies that there is job rationing of some sort in effect. Consequently, workers of homogeneous skill types first queue up in the formal sector to get jobs that pay higher than their true productivity while the unsuccessful ones get absorbed in the other sectors. We keep assuming, not unrealistically, throughout this chapter that in many developing countries there is very little skill-driven heterogeneity across workers in formal factory-based production systems vis-à-vis those who are employed in the informal sector. The major distinction, which can also explain part of this wage gap (in our case it is held as an exogenously determined formal wage negotiated between the owners and the workers of the company, and in a subsequent chapter we model the act of wage negotiation explicitly), is the difference between capital–labour ratios among sectors. In fact, as we demonstrate in the next section the welfare impact of regime shifts as manifested through withdrawal of high protection, quite common in developing countries during transition from near-autarky to relative free trade, and by decisions to export more traditional goods depend crucially on such assumptions. The argument in favour of export of low-technology and low capital-intensive commodities produced under the auspices of the unorganized sector is also well founded in view of traditional and agricultural goods that the countries in the South still export substantially.

EXOGENOUS SHOCKS

In this section, we offer two different specifications regarding the change in the structure of protection that the industries enjoy. First, let us consider that the formal and informal sectors are both protected at non-uniform rates. Then following trade liberalization, the formal sector in the country faces a tariff cut, with all other things remaining unchanged. We construct the following proposition based on such a change, with Ω defined as the level of welfare in the country. We subsequently discuss two more exogenous shocks and present the welfare implications in comparable forms in Propositions 6.2 and 6.3.

PROPOSITION 6.1.   *A tariff cut in the formal sector leads to a change in the national welfare, such that:*

$$\frac{d\Omega}{dt_F} \underset{>}{\overset{\leq}{=}} 0, iff \left\{ (\bar{w} - w)\frac{dL_F}{dt_F} + t_F P_F^* S_{FF} + t_I P_I^* S_{IF} \right\} \underset{>}{\overset{\leq}{=}} 0$$

Proof.   See Appendix 6A for detailed algebraic proof.

We provide a brief intuitive explanation here. As the tariff rate is lowered, return to capital falls and the formal sector contracts. Capital moves out of the formal sector and is employed in the informal sector. Informal/rural wage, w goes up in consequence. However, the agricultural sector contracts, since $(\bar{w} - w)$ contraction in L_F leads to reduction in real income. On the other hand, the import demand for F goes up, and it raises the tariff revenue as the country turns to a larger import of F owing to loss of domestic production. The term $S_{FF} < 0$ captures this effect. However, as t_F goes down, demand for X_I goes down and its production goes up, reducing import demand for the informal sector. This must lower the tariff revenue in the sector by that extent. $S_{IF} > 0$ is used in the proposition to capture this effect. If the change in employment due to change in tariff, $\frac{dL_F}{dt_F} > 0$, is not very large or if the gap between formal and informal wages is not too big either, then there is a welfare gain on account of the substitution effects only, as reflected by the condition in Proposition 6.1.

Next, we postulate that the tariff on informal sector output is lowered, *ceteris paribus*. We offer Proposition 6.2 on the basis of the effect of such changes.

PROPOSITION 6.2.   *A tariff cut on the informal sector leads to a change in welfare, if the following condition holds:*

$$\frac{d\Omega}{dt_I} \overset{<}{_>} 0, iff \left\{ (\bar{w} - w)\frac{dL_F}{dt_F} + t_I P_I^* S_{II} + t_F P_F^* S_{FI} \right\} \overset{\leq}{_>} 0$$

Proof.   See Appendix 6A for detailed algebraic derivations.

Once again, we begin with an intuitive explanation. A tariff cut on the informal sector will lead to a rise in output and employment levels in the formal sector as also in the rural sector due to Rybczynski effects. In the first case, as capital moves out into the formal sector and in the second case as labour moves away from the informal sector and back to the rural sector. This generates $\dfrac{dL_F}{dt_I} < 0$. Output falls in the informal sector and demand goes up causing an increase in the import demand for the product. Accordingly, we have $S_{II} < 0$ and there is a net welfare gain from trade policy reforms if the cross-substitution effect is rather negligible. This welfare gain is stronger, the bigger is the initial gap between the formal and informal wages. However, if the cross-effect, $S_{FI} > 0$ is significant, then there is welfare loss, although the final direction of $\dfrac{d\Omega}{dt_I} \overset{>}{_<} 0$, depends upon the relative strength of the terms available in Proposition 6.2.

Finally, we consider the change in price of the rural commodity. Let the price increase by exogenous causes, such that, $P_R^* > 0$. The effect on the welfare of the small open economy is formulated as:

PROPOSITION 6.3.   *A price rise in the agricultural sector leads to a change in welfare if the following condition holds:*

$$\frac{d\Omega}{dP_R^*} \overset{<}{_>} 0, iff \left\{ (\bar{w} - w)\frac{dL_F}{dP_R^*} - M_R + t_I P_I^* \frac{dM_I}{dP_R^*} + t_F P_F^* \frac{dM_F}{dP_R^*} \right\} \overset{\leq}{_>} 0$$

Proof.   See Appendix 6A and the intuitive explanation below.

The intuitive explanation for Proposition 6.3 is: As the price of the rural commodity goes up, output and employment increase in that sector. Labour moves out of the informal sector where both output and employment decrease. An interesting result is obtained in this model, whereby wage rates do not change even if the price of the rural commodity increases. Return to capital also does not change and there is only a more than proportionate increase in the return to land following a price rise in the rural sector. Now using the equation of balanced trade, the change in the level of welfare (Ω) in the country due to a change in the price of commodity R, is captured as:

$$\frac{d\Omega}{dP_R^*} = \left\{ (\bar{w} - w)\frac{dL_F}{dP_R^*} - M_R + t_I P_I^* S_{IR} + t_F P_F^* S_{FR} \right\} \qquad (6.7)$$

where, $S_{FR} = \frac{\delta M_F}{\delta P_R^*}$ and $S_{IR} = \frac{\delta M_I}{\delta P_R^*}$ are the substitutions in import demand due to change in price of the agricultural commodity.

An increase in P_R^* is just like a terms-of-trade improvement. Since $M_R < 0$, welfare goes up. Labour is drawn away from I into R, and on the other hand, as X_F goes up, so does L_F due to the Rybczynski effect. Hence, welfare goes up due to this effect as well. This is due to the complementarity relationship between X_F and X_R, a feature of Gruen and Corden (1970) and Jones and Marjit (1992) structures. Now, demand for I goes up due to the substitution effect while X_I contracts, $S_{IR} > 0$. This raises tariff revenue from import of I, leading to higher welfare. But X_F increases and even if demand for F rises, M_F can go down, leading to $S_{FR} < 0$, and that may be a source of welfare loss. It is straightforward to argue that if $t_R = 0$ and t_F is very high the adverse effect on welfare for S_{FR} being negative can be substantial.

Now, simplifying equation (6.7) we arrive at a new form:

$$\frac{d\Omega}{dP_R^*} < 0 \ iff \ t_F > -\frac{(\bar{w} - w)\frac{dL_F}{dP_R^*} - M_R + t_I P_I^* S_{IR}}{P_F^* S_{FR}} \qquad (6.8)$$

Once again, if $S_{FR} < 0$ and $S_{IR} < 0$, $\bar{w}$ is close to w and M_R is relatively low, high tariffs in F should make the terms-of-trade effect turn negative. Usually, the better terms-of-trade is welfare-improving. But in this case the complementarity effect induces the import-competing sectors to grow as well following improvements in the terms-of-trade. In a typical full-employment model without exogenously imposed wage floors one holds $\bar{w} = w$. In that case, with $t_I = 0$, the result is more likely to occur as the condition boils down to:

$$\frac{d\Omega}{dP_R^*} < 0 \ iff \ t_F > \frac{M_R}{P_F^* S_{FR}} \qquad (6.9)$$

However, the wage differential in (6.8) captures the positive welfare effect of improvement in employment in the formal sector.

A MODEL WITH OPEN UNEMPLOYMENT

Despite the fact that we present identical economic scenarios, we deploy slight variations in the symbolization in order to facilitate distinct treatments. Consider a three-sector economy producing X (urban formal manufacturing good), Y (urban informal good), and Z (agricultural good). X and Y use capital and labour, Z uses land and labour. Labour is freely mobile between Y and Z, in the sense that workers earn the same wages, W, informally employed in both these sectors. But X offers a wage, $\bar{W}$ referred to as the formal wage in the same capacity as mentioned earlier. However, unlike before, we allow open unemployment as a feature. This implies that workers migrating from the rural to the urban area may either choose to remain unemployed while awaiting a formal job that pays $\bar{W} > W$, or (perhaps more realistically, as the ability to afford unemployment may be rather low) accept W in a typical urban informal sector job. With large labour movements between urban and rural locations (often under distress), few urban formal jobs and no institutional interventions/unemployment benefits, it automatically leads to equalization of real wages between the rural and urban informal sectors. We also assume that capital moves freely between the urban formal and informal sectors earning the same return, r.

Further, consider that X is an import-competing good enjoying tariff protection, t. On the other hand, Y, the informal manufacturing sector is assumed to produce a traded good in the benchmark model. Later we introduce the possibility that Y is a non-traded good. The agricultural good, Z, is an export good. Competitive markets and constant returns to scale technology with diminishing marginal productivities of factors are assumed. Competitive price conditions imply:

$$\bar{W}a_{LX} + ra_{KX} = P_X(1+t) \tag{6.10}$$

$$Wa_{LY} + ra_{KY} = P_Y \tag{6.11}$$

$$Wa_{LZ} + Ra_{TZ} = P_Z \tag{6.12}$$

While all other symbols carry the same connotations as before, r is the return to capital and R is rental on land.

Full employment of land and capital ensure that:

$$a_{TZ}Z = T \tag{6.13}$$

$$a_{KX}X + a_{KY}Y = K \tag{6.14}$$

where, T and K are inelastic supplies of land and capital. The Harris-Todaro migration equilibrium condition is given by:

$$\frac{\bar{W}a_{LX}X}{L - (a_{LY}Y + a_{LZ}Z)} = W \tag{6.15}$$

Note that (6.15) can be re-written as a modified 'full-employment' condition for labour:

$$\frac{\bar{W}a_{LX}X}{W} + a_{LY}Y = L - a_{LZ}Z \qquad (6.16)$$

With given prices and tariff rate, t, one can determine W, r, and R from (6.10) to (6.12). Factor prices in turn determine factor proportions. Now, from (6.13) we can determine Z. Then (6.14) and (6.16) determine X and Y. This completes the determination of equilibrium. We assume that Y is labour-intensive and X is capital-intensive, an assumption which hardly needs any justification. However, the factor intensity assumption implies:

$$\left[\frac{\bar{W}}{W} a_{LX} a_{KY} - a_{KX} a_{LY}\right] < 0$$

or,

$$\left[\frac{a_{KX}}{a_{LX}} > \frac{\bar{W}}{W} \frac{a_{KY}}{a_{LY}}\right] \qquad (6.17)$$

Note that with $\frac{\bar{W}}{W}$, the capital intensity assumption as in (6.17) is a bit stronger than the usual definition, that is:

$$\left[\frac{a_{KX}}{a_{LX}} > \frac{a_{KY}}{a_{LY}}\right] \qquad (6.18)$$

If we define (6.17) as the stronger version of intensity assumption, then the weaker version must appear:

$$\left[\frac{\bar{W}}{W} \frac{a_{KY}}{a_{LY}} > \frac{a_{KX}}{a_{LX}} > \frac{a_{KY}}{a_{LY}}\right] \qquad (6.19)$$

Under the weaker version, the informal sector becomes effectively the capital-intensive sector. Equation (6.19) accommodates a kind of factor intensity reversal if W goes down way below $\bar{W}$, i.e., wider is the formal–informal wage gap. Hence, we shall continue with (6.17) and any possible factor intensity reversal is assumed away.

Reduction in Tariffs

Let us trace the changes in equilibrium as the tariff barrier on the formal sector, t, is reduced. A decline in t reduces r, increases W and reduces R. This follows directly from equations (6.10) to (6.12). A decline in R makes people use land more intensively and with a given T that reduces Z [from (6.13)] and subsequently, a_{LZ}. As the RHS in (6.16) increases with a decline in $a_{LZ}Z$, the LHS on the other hand, undergoes a fall due to a decline in $\dfrac{\overline{W}}{W}$. Also (a_{KX}, a_{KY}) increases with an increase in $\dfrac{\overline{W}}{r}$ and $\dfrac{W}{r}$. Hence, the labour constraint (6.16) becomes less binding while the capital constraint (6.14) becomes more binding. This leads to the well-known Rybczynski type result increasing the labour-intensive sector Y (urban informal sector) and contracting the capital-intensive sector, X (the urban formal manufacturing good).

Now, from (6.16) we can write total employment as:

$$L_E = a_{LX}X + a_{LY}Y + a_{LZ}Z = L - \frac{\overline{W}a_{LX}X}{W} + a_{LX}X = L - a_{LX}X\left(\frac{\overline{W}}{W} - 1\right)$$

$$(6.20)$$

By now we know that $a_{LX}X$ must have gone down and $\dfrac{\overline{W}}{W}$ also has gone down. Therefore, L_E must increase. We can now write the following proposition:

PROPOSITION 6.4.   *Under the stronger factor intensity ranking a decline in tariffs must increase total employment*

Proof.   See Appendix 6B.

The exact proof is given in Appendix 6B. Note that a downsized urban formal sector, with an expanding urban informal sector and rising informal wages must reduce open unemployment in the economy. A decline in tariffs not only contracts formal manufacturing, but also traditional agriculture. The existing set of informal and rural workers must gain as W is higher now. Displaced workers from the formal sector lose as they were getting $\overline{W}$ previously. A rise in the set of workers in the 'open unemployed' group must now find it even more difficult to find jobs and consider joining the informal sector offering higher wages in transition.

Typically, a drop in t will reduce the expected wage rate in the urban formal sector and this has a tendency to reduce open unemployment. But in the standard H-T framework people migrating to agriculture depresses the wage rate in agriculture. Therefore, the effect on expected wage rates is ambiguous, and this is also so for unemployment. However, in our framework W in fact goes up as displaced capital from the formal sector relocates in the informal sector. This is a rather necessary condition when there is not much of a change in P_Y. Here, a drop in t unambiguously reduces total unemployment or increases total employment. It is the increase in informal wages which is a striking outcome because conventional wisdom will be a drop in W as more people crowd into the informal segment. But as capital leaves the formal sector and r goes down, capital–labour ratios in each sector go up, driving up W. Not only are the displaced workers from the formal sector absorbed in Y but higher W also attracts more agricultural workers to the informal sector raising overall employment. Also note that the average wage which is a weighted average of formal wage $\bar{W}$ and W is given by:

$$W_a = \bar{W}\frac{L_X}{L} + \frac{W(L_Y + L_Z)}{\bar{L}} = \bar{W}\frac{L_X}{L} + \frac{W\left[L - L_X\left(\dfrac{\bar{W}}{W} - 1\right) - L_X\right]}{L}$$

$$= W + \frac{L_X}{L}\left[\bar{W} - W\left(\frac{\bar{W}}{W} - 1\right) - W\right] = W \qquad (6.21)$$

Clearly, the average wage is nothing but W itself. Hence, the average worker must gain from a tariff reform. Therefore, a rise in W must mean a rise in W_a and hence the welfare level of an average worker.

The Non-traded Informal Sector

If the urban informal good, Y, is non-traded, we need a separate equation for determining the equilibrium P_Y by balancing demand and supply in this sector. Let us look at the sequence of outcomes following a decline in tariff in such a context. In our earlier analysis Y definitely expands due to the assumption of factor intensity ranking between X and Y. Now an increase in Y reduces P_Y to clear the market for the informal good and a decline in P_Y tends to reduce W, offsetting the positive effect on employment.

However, a decline in t and a decline in P_Y have opposite effects on demand for Y. What we have shown in Appendix 6B suggests that a high elasticity of substitution in demand (μ_2) will be a sufficient condition to reinstate our earlier result. In fact, it is well-known that if $\mu_2 \to \infty$ then, $\hat{P}_Y \to 0$, that is, in the limit it replicates the case with a traded informal sector. More generally, even if W goes down, strong elasticity of factor substitution in X, given by σ_X, will mean an increase in employment. Nevertheless, there is every possibility that informal wages will go up.

We would like to emphasize the process of transition, whereby a high σ_X reduces $a_{LX}X$ significantly and workers with depressed wages do not hang around in the hope of jobs and resort to offers from sector Y. This must lower open unemployment in the system, and in fact has larger implications for the entire economy. For example, the riddle of jobless growth in many developing countries in recent decades could find an answer to this issue in addition to the much discussed total factor productivity growth. Interestingly, the increase in informal wages is tantamount to factor productivity growth in that sector as well and in this case it is aided by relocation of capital between the formal and informal sectors. On account of the apparent invisibility of such employment growth to formal authorities in labour bureaus the informal sources often remain obscure.

PROPOSITION 6.5.   *If Y is the urban non-traded sector, a decline in tariffs will increase total employment provided that σ_X and μ_2 are strong enough.*

Proof.   See derivation of (6B.11) in Appendix 6B.

RELATED DISCUSSION

Since we discussed two variations of the model dealing with international trade and its impact on informal wages and employment operating through exogenous changes in the neighbourhood of steady state equilibria, we bring in possible structural alterations in the same sequence as the main models. Instead of full blown models, this would take the shape of elaborate thought experiments.

Let us now reconstruct the results of our first structure with an assumption where the informal sector is absent from the model. If there is no informal sector, what we have is a standard specific factor model *a' la* Jones (1971) with only one difference. Here people try to find jobs in the formal sector and only those who are unemployed get absorbed in agriculture.

A tariff cut in sector F will give the usual results. Output in X_F falls, consequently L_F falls, while M_F rises. This is very similar to what we have in our model except the cross-effect on I. However, with I in place, an improvement in X_I absorbs labour and helps to raise w as r falls. But without I, w must fall as labourers crowd into the rural sector. If $t_I > 0$, a decline in M_I is a source of welfare loss in our model, which cannot be captured in the structure without inclusion of the informal sector. If the informal sector produces an import-competing product as argued earlier, and is protected from external competition, expansion in informal output increases distortion.

A rise in P_R^* in the two-sector model leads to an increase in welfare due to terms-of-trade effect, as well as by the volume of trade effect as M_F goes up. However, as L_F falls, it hurts welfare. What our model suggests is that with the informal sector in place, a complementarity result emerges, which may in fact reduce M_F, since X_I contracts. Such a result occurs only because X_I contracts and helps the other protected sector to expand.

Finally, how do the real incomes of labourers get affected through policy reforms? A decline in t_F increases w and consequently the real incomes of existing workers in the informal and agricultural sectors. Nevertheless as L_F drops, workers are pushed out of the formal sector. These workers suffer real income loss. Typically, a tariff cut redistributes income in face of the 'outsiders' who do not receive the patronage of labour unions. A decline in t_R reduces the real income of the informal workers and increases that of the unionized workers, since $\bar{w}$ is fixed and other prices are held constant. So, as P_R^* increases, real incomes of the workers already employed in the formal and informal sectors, go down. At the same time, there is labour outflow from the informal to the formal sector measured by dL_F. Their real income increases if and only if $\left(\dfrac{\bar{w} - w}{w}\right) > P_R^*$.

It should be pointed out in this connection that the proposed structure is quite robust to reorganization. In the absence of a distinction between wage rates in the informal and rural sectors, there remains no reason to distinguish between these two sectors. In fact, there is no obstacle in the model in combining the informal and rural sectors. In that case, all characteristics of the model reduce to the standard $2 \times 2 \times 2$ model of trade. This argument can be tested as follows: Let's add initial tariff (t_R) to the rural sector as it is initially in the formal and informal sectors. Then evaluate the effect of trade liberalization in the rural sector ($dt_R \neq 0$) on welfare ($d\Omega$), thus adding another proposition. The result turns out to be a special case of Proposition 6.2, which evaluates the welfare effect of trade liberalization on the informal sector. This is due to the fact that the rural sector is just the informal sector without capital. In fact, this added proposition would be a generalization of Proposition 6.3. Alternatively, if we drop the rural sector from the model, the comparative results in Propositions 6.1, 6.2 and 6.3 regarding the formal and informal sectors remain unchanged. Although it is true that the informal and rural sectors are very similar, there is one important difference. A rise in agricultural price does not help informal workers, while a rise in the price of the product produced in the informal sector 'must increase' w.

For the second model, on the other hand, it is well-known in the H-T framework that employment and aggregate labour income may move in opposite directions following a policy change. Aggregate labour income in our model is given by:

$$\overline{W} a_{LX} X + W(a_{LY} Y + a_{LZ} Z) = WL \qquad (6.21)$$

In this structure, regardless of the consequences on employment, aggregate labour income increases with an increase in W. What we have shown here is that a decline in t can simultaneously increase employment and raise W, provided condition (6B.11) holds. If P_Y is relatively sticky, W must increase with a fall in t alone; and conversely, if P_Y is rather sensitive W can still go up [see (6B.11) in Appendix 6B].

The weaker factor-intensity ranking condition, $\dfrac{\overline{W}}{W} \dfrac{a_{KY}}{a_{LY}} > \dfrac{a_{KX}}{a_{LX}}$ leads to a capital intensive informal sector, as a substantial wage gap $\dfrac{\overline{W}}{W}$ makes a worker's share of average cost in X quite high relative to that in the informal sector. Therefore, a drop in t may actually increase X and reduce Y.

And yet, L_E may increase considerably, since a rise in W will always have a positive effect on total employment by raising the opportunity cost of open unemployment. As there is general consensus that the informal sector is labour intensive as compared to the formal sector, we prefer to retain the stronger factor intensity assumption, perceived as the usual factor intensity ranking.

Another point to note in this context is that a rise in the effective price of Z either through an increase in prospects for exports or through an increase in productivity, is quite likely to increase unemployment. A rise in P_Z does not change W, although an increase in Z owing to this positive price inducement reduces total labour available for production of X and Y. Since X is capital-intensive, due to the Rybczynski effect, X goes up and L_E goes down. The informal sector contracts but the formal sector expands and it offers a positive signal to many people to wait for formal jobs. Obviously, this increases the extent of open unemployment.

One issue that seems to be left open in this kind of construct is reflections on the pattern of trade. Let us briefly comment on the issue at this juncture. We have discussed at length that as t goes down, both X and Z contract. In other words, the import-competing sector and the export sector both plummet. A natural query then is: What would sustain the balance of trade? Of course, as $P_X(1 + t)$ and P_Y drop relative to that of P_Z, export surplus may still increase. If not, the consequent income effect will guarantee that the adjusted consumption level shall satisfy the balance of trade constraint. A simple extension of the basic model with heterogeneous labour inputs shall make it more realistic.

Consider a situation where in addition to what we have already assumed, there is also another sector that uses skilled labour and capital and produces an export commodity. A drop in t, by reducing r will increase skilled wage and skilled output of the exportable. This can be added to the above framework without having to alter any of our basic results. Skilled labour, just as capital, can be assumed to be a scarce input and fully employed. An additional, and fairly interesting, result that one obtains with the extended model has to do with the worsening unskilled/skilled wage gap following a drop in t if the capital's share in the average cost is greater in the skilled sector than in the unskilled sector.

However, reverting back to the earlier model without the added complexities, one can recall the policy of subsidizing employment in the urban formal sector. In traditional Harris-Todaro literature it was demonstrated that the effect of a wage subsidy can lead to an increase in unemployment. Basu (1997) discusses this in great detail, although the paradox does get resolved when agriculture is decomposed into two sub-sectors and urban wage subsidy helps the labour-intensive segment (see, for example, Marjit 1991). Interestingly, in this chapter any attempt to raise formal sector employment by an artificial wage subsidy *must* lead to *greater unemployment* on the whole. The mechanism is quite symmetric to the one discussed earlier.

A wage subsidy must raise the return to capital, that is, r. That in turn reduces informal and rural wage rates. As capital constraint becomes less binding and labour constraint gets tighter, X must expand and Y must contract. From (6.20) it is straightforward to argue that total employment in X will increase and relative urban wages will also increase reducing aggregate employment.

* * *

Let us summarize the basic findings of this chapter. As explained with the first set of assumptions and the related model, in the presence of the informal sector in the economy, a tariff cut on formal sector output might not be welfare-improving. For this to be unambiguously welfare-improving, it requires both a negligible cross-substitution effect in the other sectors and a negligible employment effect in the formal sector. Secondly, a reduction in tariff in the informal sector increases welfare, as long as input demand in the formal sector expands.

This may be jeopardized by a rise in X_F. If cross-effects are ignored, i.e., if t_F is very low, welfare unambiguously rises following a tariff cut in the informal sector. Finally, the rise in price of the agricultural commodity will also be strictly welfare-improving as long as the fall in import demand for the formal good due to $P_R^* > 0$ is negligible. There would nevertheless be a striking possibility that the welfare level in the economy is reduced when there is a fall in import demand for the formal commodity owing to an increase in the price of the agricultural good.

The purpose of this analysis was to provide a simple general equilibrium framework for developing countries characterized by the informal sector, and offer usual trade policy experiments in this set-up. Tariff cuts have ambiguous results even if it is a full-employment competitive model, because of wage differentials and the presence of the cross-effects in consumption and production. Typically, when either t_F or $t_I = 0$, the welfare effect of a tariff cut is usually positive. But with pre-existing high tariffs in other sectors and complementarity in production, welfare results can go either way.

Generally speaking, therefore, this chapter addressed one of the most controversial issues in the trade policy of developing nations. Does trade increase employment? While the first model discussed overall welfare implications, the second model offered a direct relationship. There, it was argued that a decline in tariff helps create jobs in the informal sector and increases informal wages simultaneously when workers are retrenched from the formal sector. Further, this may be accompanied by a decline in rural employment. Nevertheless, the model predicts that overall employment must increase. The inclusion of an urban informal sector is justified by the fact that in the absence of such sectors in a model discussing aspects of labour market characteristics in a typical developing country, a large part of intricate and involved outcomes are completely neglected. That a drop in t reduces urban employment and reduces W, would simply lead to open unemployment in models without an urban informal sector. Albeit there will be offsetting effects on open unemployment, rural workers would definitely be worse-off and overall unemployment could easily go up. It is the role played by the informal sector that drives results capable of contesting conventional wisdom. It draws in capital, preserves and raises employment and also allows informal wages to increase. Under the circumstances, if people still leave rural areas, open unemployment does not burden the economy.

Thus, our second set of results is sensitive to the assumption of capital mobility. As a counterfactual, if no mobility of capital is allowed, then the endowment and price equations are not separable and we need full-employment conditions for both types of capital, land and rural–urban migration relationship to solve for individual factor prices. It requires the system of equations to solve simultaneously. Now, a drop in t reduces employment in X and capital cannot move out, so W must fall in equilibrium, leading to an increase in aggregate unemployment.

However, as a middle path if one allows some degree of capital mobility then the results still hold and the stronger assumption of free and full capital mobility can be suitably relaxed. In other words, the structure demands as a sufficient condition partial release of capital from X only to the extent that the K/L ratio in Y goes up when some workers also relocate to Y from X. One can model the adjustment by defining a critical level of elasticity of mobility of capital beyond which W will actually increase. This is in fact a reiteration of the elasticity condition derived and discussed in Chapter 5 with additional inferences when formal and informal commodities are traded globally.

Finally, it would be easy to graft a sector that produces skilled manufacturing goods or services by using skilled labour and capital, on to the specified framework in the second model. Interestingly, withdrawal of tariff from the import-competing sector does not alter anything except that this added sector, presumably an export sector, will also benefit simply owing to a lower return per unit of capital employed therein. In that case, several comparative static experiments will yield results where the skilled and informal sectors will demonstrate a degree of complementarity in production. A general theoretical discussion on such issues is available in Marjit (2005).

APPENDIX 6A

Proof of Proposition 6.1.

'∧' denotes percentage changes in the variables.

From equation (6.1):

$$\hat{r} = \frac{dt_F}{\theta_{KF}} < 0 \quad \text{as, } dt_F < 0.$$

From equation (6.2) substituting $\hat{r}$:

$$\hat{w} = -\frac{dt_F}{\theta_{KF}} \frac{\theta_{KI}}{\theta_{LI}} > 0$$

And finally from equation (6.3):

$$\hat{\tau} = \frac{dt_F}{\theta_{KF}} \frac{\theta_{KI}}{\theta_{LI}} \frac{\theta_{LR}}{\theta_{TR}} < 0$$

Differentiating and manipulating equations (6.4) and (6.5) (see Jones 1965):

$$\hat{X}_F = \frac{1}{\Delta} \left\{ \hat{w}(\lambda_{KI}\sigma_R \frac{\lambda_{LR}}{\theta_{TR}} + \lambda_{KI}^2 \theta_{LI}\sigma_I + \lambda_{LI}\theta_{KI}\sigma_I) - \right.$$
$$\left. \hat{r}(\lambda_{KI} + \lambda_{LI})(\lambda_{KF}\theta_{LF}\sigma_F + \lambda_{KI}\theta_{LI}\sigma_I) \right\}$$

and

$$\hat{X}_I = \frac{1}{\Delta} \left\{ \hat{w}(\lambda_{KF}\sigma_R \frac{\lambda_{LR}}{\theta_{TR}} + \lambda_{KF}\lambda_{LI}\sigma_I + \lambda_{LF}\lambda_{KI}\theta_{LI}\sigma_I) - \right.$$
$$\left. \hat{r}(\lambda_{KF}\theta_{LF}\sigma_F + \lambda_{KI}\theta_{LI}\sigma_I) \right\}$$

where, $\Delta = \left\{ \lambda_{LF}\lambda_{KI} - \lambda_{KF}\lambda_{LI} \right\} < 0,$ and accordingly $\hat{X}_F < 0, \hat{X}_I > 0.$

Next, from equation (6.6):

$X_R = \dfrac{\bar{T}}{a_{TR}}.$ Therefore, $a_{LR}X_R = \dfrac{a_{LR}\bar{T}}{a_{TR}}.$ This leads to the following equation:

$$\hat{a}_{LR} + \hat{X}_R = \hat{a}_{LR} - \hat{a}_{TR} = -\sigma_R(\hat{w} - \hat{\tau}) \tag{6.1.1}$$

Or, $\hat{w} - \hat{\tau} = \dfrac{\hat{w}}{\theta_{TR}}$

such that,

$$\hat{L}_R = \hat{a}_{LR} + \hat{X}_R = -\sigma_R \left(\frac{\hat{w}}{\theta_{TR}} \right) < 0 \tag{6.1.2}$$

Also,

$$\hat{X}_R = -\sigma_R \left(\frac{\theta_{LR}\hat{w}}{\theta_{TR}} \right) \tag{6.1.3}$$

We use the above results to arrive at the change in the welfare parameter. From the condition of balanced trade:

$$P_F^*(1+t_F)dD_F + P_I^*(1+t_I)dD_I + P_R^* dD_R - t_F P_F^* dD_F - t_I P_I^* dD_I$$

$$= P_F^*(1+t_F)dX_F + P_I^*(1+t_I)dX_I + P_R^* dX_R - t_F P_F^* dX_F - t_I P_I^* dX_I$$

which leads to:

$$d\Omega = P_F^*(1+t_F)dX_F + P_I^*(1+t_I)dX_I$$
$$+ P_R^* dX_R + t_F P_F^* dM_F + t_I P_I^* dM_I \tag{6.1.4}$$

where, $d\Omega = P_F^*(1+t_F)dD_F + P_I^* dD_I + P_R^* dD_R$

Now, $P_F^*(1+t_F)dX_F + P_I^*(1+t_I)dX_I + P_R^* dX_R = (\bar{w} - w)dL_F$

As, $dL_F = -(dL_I + dL_R), d\bar{K} = 0, d\bar{T} = 0$.

Thus,

$$d\Omega = (\bar{w} - w)dL_F + t_F P_F^* dM_F + t_I P_I^* dM_I \tag{6.1.5}$$

Let us now define the import demand function as:

$$M_F = M_F \left(\frac{P_F^*(1+t_F)}{\bar{w}}, \frac{P_I^*(1+t_I)}{\bar{w}}, \frac{P_R^*}{\bar{w}}, \Omega \right) \tag{6.1.6}$$

Differentiating equation (6.1.6):

$$dM_F = S_{FF}dt_F + \mu_F d\Omega \text{ and } dM_I = S_{IF}dt_F + \mu_I d\Omega$$

where, $S_{FF} = \dfrac{\delta M_F}{\delta t_F}$ and $S_{IF} = \dfrac{\delta M_I}{\delta t_F}$, $\mu_F = \dfrac{\delta M_F}{\delta \Omega}$ and $\mu_I = \dfrac{\delta M_I}{\delta \Omega}$.

Substituting the above in equation (6.1.5):

$$d\Omega = (\bar{w} - w)dL_F + t_F P_F^* S_{FF}dt_F + t_F P_F^* \mu_F d\Omega$$
$$+ t_I P_I^* S_{IF}dt_F + t_I P_I^* \mu_I d\Omega$$

Or,

$$d\Omega = \frac{(\bar{w} - w)dL_F + t_F P_F^* S_{FF}dt_F + t_I P_I^* S_{IF}dt_F}{1 - t_F P_F^* \mu_F - t_I P_I^* \mu_I}$$

Now, as $\mu_F = \dfrac{m_F}{(1+t_F)P_F^*}$, $\mu_I = \dfrac{m_I}{(1+t_I)P_I^*}$, it follows that

$$0 < (1 - t_F P_F^* \mu_F - t_I P_I^* \mu_I) < 1$$

Therefore, $\dfrac{d\Omega}{dt_F} \underset{>}{\overset{<}{=}} 0$, iff $\left\{ (\overline{w} - w)\dfrac{dL_F}{dt_F} + t_F P_F^* S_{FF} + t_I P_I^* S_{IF} \right\} \underset{>}{\overset{<}{=}} 0$. QED

Proof of Proposition 6.2.

From equation (6.1), $\hat{r} = 0$ and from equation (6.2), $\hat{w} = \dfrac{dt_I}{\theta_{LI}} < 0$ as $dt_I < 0$.

Again, from equation (6.3), $\hat{\tau} = -\dfrac{dt_I}{\theta_{LI}} \dfrac{\theta_{LR}}{\theta_{TR}} > 0$. The employment and

output levels in the agricultural sector are:

$$\hat{L}_R = -\sigma_R \left(\dfrac{\hat{w}}{\theta_{TR}} \right) > 0, \hat{X}_R = -\sigma_R \left(\dfrac{\theta_{LR}\hat{w}}{\theta_{TR}} \right) > 0$$

From equations (6.4) and (6.5), we solve for $\hat{X}_F > 0$ and $\hat{X}_I < 0$, subject to $\Delta < 0$.

Accordingly, $\hat{L}_F > 0$, and $\hat{L}_I < 0$.

Now, using the condition of balanced trade and from above we get:

$$d\Omega = (\overline{w} - w)dL_F + t_F P_F^* dM_F + t_I P_I^* dM_I \qquad (6.2.1)$$

The import demand function for I is similarly written as:

$$M_I = M_I \left(\dfrac{P_F(1 + t_F)}{\overline{w}}, \dfrac{P_I^*(1 + t_I)}{\overline{w}}, \dfrac{P_R^*}{\overline{w}}, \Omega \right)$$

Differentiating, $dM_I = S_{II} dt_I + \mu_I d\Omega$, and $dM_F = S_{FI} dt_I + \mu_F d\Omega$

where, $S_{II} = \dfrac{\delta M_I}{\delta t_I}$ and $S_{FI} = \dfrac{\delta M_F}{\delta t_I}$; $\mu_I = \dfrac{\delta M_I}{\delta \Omega}$, and $\mu_F = \dfrac{\delta M_F}{\delta \Omega}$,

we get

$$d\Omega = \dfrac{(\overline{w} - w)dL_F + t_F P_F^* S_{II} dt_I + t_F P_F^* S_{FI} dt_I}{1 - t_F P_F^* \mu_F - t_I P_I^* \mu_I} \qquad (6.2.2)$$

As before, with $0 < (1 - t_F P_F^* \mu_F - t_I P_I^* \mu_I) < 1$

$$\dfrac{d\Omega}{dt_I} \underset{>}{\overset{<}{=}} 0 \quad iff \quad \left\{ (\overline{w} - w)\dfrac{dL_F}{dt_I} + t_I P_I^* S_{II} + t_F P_F^* S_{FI} \right\} \underset{>}{\overset{<}{=}} 0. \text{ QED}$$

Proof of Proposition 6.3.

From equation (6.1), $\hat{r} = 0$ and from equation (6.2), $\hat{w} = 0$ as $dP_R^* > 0$ affects return to land alone.

So, from (6.3), $\hat{\tau} = \dfrac{\hat{P}_R^*}{\theta_{TR}} > 0$.

Also, $X_R = \dfrac{\overline{T}}{a_{TR}}$, and $\hat{L}_R = \hat{a}_{LR} + \hat{X}_R = \hat{a}_{LR} - \hat{a}_{TR} = \sigma_R \left(\dfrac{\hat{P}_R^*}{\theta_{TR}} \right) > 0$

Changes in the output levels in all the sectors are given as:

$$\hat{X}_R = \sigma_R \left(\frac{\theta_{LR}\hat{P}_R^*}{\theta_{TR}} \right); \hat{X}_F = -\frac{1}{\Delta} \left\{ \lambda_{LR} \frac{\sigma_R}{\theta_{TR}} \hat{P}_R^* \right\} > 0;$$

$$\hat{X}_I = \frac{1}{\Delta} \left\{ \frac{\lambda_{KF}}{\lambda_{KI}} \lambda_{LR} \frac{\sigma_R}{\theta_{TR}} \hat{P}_R^* \right\} < 0$$

where, $\Delta < 0$.

Consequently, $\hat{L}_F > 0$, $\hat{L}_I < 0$ and $\hat{L}_R > 0$.

Now, differentiating the condition of balanced trade, we get:

$$d\Omega = (\overline{w} - w)dL_F - dP_R^* M_R + t_F P_F^* dM_F + t_I P_I^* dM_I \quad (6.3.1)$$

which leads to:

$$\frac{d\Omega}{dP_R^*} \underset{>}{\overset{\leq}{}} 0, iff \left\{ (\overline{w} - w)\frac{dL_F}{dP_R^*} - M_R + t_I P_I^* \frac{dM_I}{dP_R^*} + t_F P_F^* \frac{dM_F}{dP_R^*} \right\} \underset{>}{\overset{\leq}{}} 0. (6.3.2)$$

APPENDIX 6B

Proof of Propositions 6.4 and 6.5.

Effect of a change in tariff:

Using (6.13) and (6.16) we derive

$$\frac{\overline{W}a_{LX}X}{W} + a_{LY}Y = L - \frac{a_{LZ}}{a_{TZ}}T \quad (6B.1)$$

Differentiating the above relation and (6.14), we get the equations of proportional changes denoted by '∧'.

$$\lambda_{LX}\hat{X} + \lambda_{LY}\hat{Y} = \delta_L \hat{W} \quad (6B.2)$$

$$\lambda_{KX}\hat{X} + \lambda_{KY}\hat{Y} = -\delta_K \hat{W} \quad (6B.3)$$

where, $\delta_L, \delta_K > 0$.

Derivations here follow Beladi and Marjit (1996). Now from competitive price conditions we get, $\hat{r} = \dfrac{\hat{\rho}}{\theta_{KX}}$, where, $\rho = (1+t)$

Therefore,

$$\hat{W} = \frac{\hat{P}_Y - \dfrac{\theta_{KY}}{\theta_{KX}}\hat{\rho}}{\theta_{LY}} \tag{6B.4}$$

$$0^{\wedge} > W \text{ as } 0^{\wedge} < \tau$$

Therefore we have:

$$\hat{X} = \frac{1}{|\lambda|}\begin{vmatrix} \delta_L \hat{W} & \lambda_{LY} \\ -\delta_K \hat{W} & \lambda_{KY} \end{vmatrix} = \frac{1}{|\lambda|}(\delta_L \lambda_{KY} + \delta_K \lambda_{LY})\hat{W}$$

where, $|\lambda| = \left[\dfrac{\overline{W}a_{LX}a_{KY}}{W} - a_{KX}a_{LY}\right] < 0$

(by stronger factor intensity assumption), hence:

$$\hat{Y} = \frac{1}{|\lambda|}\begin{vmatrix} \lambda_{LX} & \delta_L \hat{W} \\ \lambda_{KX} & -\delta_K \hat{W} \end{vmatrix} = \frac{-\hat{W}}{|\lambda|}(\delta_L \lambda_{KX} + \delta_K \lambda_{LX})\hat{W} = \hat{W}.A, \quad A > 0,$$

So that,

$$\hat{Y} = \frac{\hat{P}_Y - \dfrac{\theta_{KY}}{\theta_{KX}}\hat{\rho}}{\theta_{LY}}.A = \frac{\hat{P}_Y}{\theta_{LY}}.A + \frac{\theta_{KY}}{\theta_{KX}\theta_{LY}}(-\hat{\rho}).A \tag{6B.5}$$

Note that when Y is a traded good and P_Y is given, $\hat{X} < 0$, $\hat{Y} > 0$. If Y is a non-traded good, demand for Y and supply of Y must equate locally. Let us therefore postulate a demand function for Y:

$$\hat{Y}_D = \mu_1\hat{\rho} - \mu_2\hat{P}_Y \tag{6B.6}$$

A change in ρ has both income and substitution effects on demand for Y. While the substitution effect is negative, that is, a drop in ρ reduces Y_D, the income effect can go either way. μ_1, captures both these effects. μ_2, however, is own price effect and in general equilibrium models, any change in P_Y will render an income effect as well. We will assume that the substitution effect dominates and μ_1 and μ_2 are positive.

Equating (6B.5) and (6B.6) we get the equilibrating change in P_Y as:

$$\frac{\hat{P}_Y}{\theta_{LY}}.A + \frac{\theta_{KY}}{\theta_{KX}\theta_{LY}}(-\hat{\rho}).A = \mu_1\hat{\rho} - \mu_2\hat{P}_Y \tag{6B.7}$$

or,

$$\hat{P}_Y = \left\{ \frac{\hat{\rho}\left[\mu_1 + \dfrac{\theta_{KY}A}{\theta_{KX}\theta_{LY}}\right]}{\mu_2 + \dfrac{A}{\theta_{LY}}} \right\} < 0 \qquad (6B.8)$$

Therefore:

$$\hat{W} = \frac{\hat{\rho}\left[\mu_1 + \dfrac{\theta_{KY}A}{\theta_{KX}\theta_{LY}}\right]}{\left(\mu_2 + \dfrac{A}{\theta_{LY}}\right)\theta_{LY}} - \frac{\theta_{KY}}{\theta_{KX}}\hat{\rho} = \hat{\rho}\frac{\mu_1\theta_{KX}\theta_{LY} + \theta_{KY}A}{(\mu_2\theta_{LY} + A)\theta_{KX}\theta_{LY}} - \frac{\hat{\rho}\theta_{KY}}{\theta_{KX}\theta_{LY}}$$

Or, $\hat{W} = -\dfrac{\hat{\rho}}{\theta_{KX}\theta_{LY}}\left[\theta_{KY} - \dfrac{\mu_1\theta_{KX}\theta_{LY} + \theta_{KY}A}{(\mu_2\theta_{LY} + A)}\right]$

So, rearranging

$$\hat{W} = -\frac{\hat{\rho}}{\theta_{KX}\theta_{LY}}\left[\frac{\theta_{LY}\left(\mu_2\theta_{KX} - \theta_{KX}\mu_1\right)}{\left(\mu_2\theta_{LY} + A\right)}\right] \qquad (6B.9)$$

Therefore, $\hat{W} > 0$, if, $\mu_2 > \dfrac{\theta_{KX}}{\theta_{KY}}.\mu_1$

We now look at the effect of a decline in t on total unemployment, through L_E.

$$L_E = a_{LX}X + a_{LY}Y + a_{LZ}Z = L - \frac{\overline{W}a_{LX}X}{W} + a_{LX}X$$

$$= L - a_{LX}X\left(\frac{\overline{W}}{W} - 1\right)$$

Therefore, $\hat{L}_E > 0$, iff, $\left[a_{LX}X + \left(\dfrac{\overline{W}}{W} - 1\right)\right] < 0$

Or, $\hat{L}_E > 0$, iff, $\left[\left\{-\theta_{KX}\sigma_X(-\hat{r}) + \hat{W}.B\right\} - \hat{W}\dfrac{\dfrac{\overline{W}}{W}}{\left(\dfrac{\overline{W}}{W} - 1\right)}\right] < 0,$

where, $B = \dfrac{1}{|\lambda|}(\delta_L\lambda_{KY} + \delta_K\lambda_{LY}) < 0$

Hence, $\hat{L}_E > 0$, *iff,* $\sigma_X \cdot \hat{\rho} + \hat{W} \left\{ B - \dfrac{\dfrac{\overline{\overline{W}}}{\overline{W}}}{\left(\dfrac{\overline{\overline{W}}}{\overline{W}} - 1 \right)} \right\} < 0$ (6B.10)

It is now readily available from (6B.10) that since $\hat{\rho} < 0$ and $B<0$, $\hat{L}_E > 0$, if, $\hat{W} > 0$.

We have already noted that for $\hat{P}_Y = 0$, it is still the case that $\hat{W} > 0$ as $\hat{\rho} < 0$.

Therefore, $\hat{L}_E > 0$ must hold when ρ goes down—constituting the main proposition of the second model in this chapter. The general expression for (6B.10) is given by (after substitution for $\hat{W}$):

$$\sigma_X \hat{\rho} - \hat{\rho} \left[\frac{(\mu_2 \theta_{KY} - \theta_{KX} \mu_1)}{\theta_{KX}(\mu_2 \theta_{LY} + A)} \right] \left\{ B - \frac{\dfrac{\overline{\overline{W}}}{\overline{W}}}{\left(\dfrac{\overline{\overline{W}}}{\overline{W}} - 1 \right)} \right\}$$

$$= \hat{\rho} \left[\sigma_X - \left[\frac{(\mu_2 \theta_{KY} - \theta_{KX} \mu_1)}{\theta_{KX}(\mu_2 \theta_{LY} + A)} \right] \left\{ B - \frac{\dfrac{\overline{\overline{W}}}{\overline{W}}}{\left(\dfrac{\overline{\overline{W}}}{\overline{W}} - 1 \right)} \right\} \right]$$

Therefore as $\hat{\rho} < 0$, $\hat{L}_E > 0$ *iff:*

$$\sigma_X > \left[\frac{(\theta_{KY} \mu_2 - \theta_{KX} \mu_1)}{\theta_{KX}(\mu_2 \theta_{LY} + A)} \right] \left\{ B - \frac{\dfrac{\overline{\overline{W}}}{\overline{W}}}{\left(\dfrac{\overline{\overline{W}}}{\overline{W}} - 1 \right)} \right\}$$ (6B.11)

Since the bracketed term in RHS of (6B.11) is negative, a sufficient condition for an increase in employment following a decline in t is given by:

$$\frac{(\theta_{KY} \mu_2 - \theta_{KX} \mu_1)}{\theta_{KX}(\mu_2 \theta_{LY} + A)} > 0$$

which is also the condition for an increase in W. QED

7　The Extended Heckscher-Ohlin Framework with the Informal Sector

We are keen on demonstrating that a majority of the results derived so far are equally tenable in the extended form Heckscher-Ohlin trade theoretic models. This chapter, therefore, provides a set of examples where formal and informal sector production/service activities coexist for similar product/service categories where labour is fully mobile and capital as an input is classified into several specific-factor categories within and outside formal production facilities. The two models that we develop in this chapter are fairly appropriate representations of the true dualistic (formal–informal) production patterns in most developing countries.

Using an extended 2 × 2 Heckscher-Ohlin-Samuelson (HOS) structure with a formal–informal production organization for the same commodity, we show that a tariff cut in the import-competing sector increases both informal wages and employment under fairly reasonable assumptions. An increase in the price of the export commodity will also increase informal wages, although aggregate informal employment unambiguously falls even if the informal export sector is labour-intensive. Further, the formal–informal segmentation of each sector opens up an interesting, hitherto unexplored, possibility that the informal export sector may contract despite a price increase in this sector. Change in the overall size of the export sector is also ambiguous and conditional on the relative strengths of the changes in these two segments. We derive and analyse these effects with the help of a model that is referred to as the 'first model'.

Further, under similar specifications, if unionized wage adjusts to a cost of living index and coexists with a purely market driven informal wage, the well-known Stolper-Samuelson type results hold without any assumptions on factor intensity rankings. The proposed results are exposited through the 'second model' in this chapter.

Stallings and Peres (2000) discuss a related issue on trade and income inequality in developing countries, whereby a decline in informal wages implies further impoverishment of a low-income labour force. Earlier, the impact of trade on income inequality in the developing world was discussed by Attanasio et al. (2004), Hanson and Harrison (1999), Feenstra and Hanson (2001), Goldberg and Pavcnik (2003), Marjit and Acharyya (2003), and Marjit et al. (2004) among others. Further, the institution of dual labour markets and associated issues of interest in developing country labour markets have been raised in Agenor (1996), Agenor and Montiel (1996), Harrison and Leamer (1997), and Saint-Paul (1996).

This chapter is an improvement over existing results in the sense that we rule out: (i) vertical linkage and (ii) the issue of capital mobility, although, the unifying link between the present study and the rest is that they discuss similar problems, that is, the effect of contraction in a previously protected formal sector on the changes in informal competitive wages.

In addition, the description of the sectors as formal or unionized and informal or non-unionized remains the same.[1] To focus on wages and employment in the informal labour market, we take a very conventional route of defining the formal sector as unionized. Trade unions make sure that wages are decided through negotiations. We have already elaborated this approach in earlier chapters. What we offer here, however, is a traditional HOS 2×2 framework with each good being produced both in the formal and informal sectors, and yet we obtain a result which suggests that the informal sector, crowded by an influx of retrenched workers from the formal segment, can still exhibit rise in wages. It allows one to use full-employment models in a wage-differential framework. With this backdrop our study formulates the first model, a close analogue of the standard HOS structure, and proves that a decline in tariff rate should increase informal wages in a developing economy.

Finally, with regard to the cohesiveness of unionized wages to the cost of living index, as proposed earlier, we revisit the well-known Stolper-Samuelson (henceforth, S-S) theorem and its unconditional applicability when there are adjustments owing to exogenous shocks. Albeit the Stolper-Samuelson theorem is not necessarily agreeable to empirical evidence in many cases, there should be little doubt that the theorem constitutes the cornerstone of neo-classical trade theory. Time and again, there have been considerable debates on the close association between trade and income distribution and the S-S theorem has been at the heart of it. A paper by Jones and Engerman (1996) emphasizes the contribution of this famous result in view of several such debates.

Now, the second model in this chapter allows wage indexation for members of the labour union in an otherwise segmented labour market characterizing a developing country. It establishes that the internal redistribution in the country subject to changes heralded by international trade strongly replicates the well-known theorem. In other words, it would imply that the formal–informal wage gap, and the ratio of returns between labour and capital follow expected directionality, with an added feature that the results are independent of prior intensity assumptions. In an earlier attempt, Jones and Marjit (1985) discussed sustenance of the celebrated theorem in multiple dimensions. Further, Marjit (1987) provided a multi-country Ricardian analogue of the HOS model where the world production structure naturally leads to S-S results, similarly without assumptions on factor intensity. None of these, however, routed the analysis through a channel that offers substantial complexities in terms of production organization in developing countries. This is what the second model in this chapter claims as novel and interesting.

This model, therefore, describes a framework that incorporates a fixed-wage, unionized (or organized) sector, with the nominal wage tuned to the cost of living parameters. In addition, assume that there is an informal sector with a competitively determined and flexible wage sector. Assuming that the production functions display neo-classical characteristics, we hold that capital as an input is employed in both these sectors and readily relocates to the one offering relatively higher return per unit. Production functions exhibit constant returns to scale and diminishing marginal productivities. Markets are competitive, and commodity prices are exogenous owing to the assumption of a small open economy. We show that in such a structure a S-S type relationship exists between returns to capital and the informal wage rate, on the one hand, and commodity prices, on the other, and that such a relationship does not depend on the assumption of factor intensity—a very basic requirement of the standard S-S result. This structure is also amenable to interpretations under specific factor models as developed in Jones (1971) and Samuelson (1971).

THE FIRST MODEL AND ITS EQUILIBRIUM

Let us consider a two-sector small open economy producing X, an import-competing good and Y an export good with neo-classical technology. Each sector has a formal and informal segment. The formal segment has contracted workers with fixed wages, higher than those paid in the informal segment.[2] Formal wages are always higher than informal wages because labour laws allow various benefits to formal workers but not to informal workers. Second, the micro-theoretic foundation of the dual wage system, established in Goldberg and Pavcnik (2003) can be applied here as well.

As we have argued throughout this book, joining the informal sector is subject only to unavailability of formal industrial jobs in the urban areas of developing countries. As wage is allowed to adjust, there is usually no open unemployment in the real cases, which finds appropriate representation in these models. The other important assumption in this chapter is that capital can move freely within the informal segment and equalize returns. But there is no mobility of capital between the formal and informal segments. Within the formal segment also, let us assume capital to be sector-specific. It turns out that the first assumption is far more crucial than the second. We shall take up the second when we discuss the detailed working of the model. Violation of the second assumption should not jeopardize our result.

In fact, there is more to it than casual empiricism. The interest differential between the formal and informal sectors is relatively inelastic suggesting that the flow of capital is not without frictions. In fact, the assumption behind such general immobility of capital between the formal and informal sectors is rather generic principally owing to the lack of transparency and legal status of the latter organization. Therefore, despite sufficient incentives for formal capital to relocate to the low-wage informal segment, bank loans and other formal sources of credit need compliance with legal status and collaterals, which most informal units would not be able to satisfy. Possibilities of punitive actions/closures/evictions on these units via state policies render formal investments extremely risky. Additionally, of course, there could be other standard issues like moral hazard and other forms of costs that restrict easy flow of capital from formal to informal sectors.[3] Moreover, there is a theoretical motivation behind this assumption. In the first model of this chapter we deliberately close the avenue for such a mechanism to operate and still obtain the improved results. Nevertheless, we discuss some mobility issue later in the chapter.

Given these assumptions and that of a competitive small economy, we set up the following equations.

The competitive price conditions are:

$$a_{LX}\bar{w} + a_{KX}r_X = P_X(1+t) \tag{7.1}$$

$$\tilde{a}_{LX}w + \tilde{a}_{KX}R = P_X(1+t) \tag{7.2}$$

$$a_{LY}\bar{w} + a_{KY}r_Y = P_Y \tag{7.3}$$

$$\tilde{a}_{LY}w + \tilde{a}_{KY}R = P_Y \tag{7.4}$$

Full-employment conditions:

$$a_{LX}X + a_{LY}Y + \tilde{a}_{LX}\tilde{X} + \tilde{a}_{LY}\tilde{Y} = L \tag{7.5}$$

$$a_{KX}X = K_X \tag{7.6}$$

$$a_{KY}Y = K_Y \tag{7.7}$$

$$\tilde{a}_{KX}\tilde{X} + \tilde{a}_{KY}\tilde{Y} = \tilde{K} \tag{7.8}$$

where, P_i is the price of ith good, $i = X, Y$; $\bar{w}$ is the formal wage and w the informal wage; $r_i(i = X, Y)$ is return to capital specific to the formal segment, while R is return to capital specific to the informal segment; $a_{ij}(\tilde{a}_{ij})$ is the input–output coefficient in the formal (informal) segment; L is the inelastic supply of labour; and $\tilde{K}$ is the stock of informal capital, whereas $K_i(i = X, Y)$ is the stock of formal capital. Goods X and Y are produced in the formal sector, while $\tilde{X}$ and $\tilde{Y}$ are produced in the informal segment of the economy. If $r_X = r_Y$, that is, we assume mobility of capital within the formal segment, it is likely that either (7.1) or (7.3) will not bind. To avoid the case of complete specialization we assume $r_X \neq r_Y$. But there are more subtle and profound institutional reasons behind this assumption.

ANALYSIS OF THE FIRST MODEL

Decline in 't'

Let us now consider the case of a fall in the tariff rate, t. A decline in t marks the initiative of trade reforms. This will reduce r_X, reduce a_{LX}, and in turn, raise a_{KX}. It is obvious from (7.6) that all of this causes X to go down. Note that there will be no effect on Y as P_Y is held fixed. Therefore, from (7.5) it is straightforward to conclude that aggregate informal employment, that is, $(\tilde{a}_{LX}\tilde{X} + \tilde{a}_{LY}\tilde{Y})$ must increase. In the meantime, formal workers lose jobs and move to the informal segment. Based on this outcome, we have the following proposition.

PROPOSITION 7.1.   *Even if there is a rise in aggregate informal employment, informal wage w will rise if and only if, $\tilde{X}$ is capital-intensive relative to $\tilde{Y}$*

Proof.   This is a distinct implication of the Stolper-Samuelson theorem once we consider equations (7.2) and (7.4). As t goes down, R must go down and w must go up, given P_Y, if and only if $\tilde{Y}$ is labour-intensive. This assumption will go well with our intuition. If the import-competing good in a developing country is capital-intensive, and if there is no reversal of intensity rankings between the formal and informal segments within a particular sector, it is natural to presume that the informal segment of the export sector is labour-intensive compared to the informal segment of the import-competing sector.

The Rybczynski analogue of this result would imply higher $\tilde{Y}$ and lower $\tilde{X}$. Both X and $\tilde{X}$ go down and Y does not change. Therefore, $\left[\dfrac{Y + \tilde{Y}}{X + \tilde{X}} \right]$ must go up. This is the standard aggregate output effect of a relative price change. As long as the relative price of the capital-intensive good falls, wages improve. What is striking is that such a process releases labour from the formal to the informal segment, creating excess supply of labour in the informal sector. But the excess supply does not depress wages because increasing output of the labour-intensive good absorbs the excess number of workers. Factor price adjustment is independent of endowment changes as long as the endowment ratio in this segment lies in the cone of diversification, a well-known property of the HOS system. Therefore, informal wages go up even if more people find jobs in the informal sector.

Note that a decline in t may induce wage renegotiations. Suppose, $\bar{w}$ is also reduced following a tariff cut. This will contain the decline in the rate of interest on capital, although it is obvious that, $\hat{r}_X < 0$ for $\hat{\bar{w}} \leq \hat{t}$. Hence, our results will remain unchanged.[4]

Increase in 'P_Y'

Next, consider an increase in the price of the export good, such that, $\hat{P}_Y > 0$. For the formal segment of sector Y, this would imply an increase in r_Y, and subsequently an increase in Y and a_{LY}. Employment in the formal segment of Y must increase on account of this, and in the process relocate labour away from the informal segment to the formal segment of Y. On the other hand, under the assumption that $\tilde{Y}$ is labour-intensive compared to $\tilde{X}$, a rise in P_Y increases w and lowers R by the Stolper-Samuelson effect. An interesting possibility, however, exists with regard to output effects in sectors $\tilde{Y}$ and $\tilde{X}$. Contrary to conventional wisdom, an increase in the price of the export good Y may in fact lead to a contraction in the informal segment of this sector. Although the formal segment of Y unambiguously expands, the overall size of sector Y may still contract due to a possible adverse impact on its informal segment.

Intuitively, two cross-effects work within this sector in creating such a possibility. On the one hand, expansion in the formal segment of Y draws labour away from its informal segment and may lead to a contraction in output. On the other hand, price effect in sector Y directly favours an expansion of output in both the segments of this sector. The formal segment of sector X, however, remains unaffected since there has been no change in the price of commodity X. Therefore, $(a_{LX}X + a_{LY}Y)$ must increase while aggregate informal employment, $(\tilde{a}_{LX}\tilde{X} + \tilde{a}_{LY}\tilde{Y})$ must fall. The following proposition is immediate.

PROPOSITION 7.2.   *A rise in the price of Y unambiguously lowers aggregate informal employment and raises informal wages and may contract aggregate output of sector Y, if it is relatively capital-intensive compared to $\tilde{Y}$*

Proof.   A detailed mathematical proof is provided in Appendix 7A.

CAPITAL MOBILITY IN THE FORMAL SEGMENT

As we have stated earlier, equations (7.1) and (7.3) both should not hold simultaneously with $r_X = r_Y$. Suppose they do not and without any tariff (that is, at, $t = 0$), $r_Y > r_X$. Therefore, t must be adjusted for the formal import competing sector to survive. This creates another problem because now there are three full employment conditions to solve for four output levels. We assume that the government decides on the allocation of K_X and K_Y in these sectors through a maze of licenses and quantitative restrictions. This solves the problem of the determination of equilibrium.

Suppose now 't' falls *ceteris paribus*. This will completely wipe out the X sector. All formal capital will flow into Y. So X goes down and Y goes up. It is obvious that w will increase anyway since (7.2) and (7.4) are not disturbed. The Rybczynski effect is not so unambiguous now. If $a_{LY}Y$ increases substantially, $\tilde{X}$ may go up and $\tilde{Y}$ may go down. But there will be standard forces working against this result.

This is essentially a 'jump'. If a substantial amount of locked-in capital from sector X goes to sector Y, output in Y will increase substantially.

Note that r in Y does not change. But such r cannot be sustained in sector X. Therefore, a_{LY} will not change. If the rise in Y is substantial, then informal workers will be pulled back into the formal segment. But as w rises and R falls, $(\tilde{a}_{LX}, \tilde{a}_{LY})$ will also go down reducing the requirement of labour in the informal pool. Thus, two effects will dictate the impact of employment in the formal and informal sectors. This will also dictate the impact on $(\tilde{X}, \tilde{Y})$. It is possible that while Y expands, $\tilde{Y}$ goes down. In fact, it is more likely that bigger is the rise in Y, greater is the negative effect on $\tilde{Y}$, since now, the labour constraint becomes more binding.

THE SECOND (UNIONIZED) MODEL

As we have identified the possibility of wage indexation for union members, this section devotes itself to this treatment. We define $\overline{W}_X$, as the unionized wage rate for workers in the formal sector X. Conversely, W_Y is the informal wage received by those in sector Y, also depicting the output levels when commodity prices are given by P_X and P_Y, and determined endogenously. For all practical purposes, we assume $\overline{W}_X > W_Y$.

As before, the competitive equilibrium conditions in the commodity markets imply:

$$a_{LX} \overline{W}_X + a_{KX} r = P_X \tag{7.9}$$

$$a_{LX} W_Y + a_{KY} r = P_Y \tag{7.10}$$

The wage indexation leads to adjustment of W_X to a cost of living index, that is:

$$\hat{\overline{W}}_X = \alpha \hat{P}_X + (1-\alpha)\hat{P}_Y, \quad 0 < \alpha < 1 \tag{7.11}$$

where, α represents the share of expenditure on X, and $(1-\alpha)$ represents expenditure share on Y. Full employment conditions imply that:

$$a_{LX} X + a_{LY} Y = \overline{L} \tag{7.12}$$

and,
$$a_{KX} X + a_{KY} Y = \overline{K} \tag{7.13}$$

As it is standard for these types of models, a_{ij}'s depends only on factor price ratios by the assumption of constant returns to scale. Consequently, P_X and P_Y, $\overline{W}_X$, r and W_Y will be determined from equations (7.9), (7.10) and (7.11).[5] Finally, X and Y are simultaneously determined from (7.4) and (7.5).

Based on this structure we can propose a Stolper-Samuelson result characterizing the expected relationship between changes in factor and commodity prices.

PROPOSITION 7.3.   *Given the above structure, the following rankings must hold:*

$$\hat{r} > \hat{P}_X > 0 = \hat{P}_Y > \hat{W}_Y \ and \ \hat{W}_Y > \hat{P}_Y > 0 = \hat{P}_X > \hat{r}$$

Proof. Consider $\hat{P}_X > 0$ *and* $\hat{P}_Y = 0$. From (7.3), it follows that $\hat{\overline{W}}_X = \alpha \hat{P}_X < \hat{P}_X$, whereas, differentiating (7.9) and using the familiar envelope condition, it directly implies that $\hat{P}_X$ must lie between $\hat{\overline{W}}_X$ and $\hat{r}$. Since $\hat{\overline{W}}_X < \hat{P}_X$, then $\hat{r} > \hat{P}_X > 0$. Also, as $\hat{P}_Y = 0$ and $r > 0$, $\hat{W}_Y < 0$.
This proves that the first ranking in Proposition 7.3 holds.

Now consider a case where $\hat{P}_Y > 0$ and $\hat{P}_X = 0$. As $\hat{\overline{W}}_X = (1-\alpha)\hat{P}_Y > 0$, owing to this assumption regarding price changes, $\hat{r} < 0$.

Again, as $\hat{r} < 0$ and given the above assumption on price of Y, $\hat{W}_Y > \hat{P}_Y$. This proves that the second ranking in Proposition 7.3 also holds. QED

Note that for these proofs, we do not require any assumption on intensity rankings apart from the condition that they need to be different to facilitate deterministic solutions. It is easy to verify that if $\overline{W}_X$ is independent of (P_X, P_Y) the first ranking will continue to hold, but the second one shall be violated. Essentially, we prove that Y may be deemed rather capital-intensive, but a rise in P_Y raises W_Y and reduces r.

It is interesting to note that for the Rybczynski Theorem to hold in this structure, one needs to make an explicit assumption regarding capital intensity in each sector. Consider the full-employment conditions in equations (7.4) and (7.5). Given (P_X, P_Y), factor prices are determined and so are (a_{ij}). It is obvious that a rise in K or L will change X and Y depending on the factor intensity ranking. In the S-S case, it is the wage adjustment mechanism in the organized sector that gives the unambiguous result. Since the core of the Stolper-Samuelson Theorem is the welfare effect of a change in commodity prices on the owner of each factor of production, it is natural to explore such welfare implications in the present model. As there is no inter-sectoral difference in the return to capital, the capitalist's welfare can be represented by a standard indirect utility function, which can thus be manoeuvred to establish that such owners gain (lose) with an increase in P_X (P_Y).

Let us now focus on the level of welfare accruing to workers in general. For this purpose, assume that the utility function facing each worker is homothetic and their respective expenditure functions are denoted by:

$$g(P_X, P_Y)h(u) \tag{7.14}$$

where, $h(.)$ is an increasing function of each worker's utility level u. Assume further that the union keeps the utility of each union member at a certain level, say $\bar{u}$. Without loss of generality, we can therefore rewrite, $h(\bar{u}) = 1$. Thus, we have:

$$\overline{W}_X = g(P_X, P_Y) \tag{7.15}$$

Thus, using above notation we depict $\dfrac{\delta g}{\delta P_X} \dfrac{P_X}{g} = \alpha$ and, $\dfrac{\delta g}{\delta P_Y} \dfrac{P_Y}{g} = 1 - \alpha$ with $0 < \alpha < 1$. The expected utility of a worker is given by:

$$U = \frac{a_{LX} X}{\bar{L}} \cdot 1 + \frac{a_{LY} Y}{\bar{L}} \frac{W_Y}{\overline{W}_X} \tag{7.16}$$

Subject to introduction of this reformulation, consider a change in P_X *ceteris paribus*. Rewriting (7.16) and differentiating, we get:

$$dU = -d\left(\frac{a_{LY} Y}{\bar{L}}\right)\left(\frac{1 - W_Y}{\overline{W}_X}\right) - \left(\frac{a_{LY} Y}{\bar{L}} d\right)\left(\frac{1 - W_Y}{\overline{W}_X}\right)$$

$$dU = -\lambda_{LY}(\hat{a}_{LY} + \hat{Y})\left(\frac{1 - W_Y}{\overline{W}_X}\right) + \lambda_{LY}\left(\frac{dW_Y}{W_Y} - \frac{d\overline{W}_X}{\overline{W}_X}\right) \tag{7.17}$$

where, λ_{LY} is the share of total labour force employed in sector Y. Working through the model and using derivations and results as in Jones (1965) we obtain:

$$\hat{Y} = -\frac{\left|(\hat{\overline{W}}_X - \hat{r})_{S_X} + (\hat{W}_Y - \hat{r})_{S_Y}\right|}{|\lambda|} \tag{7.18}$$

and,

$$\hat{a}_{LY} = -\sigma_Y \theta_{KY}(\hat{W}_Y - \hat{r}) \tag{7.19}$$

where, $|\lambda| = \begin{bmatrix} \lambda_{LX} & \lambda_{LY} \\ \lambda_{KX} & \lambda_{KY} \end{bmatrix}$, σ_Y is the elasticity of factor substitution in Y and (S_X, S_Y) are positive numbers denoting supply elasticity in X and Y, respectively. We know that: $(\overset{\wedge}{\overline{W}}_X - \hat{r}) < 0$. and $(\hat{W}_Y - \hat{r}) < 0$. Thus, if X is labour-intensive, and if $|\lambda| < 0$ and $\hat{Y} > 0$, then also $\hat{a}_{LY} > 0, \hat{W}_y < 0$ and $\overline{W}_X > 0$. Therefore, with $\overline{W}_X > W_Y, dU < 0$ in (7.17). On the basis of these results, the following proposition conveys the essential message.

PROPOSITION 7.4.   *If the unionized sector is labour-intensive, a rise in P_X means that workers become worse-off*

Proof. A clear intuitive appeal lies behind this proposition. As P_X increases and capital becomes expensive, the capital constraint is relaxed through factor substitution and Y sector expands in production. Labour is reallocated from the high-wage to the low-wage sector and the real wage for both types of labour—formal and informal—falls. If the unionized sector is capital-intensive, Y will fall, although $\overline{W}_X$, W_Y and a_{LY} should improve. Relationship (7.17) reveals that if the decrease in Y is too strong, then the workers must be better off. If $|\lambda|$ is close to zero, the increase in Y will be very large and workers should gain. A relatively low value of $|\lambda|$, on the other hand, implies that factor intensities are not very close to begin with.

What Proposition 7.4 indicates is that unlike factor-price behaviour, the real income changes will involve Rybczynski-type effects, reallocating labour from one sector to the other. Therefore, one needs explicit conditions on factor intensities. An increase in P_X, if X is labour-intensive, will reduce the supply of X. Hence, such an intensity assumption will be detrimental for the viability of this proposition. However, if X is capital-intensive, it will need restrictions on the magnitude of $|\lambda|$ for the welfare result. Similarly, one can work out the effects of a change in P_Y.[6]

* * *

This chapter formulated two varieties of a modified 2 × 2 HOS structure with formal and informal segments. We discussed the Stolper-Samuelson and Rybczynski type outcomes in this framework. One significant result is that even if trade reforms downsize the formal or the regulated segment, and drive labour into the informal segment, existing informal workers should gain under reasonable assumptions. Larger aggregate informal employment also implies higher informal wages. We discuss the prime results derived from each of these models in that order.

Interestingly, a cut in import tariff and a rise in export price do not have the same implications for aggregate informal employment. While a reduction in t definitely increases informal employment, a rise in P_Y increases formal sector employment. However, the wage implications are very similar. The reason behind the result is quite different from the ones discussed in Marjit (2003), which argues that capital mobility between the formal and the informal is crucial. In this chapter we restricted capital to move between the formal and informal sectors. Yet, informal wages improve along with informal employment because of the standard Stolper-Samuelson argument. Capital mobility between the formal and the informal sector becomes an important issue when we consider one formal and one informal sector, but not a pair of informal sectors as we considered in this chapter. In fact, the existence of two informal sectors that are prototypes of formal sectors, allows us to use the Stolper-Samuelson argument. In this case, even if capital does not move between the formal segment and the pair of informal sectors, it does not affect our conjectured results. Finally, the first model essentially expands a set of recent papers which argue that trade reforms can be quite helpful to the existing set of informal workers.

In the second model we proposed a wage differential model in a simple general equilibrium framework. Such a structure draws from the extensive empirical evidence available on developing countries and is very close to the standard neo-classical model. Unions can fight to absorb part of the price increase through an increase in nominal wages, a well-accepted approach in the discipline. Informal wages are entirely market-determined. With the help of the second model we demonstrated that the celebrated Stolper-Samuelson ranking holds in this set-up without any assumption on intensity ranking. An interesting implication of the analysis is that capitalists may not like a rise in the price of goods produced in the informal sector (P_Y), even if they employ a lot of capital in that sector, simply because it raises $\overline{W}_X$, and the price of goods produced in the unionized sector (P_X) does not change. In standard general equilibrium models $\overline{W}_X = W_Y$, therefore, relative demand for capital must expand if the capital-intensive sector expands. In this case, however, $\overline{W}_X$ adjusts upward whenever P_Y increases.

NOTES

1. It is intrinsic to the description of formal and informal sectors in developing countries that 'formal' sector workers use collective bargaining as a wage-setting mechanism and include employees mainly from the government and registered

private manufacturing and service firms. Historically speaking, in any country, the collective bargaining starts with the participation of industrial workers—a tradition that has spread to later evolving service sectors and has typically ignored the agricultural sector. In many developing and transition countries, however, this participation rate is not more than 30 per cent of the total workforce, (see Kar and Marjit 2001 for details). The remaining large section of workers does not get the benefit of union membership, either in terms of pay nor job protection and are not even covered by national minimum wage acts (which exist but are rarely adhered to in the poor countries due to weak governance, strategic non-intervention, and so on) and are generally referred to as informal workers. Thus, another description of a formal sector will be where minimum wage regulations are strictly enforced, whereas in the informal sector such law is not properly enforced and wages can have a free fall.

2. In this example, one can allow for renegotiation of the fixed wage. We have checked that there will not be any qualitative change in the results already obtained. For example, a renegotiation in the fixed formal wage will redistribute the effects between labour and capital depending on the intensity assumption and shall not alter the direction of the previous outcome, where formal wage does not change (see Marjit et al. 2005).

3. Thus, whatever little capital flow exists, takes the form of outsourcing of formal production/services to the informal segment (vertical linkage, see Marjit 2003) and that which can be closely monitored by its formal counterpart. While these are definitely issues that require further research, it is clearly beyond the scope of this chapter.

4. In a fixed wage model choosing one of the prices as a numeraire generates theoretical problems, since nominal movements have real effects. Consider uniform rise in P_X and P_Y. In a full-employment model it should leave all real variables unaffected. Here, it will not be the case. Both X and Y will expand, $\tilde{X}$ will also expand but $\tilde{Y}$ will contract. R and w will increase by same proportion, but not r_X, r_Y. Hence, it is important that we explicitly work out the effects of a change in P_Y.

5. Equation (7.3) is stated in terms of a percentage change. One can write, $\bar{W}_X = \bar{W}_{XO} + f(P_X, P_Y)$ by using the general version of (7.3) without any change in directionality of our analysis. $\bar{W}_{XO}$ is exogenously given, and a change in $\bar{W}_{XO}$ is only in response to changes in P_X and P_Y.

6. We are indebted to Koji Shimomura for a better understanding of the welfare implications of a price change.

APPENDIX 7A

Using equations (7.2) and (7.4), and following Jones (1965) we get:

$$\hat{w} = -\frac{\tilde{\theta}_{KX}}{\Delta_1}\hat{P}_Y > 0 \ \ where \ \ \Delta_1 = (\tilde{\theta}_{LX}\tilde{\theta}_{KY} - \tilde{\theta}_{LY}\tilde{\theta}_{KX}) < 0, \hat{P}_Y > 0$$

and $\hat{R} = \dfrac{\tilde{\theta}_{LX}}{\Delta_1}\hat{P}_Y < 0$, such that, $(\hat{w} - \hat{R}) = \dfrac{\tilde{\theta}_{LX} - \tilde{\theta}_{KX}}{\Delta_1}\hat{P}_Y = \alpha\tilde{P}_Y$

From equation (7.3), it directly follows that $\hat{r}_Y = \dfrac{\hat{P}_Y}{\theta_{KY}} > 0.$

Now using the equation for labour constraint, (7.5), we get:

$$\tilde{\lambda}_{LX}\hat{\tilde{X}} + \tilde{\lambda}_{LY}\hat{\tilde{Y}} = \lambda_{LX}\sigma_X(\hat{\tilde{w}} - \hat{r}_X) + \lambda_{LY}\sigma_Y(\hat{\tilde{w}} - \hat{r}_Y)$$

$$+\tilde{\lambda}_{LX}\tilde{\sigma}_X\tilde{\theta}_{KX}(\hat{w} - \hat{R}) + \tilde{\lambda}_{LY}\tilde{\sigma}_Y\tilde{\theta}_{KY}(\hat{w} - \hat{R})$$

$$= -\frac{\lambda_{LY}}{\theta_{KY}}\sigma_Y\hat{P}_Y + [\tilde{\lambda}_{LX}\tilde{\sigma}_X\tilde{\theta}_{KX} + \tilde{\lambda}_{LY}\tilde{\sigma}_Y\tilde{\theta}_{KX}]\alpha\hat{P}_Y = -\varphi\hat{P}_Y + \alpha\beta\hat{P}_Y$$

$$= (\alpha\beta - \varphi)\hat{P}_Y$$

Finally, from equation (7.8):

$$\tilde{\lambda}_{KX}\hat{\tilde{X}} + \tilde{\lambda}_{KY}\hat{\tilde{Y}} = -[\tilde{\lambda}_{KX}\tilde{\sigma}_X\tilde{\theta}_{LX} - \tilde{\lambda}_{KY}\tilde{\sigma}_Y\tilde{\theta}_{LY}](\hat{w} - \hat{R})$$

or, $\ \ \tilde{\lambda}_{KX}\hat{\tilde{X}} + \tilde{\lambda}_{KY}\hat{\tilde{Y}} = -\phi\alpha\hat{P}_Y$

Using Cramer's rule to solve for $\hat{\tilde{X}}$ and $\hat{\tilde{Y}}$:

$$\hat{\tilde{Y}} = -\frac{[\tilde{\lambda}_{LX}\phi\alpha + \tilde{\lambda}_{KX}(\alpha\beta - \varphi)}{\Delta_2}\hat{P}_Y, \ \ where,$$

$$\Delta_2 = (\tilde{\lambda}_{LX}\tilde{\lambda}_{KY} - \tilde{\lambda}_{LY}\tilde{\lambda}_{KX}) < 0$$

Thus, given $\hat{P}_Y > 0$ and $\Delta_2 < 0, \hat{\tilde{Y}} > 0$, iff, $[\tilde{\lambda}_{LX}\phi\alpha + \tilde{\lambda}_{KX}(\alpha\beta - \varphi) > 0$

Simplifying which, $\hat{\tilde{Y}} > 0$, iff, $\left(\dfrac{\varphi - \alpha\beta}{\alpha\phi}\right)\left(\dfrac{\tilde{\lambda}_{KX}}{\tilde{\lambda}_{LX}}\right) < 1.$

Also, from equation (7.7):

$$\hat{Y} = -\hat{a}_{KY} = -\sigma_Y\theta_{LY}(\hat{\tilde{w}} - \hat{r}_Y) = \sigma_Y\frac{\theta_{LY}}{\theta_{KY}}\hat{P}_Y > 0$$

Therefore, change in the size of sector Y is given by Y_A (aggregated over formal and informal sector outputs):

$$\hat{Y}_A = s_Y \hat{Y} + (1 - s_Y)\hat{\tilde{Y}},$$

where, s_Y = Share of formal sector in aggeragte output of Y,

Thus,

$$\hat{Y}_A = s_Y \hat{Y} + (1 - s_Y)\hat{\tilde{Y}} = s_Y \sigma_Y \frac{\theta_{LY}}{\theta_{KY}} \hat{P}_Y -$$

$$(1 - s_Y)\frac{[\tilde{\lambda}_{LX}\phi\alpha + \tilde{\lambda}_{KX}(\alpha\beta - \varphi)]}{\Delta_2} \hat{P}_Y$$

such that, $\hat{Y}_A > 0$, *iff*, $s_Y \left\{ \sigma_Y \frac{\theta_{LY}}{\theta_{KY}} + \frac{[\tilde{\lambda}_{LX}\phi\alpha + \tilde{\lambda}_{KX}(\alpha\beta - \varphi)]}{\Delta_2} \right\} >$

$$\frac{[\tilde{\lambda}_{LX}\phi\alpha + \tilde{\lambda}_{KX}(\alpha\beta - \varphi)]}{\Delta_2}.$$

Simplifying, $\hat{Y}_A \underset{<}{\geq} 0$, *iff*, $\left\{ \frac{\theta_{LY}}{\theta_{KY}} \underset{<}{\geq} \frac{[\tilde{\lambda}_{LX}\phi\alpha + \tilde{\lambda}_{KX}(\alpha\beta - \varphi)]}{\Delta_2} \right\}$

$$\left(\frac{1}{s_Y \sigma_Y} - 1 \right).$$ QED

II
EMPIRICAL RESEARCH AND
FINDINGS ON INFORMAL SECTOR

8   Empirical Evidence for India

In recognition of the fact that a contemporary discussion of the informal sector as we have developed it so far remains incomplete without invoking adequate empirical evidence, we devote this and the subsequent chapters in Part II of this book towards such corroboration. However, it is best to admit that relating, for example, informal wages and trade liberalization via inter-sectoral capital mobility is a more difficult job empirically, than it is theoretically. The empirical structure is largely dependent on the availability and reliability of data on the informal sector. For India there exist surveys of informal units by NSSO—usually five-yearly samples drawn from almost all the provinces and union territories (that is, centrally/federally administered regions such as Delhi) in the more recent years. The survey covers average yearly wages, employment, major occupational categories by broad industry types, gender, fixed assets, and value added of the informal units classified as NDMEs and OAEs, both rural and urban in either case. The sample size varies from less than 100 units in relatively remote locations to more than 10,000 in major cities. Given this, our next concern is which variables to use that will serve the focus of this chapter best. To this end we take up only urban NDMEs given their strong inter-linkage with the urban formal sector for five consecutive rounds, 1984–5, 1989–90, 1994–5, 1999–2000 and 2000–1, for 17 states in the first period as per availability, which extends to all states and union territories for the remaining time period. We intend to show that the period of gradual trade liberalization in India, that is, the post-1991 decade, which led to the closure of many formal and traditional industries releasing unskilled labour in large numbers coincides significantly with annual (real) growth in: (i) urban informal wage (IW), (ii) urban informal fixed assets (as a proxy for capital formation, FA), and (iii) urban informal value added (VA). The latter two variables are used to explain the movement of the first.

The logic behind such modelling results from the observation that trade liberalization drives capital and labour into the informal sector and yet wages rise across states, steeply for some and moderately for the rest, leading to an average annual real wage growth of 10 per cent, somewhat contrary to conventional wisdom (see Figure 8A.1, Appendix 8A). The next section is devoted to exploring this relationship. As highlighted, the scarcity of secondary data often necessitates primary surveys to comprehend the condition of wages and employment in the informal sector. In a recent engagement, we accumulated some data on the production organization between the formal and informal producers/traders in rural locations in West Bengal. Several issues that are entangled in such a relationship along with the implications of structural changes that the country has generally witnessed are also discussed in this chapter. The chapter also traces the channels for capturing the organizational structures between formal and informal industries, explores marketing procedures and discusses regime shifts in traditional practices.

Maiti and Marjit (2008) offers an interesting discussion on garments and other handicrafts made from handlooms, brassware, hornware, clay works, conch shells, and similar items in rural West Bengal and finds a declining trend in favour of cooperative units due to greater intrusion of market forces in the post-reform period in India.

REFORMS AND INFORMAL WAGES IN INDIA

What could possibly explain the post-reform average increase in wages if more unskilled labour, which was formerly part of the organized sector flows into its informal counterpart due to contraction of formal industries and consequent unemployment? We use the available data and estimate annual growth in real wages (deflated by the 1989–90 consumer price index of India) in NDMEs with respect to annual growth in real FA and real VA in those units. A rise in FA, an equivalent to capital formation, is expected to affect informal wages positively as would a rise in the value added of each such unit. We offer regression analyses over yearly cross-sections for each round of data and subsequently pool the data for all the available years to run a panel regression on the same set of variables to capture the overall impact on real informal wages (Figures 8A.2 and 8A.3 in Appendix 8A provide the annual growth rates of real *FA* and real *VA* respectively). Table 8A.1 (in Appendix 8A) offers detailed descriptive statistics for the variables under consideration and Table 8A.2 in Appendix 8A shows that there does not exist a substantial problem of multi-collinearity among the variables.

The first of the two explanatory variables, informal fixed assets (real *FA*) grew at a temperate rate between 1984–5 and 1989–90 for many states (Figure 8A.2, Appendix 8A), although Assam (AS), Haryana (HY), Kerala (KE), Tripura (TR) and West Bengal (WB) registered negative growth. However, during 1989–90 and 1994–5, immediately after the reforms took effect in India, informal fixed assets showed high growth rate in most of the states while some reported negative growth (BH, HP, LA, ME, and so on). Between 1994–5 and 1999–2000 informal fixed assets grew positively (10 to 150 per cent) for 29 out of the 30 locations in India, with the exception of Manipur (MA). For some of the states, however, the growth in real fixed assets fell during 1999–2000 and 2000–1.

The second explanatory variable, real value added (*VA*) also registered a negative trend for all states, except Gujarat and West Bengal, during 1984–5 and 1989–90. It underwent a turnaround in the post-reform period, when most states and union territories showed a significant increase in value added. Finally between 1999–2000 and 2000–1 it reported negative growth rates in most states.

The dependent variable in our model, the growth rate of real informal wage (*IW*) shows negative growth for all the states between 1984–5 and 1989–90 (Figure 8A.1, Appendix 8A). The trend shifted substantially in favour of informal workers in the period immediately following the introduction of economic reforms in India. All the states, including GJ, MH, OR (22 per cent), TN, RJ (32 per cent), and AP (38 per cent) showed significant positive annual growth in informal wages. Between 1994–5 and 1999–2000, 29 out of the 30 locations, except WB (–2 per cent) showed moderate positive annual growth in informal wages and the post-reform average annual growth in informal wages was recorded at between 15–20 per cent with a variance of 26 per cent between the states.

Using the simple empirical model:

$$w_t = \alpha_t + \beta_1(FA)_t + \beta_2(VA)_t + \varepsilon_t \qquad (8.1)$$

where, *a* is constant, *w* is real informal wage, *t* is year, ε the error term and the rest as defined, we offer results from a generalized least square regression (Table 8A.3, Appendix 8A), after correcting for the presence of heteroscedasticity in the error terms. Between 1984–5 and 1989–90 (denoted as 1989–90 in Table 8A.3, Appendix 8A), all the elements significantly explain changes in informal real wages. Notably, the intercept term is negative. Admittedly, the explanatory power of the regression (adjusted R-squares) analysis declines over. Note that, the explanatory power of the regression analysis (adjusted R-squares) declines over time.

Subsequently, we offer a pooled (a pseudo panel) regression for these variables:

$$w_{it} = \alpha + \beta X_{it} + \varepsilon_{it} \tag{8.2}$$

where, w_{it} = real informal wage pooled for i states and t periods, $i = 1..N$, the number of states, β is the coefficient vector for the explanatory variables (X), $t = 1..T$ the time periods and ε follows $N(0, \sigma^2)$. The findings are reported in Table 8A.4 in Appendix 8A. The panel regression tests for whether the fixed effects (FE) or the random effects (RE) model is consistent with the data, given that FE/RE is the natural choice over the classical regression (CR) model since the value of the Lagrange Multiplier is very large. Further, between FE and RE the results from the Hausman test suggest that FE is the appropriate model to use. Consequently, we use the methodology of Least Squares Dummy Variables after correcting for heteroscedasticity. According to this model, however, the real FA is not significant, although with a positive impact on real IW. Real VA, on the other hand, is positive and highly significant (at the 1 per cent level) in explaining the increase in real IW. The panel regression is consistent with cross-section results, in that the real VA continues to be significant in explaining real informal wages while FA is not, although the general direction is positive as expected.

Albeit we did not provide a fuller empirical account, the data from NSSO also reveals that own account enterprises or self-employed units within the informal sector also experience positive growth in prices, output and participation. These empirical features characterizing the informal sector are reflected in the short theoretical model. In fact, theory predicts that the wages of informal workers should increase and the informal industrial commodity should expand production if the formal import competing sector contracts due to withdrawal of trade protection. The growth in value added and fixed assets in the NDMEs are approximations to this end. We now move on to localized issues in the production relations between the formal and informal units and deal with a case where the changes ushered in through greater openness deliver palpable implications for the organizational characteristics therein.

EXPORT MARKET AND PRODUCTION ORGANIZATION BETWEEN RURAL FORMAL AND INFORMAL INDUSTRIES[1]

This section offers a micro-level analysis of informalization on the basis of primary data from rural West Bengal. Since the mid-1980s India started the process of liberalizing her economy and since 1991 the process has been vigorously stepped up. The 'first generation reforms' emphasized on growth by encouraging conditions for private sector investment through reduction of taxes, opening up of foreign trade and investment, and fostering other deregulatory policies. The Ninth Five-Year Plan emphasized the acceleration of economic growth through speeding up the liberalization process and spoke of modernization and formalization as a corollary to this growth process by making it more market-friendly.

As in almost every other case, inviting significant changes in the way an economy and the larger society functions must transit through several contentious steps. In large and heterogeneous countries such as India, measuring the extent of tension between groups, communities, classes, religions, and occupations can in fact appear an unfathomable exercise in theory and empirics. Although much has been written on the economic, sociological, and political aspects bordering interests of selective groups and lobbies, the essential tension that exists between forces in a dual labour market has been somewhat neglected.

Here we endeavour to answer a few questions that might add to the terse literature on formal–informal interactions through the production organization. First, what are the characteristics of the formal and informal production organization? Second, how is the formal–informal production reorganization functioning in response to liberalization policies and greater market exposure, and to what extent? Third, what are the reasons behind rising segregation within the formal–informal production organization? This section provides an analysis of the formal–informal division of the production organization due to economic policy changes since the early 1990s in the Indian economy with reference to some manufacturing industries in West Bengal. Hence, it is a micro-statistical exercise to generate some direct understanding of the evolving process.

It is well-known that important policy changes have taken place since the opening up of trade (reduction in tariff and interest rates) and revision of financial limits facing production units under small-scale and cottage industries. In spite of growing competition from large-scale industries and MNCs, these policies create, to some extent, favourable conditions for the development of small-scale and rural industries, which gain by taking advantage of increasing demand from the national and overseas markets for crafts and aesthetic value oriented goods (handmade goods). As a consequence, units which have access to sufficient capital and marketing outlets expand fast. On the other hand, due to organizational differences and structural backwardness, larger production units get tied to *mahajan*s (the local term for moneylenders), traders, or master enterprises to canalize products to the national and overseas markets.

Transfer of production units from formal to informal categories arises basically owing to cost considerations involving formal wages and administrative and transaction costs in the formal units. As demand expands, specialization over stages of production gets intensified according to diversification in consumer demand. In addition, possible expansions are based on several allied considerations ranging from adherence to labour laws and compliance with legal requirements in running a factory set-up. As an alternative, if the expansion is made effective via outsourcing to the informal sector, then many of these legal requirements can be bypassed. Although such straight jacketing of the concept of fragmentation may not be valid everywhere, functionally it is often the case as we now argue.

The prevailing theories of firm organization cannot explain the existence of informal production organizations (like units under the putting out and subcontracting system at a relatively low scale). These studies establish the superiority of a firm organization over a non-firm organization like the putting out system (Alchian and Demsetz 1972; Coase 1937; Knight 1946; Simon 1991; Williamson et al. 1975). However, at the same time different forms of non-firm organizations have developed to reduce transaction costs in different ways or to tackle constraints of the organizational design. Through subcontracting, master enterprises or traders save administrative as well as supervision costs. Moreover, entrepreneurs residing in distant or remote rural areas face information gaps regarding markets and technology. Often, some intermediaries come up to gather information about market sources, product designs, types of products, and so on, and help bridge these gaps. Artisans with small capital stocks and drawing on their traditional hereditary skills become more dependent on these intermediaries providing services in exchange for a part of the profit. Besides, surplus rural masses are usually forced to search for alternative employment opportunities in lean seasons and usually engage in small-scale and cottage industries at the household level (Maiti 2004).

This may be deemed as a procedure which creates greater tie-ups between small producers and intermediaries as the outside market expands. This is related, in a different context, to a study by Marjit and

Roychowdhury (2004), which suggests that an expansion of market size usually leads to 'buy-outs' of existing joint ventures.

Database and Methodology

Given the limitations of the secondary data, a detailed primary survey was designed. The districts of West Bengal have different and diverse types of crafts and rural industries distributed over blocks, regions and villages. No secondary source provides the actual figures of industries by types at a decentralized level. Keeping these limitations in mind, this section tries to offer an appropriate sample design—a multi-stage stratified random sampling.

Sample Design

West Bengal was purposively chosen due to its significant rural industrial growth, a glorious crafts heritage and high population density.

Stage I: Selection of Districts

The districts of West Bengal have different agro-climatic and socio-economic characteristics. They also have a distinct handicraft heritage. Four districts were selected on the basis of stratified random sampling. The districts were segregated into two strata—the rural industrially-advanced and the rural industrially-backward districts on the basis of percentage share of workers in the main occupations[2] engaged in rural manufacturing, processing and repairing units (including home-based and non-home-based industries). A district with more than 8 per cent workers in rural industries was considered a relatively advanced district, and backward otherwise. The apparently abstruse figure of 8 per cent is a result of the distribution of such workforce according to the Census of India (1991) and interestingly the benchmark is such that an equal number of districts lie both above and below this share. Two sample districts were drawn from each stratum based on random sampling without replacement. Sample districts, Nadia and Midnapore, constitute the advanced strata while Bankura and Purulia the backward strata (see Table 8A.5).

For each district we prepared a list of units with the help of district level officers and knowledgeable persons in the districts (at the DIC, zilla parishad, and gram panchayat levels) and subsequently, two sets of industries—a common set of industries and district-specific industries. The common set of industries included those featuring in all sample districts, for example, the handloom industry, wood and wood products industry, iron and grill factory, brass and bell metal industry, and jewellery. Industries specific to particular districts generally included clay modelling and hat weaving (in the case of Nadia district); hornware, straw mattresses, and *zari* (in the case of Midnapore district); conch shells, *docra*, and terracotta products (in Bankura district) and lac and *chhou masks* (in Purulia district). Two common industries from the *common set* and one district-specific industry from *each sample district* were randomly selected. The common industries covered handloom and brassware industries while the district-specific sample industries included clay works from Nadia, hornware from Midnapore, conch shells from Bankura, and lac work from Purulia.

Stage II: Selection of Blocks

From each sample district a list of blocks by types of industry was prepared with the help of the zilla parishad, DIC, and the Khadi Board (Board of Indian handspun and hand-woven cloth). Localized information on industrial concentration was rather important in this case given that all the blocks in the districts do not carry equal importance in terms of rural industrialization and the depth varies substantially across the geographic spread of the district under consideration. From the list of blocks created for respective industry types, one block was randomly selected. Santipur, Krishnanagar, and Krisnaganj-I were sample blocks from Nadia district; Tamluk, Mahishadal, and Panskura II from Midnapore district; Nakura II and Indpur from Bankura district; and finally, Puncha, Manbazar I, and Balarampur from Purulia district.

Stage III: Selection of Village or Village Cluster[3]

Similarly, it is easily understood that given the small-scale nature of these industries, all villages do not share significant production traits. In fact, the sampling must take a purposive turn at this juncture given the reputation of artisans in specific villages for making specific commodities. Thus, Phulia for handloom, Matiari for the brassware industry and Dhubulia for the clay industry from Nadia district were selected for the study. Panskura for handlooms, Mahishadal for brassware and Baishnabchawk for hornware were selected from Midnapore district. Kenjakura for handlooms, Mogra for brassware, and Hatagram for conch shells were also included in the sample. Further, Nuagarh for handlooms, Gopalnagar for brassware, and Balarampur for the lac industry were selected from Purulia district.

Stage IV: Selection of Unit or Artisan

At first, an organization-wise list of production units of every sample village and/or cluster of villages was prepared through a pilot survey and then 15 units from each type of production organization were selected randomly, provided they were available. In case, sufficient numbers were not available, all units that were willing to respond were included in the study. If only one production organization existed in a cluster, 30 units of that were selected.

From this sample design, 356 units, of which proprietor households comprised 149 independent units, 162 tied units, and 45 cooperative units were selected for a detailed survey. The reference period for the study was the financial year 2001–2 (April 2001 to March 2002), a decade after the initiation of the new economic policy of the Government of India.

Method of Data Collection

At first, a pilot survey was undertaken to arrive at the exact number of units under different forms of production organization in the sample village or in a cluster of villages. Then, a separate code was generated according to the nature of the production organization. Using the random number table, the exact sample unit was drawn. The survey method or personal interviews with heads of units on the basis of specially designed schedules and questionnaires was used to collect the primary data. Table 8A.14 similarly show stages of production in the units that use lac as their main ingredient. Finally, Table 8A.15 describes the overall production organization in these industries.

Stages of Production and the Formal–Informal Divisions

Among the total units surveyed, it was observed that informal characteristics, such as non-registration (also see Kulsherestha and Singh 2001), non-maintenance of accounts, male dominance in entrepreneurship, inadequate formal educational background, home-based production units, dependence on other supplementary activities, and caste driven trade practices were the most visible traits. Units displaying these characteristics functioned through several distinct stages in the production process, towards the creation of use value as well as aesthetic value for the industry as a whole, albeit the stages varied with alterations in the nature of the product and the suitable production organization. Owing to extensive division of labour in the production process specialization increased where a group of artisans performed some of the stages of the work in their own households or workshops tied with master enterprises and mahajans. Detailed production stages and activities of sample manufacturing industries are given in Tables 8A.8 to Table 8A.13 in Appendix 8A.

The data shows that diverse technologies and human skills are used in the production process across rural industries along with traditional techniques. Further division of labour is engendered through development of technology regardless of the specificity of the regions chosen (also see Jain 1986). Tied units also become specialized in certain types of work and they are assigned the whole or a part of the work by the master artisans or mahajans on a contractual basis. The instruments of production are owned/possessed by the craftsmen and the merchant capitalist/middleman (who are mostly located in the town) or the master enterprise advances circulating capital (wage funds and raw materials). Though the artisans possess tools and workshops, there is little autonomy at the disposal of such producers who are tightly controlled by the traders in two main ways. First, the proprietor artisans and mahajans get involved through a system of mutual trust and unwritten contracts (see Government of West Bengal 1975), where interest-free loans on equipment and raw materials are paid back through supply of finished products adjusted for the cost of raw materials. In the process, the entire transaction adopts a primordial flavour. Secondly, from time to time master enterprises or larger independent units supply similar raw materials or equipment as an activity of outsourcing to these units and receive back parts or the entire commodity produced outside their own production units. The second tie-up is more in the nature of subcontracting between formal and informal units.

A few relatively larger units employ hired labour more on the basis of daily wage rates. If production takes place within the homestead, both men and women actively participate. However, workers belonging to the household are not paid wages. Workers mainly perform their jobs in a workshop or factory and mobile places within the household premises. However, rural manufacturing activities do not necessarily operate in petty forms alone; rather many such units have been transformed into workshops and factory levels. But, the putting out system (see Singh 1990: 16–25) prevalent here is different from the one in Europe that was functional during the phase of capitalist development when textiles had pre-eminence. Artisans obviously have the ownership of the means of production and bear the responsibility towards loss owing to damages to tools and equipment, including cattle used in any productive activity. In a few cases, the mahajans or traders also happen to share losses. These units, seemingly independent, are really dependent on merchant capitalists for survival, and as such are designated as tied units.[4]

Apart from these, the cooperative artisans are more akin to the tied units described thus far, but they also benefit from the organization or larger society in terms of loans, bonuses, training, and cover for damages and enjoy some degree of autonomy in the production process. In the case of tied units, the surplus is shared by the merchant capitalist and the proprietor artisans. In a cooperative society, on the other hand, a certain amount of surplus is spent for administrative, managerial, and marketing purposes as the society takes on the responsibility of marketing these products.

Hence, it is evident that different forms of production organizations exist in rural industries and are broadly categorized as independent, tied, and cooperative. Independent units possess their own fixed and working capital, and entrepreneur artisans have control over the production process, types of production and marketing channels. Tied units possess fixed assets for manufacturing the product but largely depend on mahajans, contractors, middlemen, or master enterprises for raw materials. Units as a part of a cooperative also maintain fixed assets for production but they are under the management of the cooperative society supplying the main raw materials for production.

Moreover, independent units may be distinguished in terms of the use of labour. Overall, 51.7 per cent (77 units) of the independent units operate with the help of unpaid household labour, while 27.5 per cent (41 units) of such units use hired workers in addition to household labourers. The remaining 20.8 per cent (31) independent units run their production with hired labour only, and are deemed as rural Directory Manufacturing Enterprises (DMEs). Strikingly, 13 per cent tied units and 15.6 per cent units under cooperatives use hired labour to some extent in their manufacturing activities along with household labour. The remaining 87 per cent tied and 84.4 per cent cooperative units operate fully on the strength of household workers. Combining all the organizations, 72 per cent and 19.3 per cent of the units are dependent on household labour and hired labour respectively and the remaining 8.7 per cent units are operated as DMEs solely dependent on hired labour. An important point that is noteworthy in this connection is that a significant share of the units operates as factories depending on hired labour and even tied and cooperative units also employ hired labour.

ORGANIZATIONAL CHANGE

On the basis of the primary information collected over all the sample industries, we observe that 23, 21, and 12.99 per cent of the units out of the total sample remain independent, tied, and cooperative units as earlier. But the remaining 44.01 per cent units overall have undergone some transformation from one form to another during the last decade. These units have been transformed in six visible ways: independent to tied/cooperative, tied to independent/cooperative, and cooperative to independent and tied. It shows, however, that the leverage is higher for shifts in favour of tied units. Around 2001–2, 13 per cent and 17 per cent of the units became tied and shifted from their erstwhile independent and cooperative status. On the other hand, only two tied units (0.01 per cent) were transformed into independent status. Thus, on the whole, 30 per cent of the units shifted into the category of tied units. It is also important to note that around 13 per cent of the cooperative units were transformed into independent units (see Table 8A.17 in Appendix 8A).

Marketing Channels

It is easily appreciated that unless firms, smaller or larger ones, face a sustained demand for their products and services, growth at the firm-level cannot perpetuate. Viewed from the issue of marketing a product and focusing on this aspect, which our general understanding of neo-classical economics subsumes, it appears that the positive aggregate demand for a product is generated locally, nationally or from cross-border sources. While the local demand for products manufactured in rural industries may not be sufficient to keep the industries operational (mainly owing to low purchasing power among rural masses), national and foreign markets often provide the necessary coverage. However, during the period which this study essentially accounts for, there was an expansion in the source of raw materials as necessary ingredients for such commodities. For example, the Minerals and Material Trading Corporation (MMTC) of India earlier supplied foreign scrap to the artisans. But after the introduction of the Open General License (OGL), MMTC discontinued this system and presently any individual can import directly from abroad. Albeit, the legal environment helped reshape the market for input demand, there is little doubt that the artisans were not necessarily the greatest beneficiaries.

In fact, the typical problem of credit constraint that ails artisans in all possible cases, also affected the market for inputs. The void was quickly filled by traders or master enterprises, and import activity then took the shape of pure intermediation. Most of the artisans have thus become clients for purchase of raw materials at prices controlled by the traders, along with compromises on both the quality and the frequency of supply, rather distinctly from what an artisan would consider optimal. In conch shell, lac, and hornware industries, we find that the producers working from remote rural areas find it possible to market their products in the cities only via such intermediaries and have to bank on both high levels of dependence and trust. Raw materials for the conch shell industry come from coastal towns in the southern and eastern parts of India and the suppliers of raw materials are usually the purchasers of finished products to be sold in the same places. However, newer waves of information and awareness about markets beyond the world that the small artisans in backward villages are trapped in, has had a significantly positive impact on a large number of smaller firms. Some of these units have started transacting directly with export merchants or marketing agencies, which in turn deal with traders in Japan, Germany and a host of other countries.

Nevertheless, the small artisans continue to suffer from access to appropriate markets and major marketing channels for a host of products belonging to these industries. Based on their responses we enlist the following as major channels through which small artisans regularly market their products. This may not be an exhaustive list and there are certain overlaps. Furthermore, the channels are identified on the basis of functional characteristics and rarely by textbook definitions of these activities. This tells us that the informal/unorganized element in rural businesses is still extremely high and that much of it functions on the basis of mutual acquaintances and trust: (i) selling door-to-door and visiting the village markets; (ii) supplying to specific merchant outlets by prior negotiations (verbal); (iii) setting up own sales counter; (iv) entering into a contract with local traders (mostly verbal); (v) supplying to a middleman, who then takes it to a trader; (vi) supplying to large traders; (vii) supplying to a registered exporter/export agency (involves more paperwork); (viii) hiring own salesperson and spending on advertisements; (x) entering into contract with cooperative society (this is more formal in nature); (xi) being part of marketing societies; and (xii) occasionally selling in village fairs.

It is not surprising then that the small but independent artisans suffering from dearth of working capital and proper knowledge of the market face a market channel that terminates within the local levels (vendors and local retailers). Access to markets is observed to be positively influenced by the extent of working capital deployed at the firm level. Similarly, access to markets seems varied for the range of small artisan producers discussed in this chapter. (Through a number of depictions in Appendix 8A we try to buttress the point that such markets have expanded for the group compared to what it was exposed to over the better half of the last century).

* * *

It remains empirically a rather vexing task to identify appropriate channels through which the shocks borne by the formal sector permeate to its informal counterpart. This chapter offered an attempt to isolate some of the factors that could account for this formal–informal interplay of events. In fact, both the theory of capital mobility across sectors, in particular between the formal and the informal sector, along with subsequent empirical evidence bears testimony to the appeal it has on a better comprehension of similar aspects under development economics. And yet, the empirical analysis is neither complete nor inimitable in view of several other factors that have potentially strong explanatory powers if included in the analysis. This, however, does not offer an array of easy choices, typically because the theory that could lend useful insights in such cases is often absent and vice versa; further a large number of existing studies have in fact cluttered the scenario even more by invoking contrasting implications from an apparently similar set of variables but discussed at considerably low frequencies and coverage.

In a nutshell, therefore, the choice of variables in this chapter may even be treated as an experimental effort at understanding how the inter-sectoral reallocation of resources can lead to outcomes that are clearly predictable theoretically under sufficiently general conditions. This chapter also tried to set up a platform in which more rigorous empirical evidence might come up in favour of issue like reorganization within formal and informal industrial structures compared to what is observed presently. Economic reforms in a country, however, remain the unifying thread through this analysis, and might be supplemented by similar legal, economic and structural shifts that countries with large dual labour markets might be exposed to.

NOTES

1. This section is based on a study on similar aspects by Marjit and Maiti (2006).

2. Percentage shares of rural workers engaged in manufacturing, processing, and repairing to total number of workers in each occupation is obtained from the Census of India, 1991

3. Cluster means the combination of a few villages in which particular types of industrial activities dominate. Selection of one particular village could not provide a sizable number of sample units.

4. In this regard, Debdas Banerjee (1994) also provides some information.

APPENDIX 8A

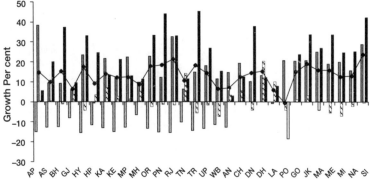

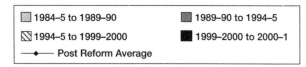

Figure 8A.1   Annual Growth Rates of Real Informal Wage

Source: NSS reports (various rounds) and own calculations.

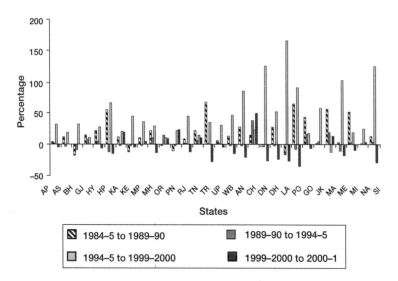

Figure 8A.2   Annual Growth Rates of Informal Fixed Assets

Source: NSS reports (various rounds) and own calculations.

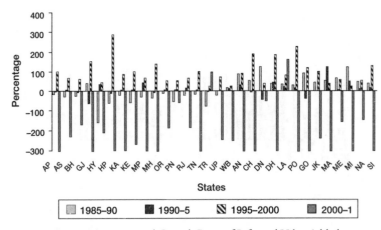

Figure 8A.3   Annual Growth Rates of Informal Value Added

Source: NSS reports (various rounds), ASI reports, GoI, and own calculations.
Notes: AP—Andhra Pradesh, AS—Assam, BH—Bihar, GJ—Gujarat, HY—Haryana, HP—Himachal Pradesh, KA—Karnataka, KE—Kerala, MP—Madhya Pradesh, MH—Maharastra, OR—Orissa, PN—Punjab, RJ—Rajasthan, TN—Tamil Nadu, TR—Tripura, UP—Uttar Pradesh, WB—West Bengal, AN—Andaman and Nicobar Islands, Ch—Chandigarh, DN—Dadra and Nagar Haveli, DH—Delhi, LA—Lakshadweep, PO—Pondicherry, GO—Goa, JK—Jammu and Kashmir, MA—Manipur, ME—Meghalaya, MI—Mizoram, NA—Nagaland, SI—Sikkim.

Table 8A.1   Descriptive Statistics for the Variables (year-wise)

Year	Variables	Mean	SD	Skew-ness	Kurt-osis	Mini-mum	Maxi-mum	Obser-vations
1989–90	IW	(–) 15.08	3.45	0.97	3.16	(–) 18.96	(–) 6.75	17
	FA	4.71	9.29	0.54	3.18	(–) 10.75	26.92	17
	VA	(–) 7.90	7.12	1.20	4.20	(–) 19.04	10.00	17
1994–5	IW	20.72	10.97	0.22	3.03	(–) 0.43	47.97	30
	FA	3.23	12.93	1.36	5.99	(–) 19.28	47.98	30
	VA	5.89	13.31	1.98	7.94	(–) 12.24	56.44	30
1999–2000	IW	1.29	7.65	1.26	4.76	(–) 9.07	25.49	30
	FA	58.50	50.32	1.35	4.16	(–) 13.24	208.01	30
	VA	42.05	32.67	1.47	4.93	3.48	140.38	30
2000–1	IW	44.18	28.51	(–) 0.52	3.30	(–) 37.11	90.74	30
	FA	(–) 10.52	35.77	0.87	4.19	(–) 69.15	99.74	30
	VA	(–) 40.18	25.04	0.82	4.42	(–) 94.69	26.49	30
All years	IW	16.16	26.84	0.81	3.20	(–) 37.11	90.74	107
	FA	15.10	43.33	1.69	7.54	(–) 69.15	208.01	107
	VA	0.92	38.68	0.59	4.54	(–) 94.69	140.38	107

Source: NSS reports and own calculations.
Note: Description of the variables: IW = Annual growth rate of real informal wage; FA = Annual growth rate of real fixed assets; VA = Annual growth rate of real value added.

Table 8A.2   Correlation Coefficient Matrix (year-wise)

1989–90	IW	FA	VA
IW	1.000	.4276	.4737
FA	.4276	1.000	.3775
VA	.4737	.3775	1.000
1994–5	IW	FA	VA
IW	1.000	.3393	.2704
FA	.3393	1.000	.0486
VA	.2704	.0486	1.000
1999–2000	IW	FA	VA
IW	1.000	.0635	.3544
FA	.0635	1.000	.1344
VA	.3544	.1344	1.000
2000–1	IW	FA	VA
IW	1.000	.1512	.4451
FA	.1512	1.000	−.2026
VA	.4451	−.2026	1.000

Source: NSS reports and own calculations.

Table 8A.3   Regression Results for Individual Time-points Corrected for Heteroscedasticity

Methodology: Generalized Least Squares
Dependent Variable: Annual Growth Rate of IW

Year	Exp. Variables	Coeff.	t-ratio	R^2	Adj. R^2	AIC	LL
1989–90	CONSTANT	(–) 11.35	(–) 6.70473*				
	FA	0.102	2.588*	0.48	0.36	5.01	(–) 39.10
	VA	0.233	5.098*				
1994–5	CONSTANT	15.89	8.846*				
	FA	0.278	2.190*	0.23	0.14	7.59	(–) 109.98
	VA	0.183	1.744**				
1999–2000	CONSTANT	(–) 3.76	(–) 1.622				
	FA	0.014	0.4587	0.16	0.06	6.961	(–) 100.42
	VA	0.083	2.041**				
2000–1	CONSTANT	69.56	5.691*				
	FA	0.152	0.8636	0.30	0.23	9.41	(–) 137.09
	VA	0.607	2.239*				

Note: * denotes significance at the 5% level and ** denotes significance at the 10% level.
Adj. R^2 = adjusted R^2
AIC = Akaike Information Criterion
LL = Log-likelihood

Table 8A.4   Unbalanced Panel Regression

Random Effects Model: $v(i, t) = e(i, t) + u(i)$

Methodology: 2-step GLS
Lagrange Multiplier Test = 157.18 (1 df, prob value =.00
(High values of LM favour FEM/REM over CR model).
Fixed vs. Random Effects (Hausman) = 2.07 (3 df, prob value = .5584)
(High [low] values of H favour FEM [REM]).

$\Rightarrow$ *RE model is inconsistent, which leads us to use a fixed effects model. The results from the LSDV (group dummy) model are:*

Least Squares with Group Dummy Variables
Ordinary least squares regression Weighting variable = none
Dependent Variable = REALIW Mean= 16.16, S.D.= 26.83
Model size: Observations = 107, Parameters = 7, Deg. Fr.= 100
Residuals: Sum of squares= 25107.46, Std. Dev = 15.84
Fit: R-squared = .6711, Adjusted R-squared = .6513
Model test: F [6, 100] = 34.01, Probability value = .00
Diagnostic: **Log-L = –443.83**, Restricted (b=0) Log-L = –503.32
Log Amemiya Probability Criterion. = 5.589, **Akaike Info. Criterion = 8.427**
Estd. Autocorrelation of e (i, t) .1392
White/Heteroscedasticity corrected covariance matrix used.
Results from Heteroscedasticty-corrected Panel (Fixed Effects) Regression
** Significant at the 1% level.

Explanatory Variable	Coefficient	Standard Error	t-ratio
REALFA	0.0304	0.0494	0.616
REALVA	0.2567**	0.0704	3.647

Table 8A.5   Socio-economic Characteristics of Sample Districts, 2001–2

Sample District	Nadia	Midnapore*	Bankura	Purulia
Area (sq. km)	3,927	14,081	6,882	6,259
Inhabited village	1,248	10,474	3,565	2,456
Population (lakh)	46.04	96.39	31.92	25.35
Density (per sq. km)	981	686	464	405
% of total state population	5.74	12.02	3.98	3.16
% of total state land area	4.42	15.87	7.75	7.05
% of SC population, 1991	29.01	16.34	31.37	19.35
% of ST population, 1991	2.35	8.28	10.34	19.23
Net sown area# (hectare)	306.9	859.9	383.3	335.8
	(78.6)	(65.0)	(55.7)	(53.9)

(*contd...*)

(*Table 8A.5 contd...*)

Sample District	Nadia	Midnapore*	Bankura	Purulia
Rural literacy rate	62.32	74.42	62.44	53.82
Male literacy	68.70	84.76	76.27	72.82
Female literacy	55.50	63.63	47.92	33.91
Road length/sq. km	0.25	0.14	0.16	0.13
Road Density (sq. km/lakh popu.)	942.82	1,699.24	341.47	783.35
Food-grain productivity (kg/hr)	2429	2305	2499	1728
Cropping intensity	242	164	145	104
Agriculture wage rate (Rs, male)	56.00	57.48	55.02	47.48
Rural industrial workers (%), 1991	12.2	9.61	7.23	7.13
Rural poverty (1993–4)	39.38	38.9	49.77	44.01
Per capita income (Rs)	10,654.68	10,252.62	9,849.34	8,809.96

Source: *Economic Review*, Government of West Bengal, 2001–2; *District Census Handbook* (Nadia, Midnapore, Bankura, Purulia), *Statistical Abstract*, Government of West Bengal, 2001–2.
Note: * Midnapore was recently divided into East Midnapore and West Midnapore. East Midnapore is relatively developed. Our sample is drawn from East Midnapore.
Figures in parentheses represent percentage share.

Table 8A.6   Number of Sample Artisans/Units

Sample Districts	Stage I Sample Industry	Stage III Sample Block	Stage IV Village Selection	Stage V Sample Units/Artisans under Production Organizations			
				Ind.	Tied	Cooper.	All
Nadia	Handloom	Santipur	Fulia	12	15	15	72
	Brassware	Krishnagang	Matiari	12	15	0	27
	Clay works	Krishnanagar I	Sadhanpara	20	0	0	20
Midna-	Handloom	Nilkunthi	Tamluk-I	15	15	0	30
pore	Brassware	Mahishadal	Ektarpur	3	15	0	18
	Hornware	Panskura II	Baishnabchawk	12	7	15	34
Bankura	Handloom	Bankura I	Kenjakura	15	15	15	45
	Brassware	Bankura I	Mogra	0	30	0	30
	Conch shell	Indpur	Hatagram	15	15	0	30
Purulia	Handloom	Purulia	Nuagarh	15	15	0	30
	Brassware	Manbazar	Gopalnagar	0	20	0	20
	Lac works	Balarampur	Balarampur	30	0	0	30
Total				149	162	45	356
				(41.85)	(45.51)	(12.64)	(100)

Source: Field survey.

Table 8A.7   Number of Registered Units

Industry	Registered	Not Registered	All
Handloom (AR)	22 (30.6)	50 (69.4)	72 (100)
Handloom (BR)	15 (20.0)	60 (80.0)	75 (100)
Brassware (AR)	8 (17.8)	37 (82.2)	45 (100)
Brassware (BR)	0 (0.0)	50 (100)	50 (100)
Clay works	5 (25.0)	15 (75.0)	20 (100)
Horn ware	7 (20.5)	27 (79.5)	34 (100)
Conch shell	6 (20.0)	24 (80.0)	30 (100)
Lac works	21 (70.0)	9 (30.0)	30 (100)
Total	84 (23.6)	272 (76.4)	356 (100)

Source: Field survey.

Table 8A.8   Number of Units Maintaining Accounts

Industry	Account Maintained	Not Maintained	All
Handloom (AR)	20 (27.8)	52 (72.2)	72 (100)
Handloom (BR)	12 (16)	63 (84)	75 (100)
Brassware (AR)	8 (17.8)	37 (75.2)	45 (100)
Brassware (BR)	1 (2)	49 (98)	50 (100)
Clayworks	4 (20)	16 (80)	20 (100)
Hornware	7 (20.6)	27 (79.4)	34 (100)
Conch shells	3 (100)	27 (90)	30 (100)
Lac works	25 (83.3)	5 (16.7)	30 (100)
Total	80 (22.5)	276 (77.5)	356 (100)

Source: Field survey.

Table 8A.9   Production Stages in Handloom Industry and Nature of Machines and Labour Used

Stage	Machine & Tools Used	Nature of Work	Type of Labour	Mode of Payment*
1. Dubbing	Big containers	Dubbing the fibre	Unskilled Household or hired labour	Daily basis
2. Drying	–	Drying in sunlight	Unskilled Household or hired labour	Daily basis

(*contd...*)

(Table 8A.9 contd...)

Stage	Machine & Tools Used	Nature of Work	Type of Labour	Mode of Payment*
3. Rolling I	*Charkha* (Handloom)	Cotton rolled on wooden mounds	Unskilled women household or contract	Piece rate
4. Rolling II	Drum	Rolling of cotton	Skilled household or hired labour	Piece rate
5. Weaving	*Maku* (Handloom), Drum/	Weaving the fibre	Skilled household or hired labour	Piece rate
6. Packing	Scissors	Separation, packing	Unskilled household or hired labour	Piece rate

Source: Field survey.
Note: *mode of payment applies mainly to hired labour; household labour is mostly unpaid.

Table 8A.10   Production Stages in Brassware Industry and Nature of Machines and Labour Used

Stage	Machine & Tools Used	Nature of Work	Type of Labour	Mode of Payment
1. Clay preparation	–	Pasting clay	Unskilled household labour	–
2. *Muchhi* & dice		Making & checking of *muchhi* & dice	Household skilled female, or daily labour	Piece rate
3. Melting	Furnaces	Melting the old metal or new mixtures	Skilled household male or hired labour	Piece rate
4. Shaping/ Casting	Hammer & accessories or press machine	Shaping the molten metal	Skilled household or hired labour	Piece rate
5. Structuring	Hammer & Accessories	Structure broken portions into proper shapes	Skilled household or hired labour	Piece rate
6. Engraving/ Designing	Hammer & Accessories	Design utensils	Skilled household or hired labour	Piece rate
7. Polishing		Polishing the designed products	Skilled household or hired labour	Piece rate

Source: Field survey.

Table 8A.11   Production Stages in Clay Works and Nature of
Machines and Labour Used

Stage	Machine & Tools Used	Nature of Work	Type of Labour	Mode of Payment
1. Clay preparation	Spade	Making clay from sand, jute fibre, straw	Unskilled male household or hired labour	Daily basis
2. Shaping	Structure	Shaping the structure	Skilled male/ female household or hired labour	Daily basis
3. Designing	Simple tools of wooden or bamboo blade	Designing doll or structure	Skilled male/ female household or hired labour	Daily basis
4. Polishing	Colour, brush	Colouring and polishing	Skilled male/ female household or hired labour	Daily basis
5. Burning	Clay-oven	Kiln-burn product	Unskilled male/ female household or hired labour	Daily basis
6. Designing & polishing	Colour, brush	Colouring and Polishing the product	Skilled male/ female labour	–

Source: Field survey.

Table 8A.12   Production Stages in Hornware Industry and Nature of
Machines and Labour Used

Stage	Machine & Tools Used	Nature of Work	Type of Labour	Mode of Payment
1. Drawing	Chalk, needle	Sketching on raw horns to design the product	Skilled male household/ hired labour	Piece rate
2. Cutting	Scissor (*karat*)	Cutting the horn according to the drawing	Skilled male household/ hired labour	Piece rate and daily rate
3. Grinding	Stone or grinder machine	Grinding the raw horn	Skilled male household/ hired labour	Piece rate and daily rate

(*contd...*)

(*Table 8A.12 contd...*)

Stage	Machine & Tools Used	Nature of Work	Type of Labour	Mode of Payment
4. Bopping	Abrasive paper, simple accessories	Rubbing the horn	Skilled male household/ hired labour	Piece rate and daily rate
5. Polishing	Motor	Polishing the horn and designing	Skilled male household/ hired labour	Piece rate and daily rate
6. Packing	Simple accessories	Packing the final product	Skilled male household/ hired labour	Piece rate and daily rate

Source: Field survey.

Table 8A.13   Production Stages in Conch Shell Works and Nature of Machines and Labour Used

Stage	Machine & Tools Used*	Nature of Work	Type of Labour	Mode of Payment
1. Cutting	Cutting machine (made by Crompton-Greaves 2 Horse Power)	Cutting raw conch shells according to size	Male, household/ hired labour	Daily rate
2. Rubbing-I	Grinder machine/ Sil, *dara, batali*, file, *bhramar*	Rub the outer layer of conch shells	Skilled male/ female, household/ hired labour	Piece rate
3. Pasting	Glue (resin, zinc oxide) wax	Pasting rubbed conch shells into required shape	Male/female, household/ hired labour	Piece rate
4. Rubbing-II or Polishing	Grinder machine/ Sil, *dara, batali*, file, *bhramar*	Rub the pasting area	Male/female, household/ hired labour	Piece rate
5. Designing	Grinder machine/ *kalan*	Design the conchs shell ring artistically	Male/female, household/hired labour	Piece rate

Source: Field survey.

Note: * Various small tools named as per local vernaculars or dialects, such as small hammers, shapers, weights, and grinders.

Table 8A.14   Production Stages in Lac Works Industry and Pattern of Machines and Labour used

Stage	Machine & Tools Used	Nature of Work	Type of Labour	Mode of Payment
1. Grinding and boiling	Crusher machine, soda	Grinding the raw lac	Household/hired male worker	Daily rate or contract
2. Straining	Crusher machine	Strain the lac	Skilled hired male worker	Daily rate or contract
3. Washing	By hand or washing machine	Wash the strained lac	Hired male worker	Daily rate or contract
4. Driving	By hand	Separate the lac	Unskilled female hired labour	Daily rate or contract
4. Melting	By hand or rope or shaping machine	Melting lac	Skilled male contract or hired labour	Daily rate or contract
5. Button making	By hand and rope or shaping machine	Producing button from molten lac	Skilled male contract labour	Daily rate or contract
6. Melting button	Furnace and container	Melting the button	Unskilled female household labour	–
7. Making & designing	Rope & accessories	Making the products as per designs	Skilled male/ female household labour	–

Source: Field survey.

Table 8A.15   Features of Production Organizations

Production Organization	Feature
Independent	Own fixed capital and working capital; own control over production process, type of products, sources of raw materials and marketing
Tied	Own fixed capital but controlled by master enterprises or contractor, *mahajans*, middlemen who supply raw materials
Units/artisans under cooperative	Own fixed capital and controlled by cooperative society

Table 8A.16   Number of Units under Different Production
Organizations for All Industries Combined

Organization Strata	Independent	Tied	Cooperative	Total
Solely on household workers	31 (20.8)	0 (0)	0 (0)	31 (8.7)
Both household and hired workers	41 (27.5)	21 (13)	7 (15.6)	69 (19.3)
Solely on hired workers	77 (51.7)	141 (87)	38 (84.4)	256 (72.0)
All	149 (100)	162 (100)	45 (100)	356 (100)

Source: Field survey.

Table 8A.17   Organizational Changes
in Industries during 10 Years
since Economic Liberalization,
1991–2001

Organizational Change	All	
1. Same as independent	82	(23)
2. Same as tied	73	(21)
3. Same as cooperative	45	(12.99)
4. Independent to tied	47	(13)
5. Tied to independent	2	(0.01)
6. Independent to cooperative	0	(0)
7. Tied to cooperative	0	(0)
8. Cooperative to independent	47	(13)
9. Cooperative to tied	89	(17)
Total	356	(100)

Source: Field survey.
Note: Numbers in parentheses indicate percentages.

9 Trade Reforms, Labour Market Reforms, Informal Wages, and Poverty

The phenomenal expansion of the third world metropolis over the last decade or so has unleashed a plethora of questions regarding in various socio-political and economic aspects. The growth and expansion, even by the most conservative estimates, has been rather skewed and has sharply widened disparity across regions or locations within a given country. The most striking comparison of the situation is visible in growing cities in the South, where coexistence of extremely rich pockets with those of stark poverty has become a reality more than ever before. Undoubtedly recent developments have largely favoured the more skilled workforce on a global scale.

A substantial portion of unskilled employment opportunities on the other hand, is generated in urban or semi-urban areas, and not surprisingly a majority of this workforce is economically marginalized. These groups are exposed to difficult and hazardous working conditions; they suffer from non-existent social security or health benefit schemes other than poorly functioning state-provided medical facilities and lack of access to information. Consequently, high incidence of poverty among these groups is quite common. Sustained improvements in the living standards of these groups can only be brought about by capital accumulation, productivity gains and wage increases. It is argued that developing countries suffer from lack of dedicated funds for poverty alleviation and impacts on poverty are often the byproduct of other policies, such as trade liberalization (Bowles 1999; Demery and Squire 1996; Dollar 1992; Topalova 2005; Winters 2000, to name a few). It has also been established that dedicated policies towards urban employment generation and poverty reduction often increase both in the presence of poverty-stricken rural sectors and high levels of rural–urban migration (see Basu 1984).

This chapter offers another look at the connection between trade liberalization and poverty reduction, with a particular focus on informal sector workers in cities and towns of the developing world. More specifically, it looks at the channel between how trade reforms affect urban informal workers and how that in turn affects urban poverty. The previous chapters in this volume have demonstrated that informal sector workers are hard pressed to accept low-paid jobs in the cities rather than wait indefinitely for formal high-paying urban employment to open up. This can significantly explain the persistence of urban poverty in many cities of the third world. In the theoretical sections in this chapter we reconstruct the conditions of the urban informal sector and subsequently use empirical results from previous chapters to reflect on the incidence and depth of poverty and the implications of reforms on both these issues. Given that country-wise data on the informal sector is hard to collect, we rely on the Indian evidence and expect that it shall offer some general characteristic not totally alien to other countries with dual labour markets.

In particular, we distinguish the urban informal sector as comprising of an industrial section that uses some amount of capital as input and another as using raw labour as the only input. To the best of our knowledge, and despite growing interest in the subject, such distinction has not been made earlier. For country examples such as that from India, the overwhelming share of workers using only physical labour towards menial occupations is too large to be clubbed as one indivisible informal unit. The occupational distribution ranges from domestic help comprising predominantly of women and child labour, domestic cooks, chauffeurs, daily wage labour in construction, cart pullers, rickshaw pullers, and the like. And yet, this is frequently considered as frictional in nature and denied due consideration in policy discussions. While the nature of occupations may certainly differ in other countries, use of manual labour to service the wealthier sections of the population is almost universal in the developing world and usually outside the purview of formal industries and service sectors. We argue that the impact of trade liberalization should be felt significantly by such groups and may even be favourable to many under plausible conditions.

The empirical section based on the first theoretical model is not an exact estimate of the predictions, but offers an aggregative look at wage movements for informal workers in India at the provincial level. The implication of informal wage movements on the extent of urban poverty in India is the prime focus in this chapter and extends the empirical results from Chapter 8. Undoubtedly, the most appropriate empirical exercise linking trade, the informal sector and poverty would be one that narrows down the focus to specific industries in both the formal and informal sectors. While this is certainly a plausible way of drawing the connection and should be tried at length, it may also be rather limited in explaining the phenomenon on a wider scale. This chapter offers a general equilibrium model relating international trade, informal sector, and poverty with a wider reach. Our theoretical result predicts that informal wages should increase if there is trade liberalization and that there would be an expansion in the urban informal industrial base. The aggregative empirical results test just this: Growth in informal wages and factors that explain it best when there is expansion in the sector. And finally, we estimate if such wage growth is capable of reducing urban poverty. The next section discusses the relation between reforms and poverty, while the section that follows offers the benchmark model and its results. The next section discusses the empirical connection between trade reforms, informal wages, and poverty and the following section develops a modified general equilibrium structure with labour market reforms. The last section provides a conclusion.

REFORMS AND POVERTY

Economic reforms and poverty in India has emerged as a topic of great interest among economists ever since India started restructuring its economic policies in the early 1990s. High rates of GDP growth in recent years have encouraged economists and policy analysts to explore whether such growth has contributed to a reduction in poverty across states. Although poverty rates in urban and rural areas have shown declining trends in general, the outcome varies considerably across states. Topalova (2005), for example, argues that tariff reduction on importable commodities has not been effective in reducing the incidence and depth of poverty across districts in India with concentration of import-competing activities. Using a specific factor model of trade, Topalova's study shows that in the presence of limited factor mobility, trade liberalization led to an increase in the extent of rural poverty in India. In a similar vein (also considering product and labour market deregulations) and in connection with the effect of trade on poverty in India, Hasan et al. (2006) provide contradictory evidence showing that the impact of trade reforms on poverty is actually more visible in states with relatively 'flexible' labour market conditions. Moreover, this is consistent with Besley and Burgess's position (2004). Flexible labour market characteristics, as exemplified and quantified by Besley and Burgess (2004) do, however, have some exceptions. According to their results, Maharashtra and Gujarat, despite being labour-friendly in terms of the conditions set out in this paper have shown impressive improvements.

This chapter intends to trace the exact link between labour market flexibility and poverty in the presence of a huge informal labour market, as would be the case with many developing countries, including India. Labour market rigidities have often been deemed responsible for production being outsourced to the unorganized sector. Per worker costs in the unorganized sector stay low due to a large stock of unskilled and semi-skilled workers competing for fewer jobs where collective bargaining is absent. Further, firms in this sector avoid various labour laws and safety requirements and keep the total labour costs lower than what formal firms spend. On the other hand, if a regional government follows pro-employer policies, then there may be greater flexibility in hiring and firing practices even within formal sectors. For India, the main labour regulation is exercised through the Industrial Disputes Act (1947), which according to the Constitution of India may be amended locally by individual states. Besley and Burgess (2004) noted that states could be classified as pro-employer, pro-labour, or neutral depending on the nature of amendments that they have sought at the state level. In pro-employer states more people are likely to find jobs in the formal sector and since labour regulations are followed in such jobs, one expects a significant negative impact on poverty. Concerning the broader question on what drives informalization among firms, a few recent papers like those by Dabla-Norris et al. (2008), Fugazza and Jacques (2004), and McKenzie and Sakho (2010) discuss possible channels. Of these, Dabla-Norris et al. (2008) find that the quality of the legal framework is crucial in determining the size of the informal sector for 80 developing and developed countries. If the legal system is functional, then the significance of taxes, regulations, and constraints are of limited importance. Further, Straub (2005) argues that compliance with formal registration procedures at a cost allows firms to benefit from key public goods, enforcement of property rights and contracts. This would ultimately enable the firms to participate in the formal credit market as well. Access to the formal credit market, according to Straub (2005), is evaluated against the relative costs of existence in either of these regimes and should be considered as a critical determinant of the choice between formality and informality. The relationship between economic reforms and informality also varies widely for African countries (see, for example, Savard and Adjovi 1997 for Benin; Sethuraman 1997; Tripp 1997; Wuyts 2001 for Tanzania; Bautista et al. 1998 for Zimbabwe; Xaba et al. 2002 for a number of countries showing steady growth in informal output and employment; Olofin and Folawewo 2006 for Nigeria; Verick 2006 for an overall account). Finally, note that the health of the informal sector is deeply related to the extent of poverty in these countries and many of these studies also discuss the connection (see Kar and Marjit 2009 for a general discussion and estimates for India).

Here we confine ourselves to the definition of income poverty only, so that people are poor if they earn low wages as is common among informal sector workers in poor countries. The workers do not have to be necessarily unemployed in order to be considered poor; they may have jobs and may still be living in stark poverty due to low market wages. It is also expected that more employer-friendly policies shall raise informal wages since increased labour demand in the formal sector must draw away workers from the pool in the informal sector. Thus, introduction of flexibility in the labour market is likely to improve informal wages and help reduce poverty.

This is, however, only one aspect of the main argument. Reality demands a description of more intricate relationships. An example of such linkages may, however, be sought through simple exercises such as inter-sectoral mobility of factor inputs like capital. It can be shown that flexibility in labour laws may benefit owners of capital in the formal sector. This in turn should pull capital into the formal sector at the cost of production and employment in the other sector.

When capital mobility is restricted, fully or partially, stringent labour market regulations are harmful for informal workers since low employment in the formal segment leads to greater crowding into the informal sector lowering wage rates. However, if capital could move freely, aggressive trade unions in the organized sector would push capital away into the informal segment thereby raising informal wages despite high employment. Hence, the interest of organized and unorganized workers should be positively related. Our emphasis is on whether labour market reforms help informal workers and if that depends on the nature of capital flows.

It seems that recent contributions on the impact of reforms in India and its relationship with labour market flexibility have overlooked a number of important aspects. First, the exact theoretical and/or empirical hypothesis regarding the relationship between labour market reforms and poverty is not suitably addressed. Second, in the presence of a vast informal labour market there is scant research on the implications of labour market adjustments on poverty and inequality. Third, various rounds of NSSO data show that real informal wages increased substantially in all the Indian states during the post-reform era with one important characteristic shift in employment patterns in most places. However, this change should not be deemed an outcome of a conscious transformation in the legal framework applicable to the labour market (see Marjit and Kar 2007). In fact, the NCEUS report (2007: 9) finds that the 8.5 million new jobs created in the formal sector in India happened without any supporting job or social security benefits. The general equilibrium implications of this have not been taken into account. We treat this change as a result of reforms in the labour and product markets and construct a benchmark model (with a variant) within a general equilibrium framework allowing for some degree of capital mobility. In this set-up product market reforms and labour market reforms have conflicting outcomes depending upon the degree of inter-sectoral capital mobility. This chapter discusses the impact of both types of reforms and derives conditions under which both will improve informal wages. Informal wages serve as a proxy for poor people's income, and not unrealistically, should be interpreted as the subsistence wage. Any drop in wages would push individuals below the poverty line. Conversely, it should be noted that given the considerably large share of employment in these sectors even small positive gains in real wages can increase the economic well-being of millions in poor countries.

THE BENCHMARK MODEL

Consider a small open economy with two formal sectors, X and Y, which produce traded commodities. X is an import-competing good manufactured with capital and skilled labour and is protected by an import tariff, t. The skilled wage is fixed at $\bar{w}_S$ by prior negotiations with the labour unions as an outcome of a bargaining process. We do not model this wage fixation explicitly in this section.[1] Commodity Y is an export item produced with skilled labour, capital and an intermediate commodity, I, which in turn is produced in the informal sector. Since Y is traded at exogenously given world prices the price of commodity

I, P_I is determined from its fixed-coefficient production relation with Y. The production of I requires use of capital, and unskilled labour available in large stock, which receives a wage $w < \bar{w}_S$. This, we argue, is the subsistence wage that allows the workers to live on or just below the urban poverty line and any improvement is expected to pull them above or closer to the same.

We consider I as one of the several intermediates ranging from leather and rubber products to electronic equipment produced under informal arrangements. Such commodities are often sold by formal export industries after appropriate value additions. The third commodity we consider is non-traded, uses unskilled labour as the only input and represents very low-skilled activities, such as domestic help or small vendors with little or no use of capital. It may be considered an informal service sector. The price relations for a competitive market accommodating these commodity types are given by equations (9.1) to (9.4). All the factors of production are fully employed as shown by equations (9.5) to (9.8). The typical nature of the urban informal sector allows us to consider a full-employment competitive model of this nature, since for all practical purposes the reservation wage for unskilled informal workers in poor countries is quite low. For the relatively unskilled workers who do not succeed in getting formal employment, informal employment offers the only available alternative. Moreover, in this model, while capital is homogeneous and moves freely between all the sectors, labour is heterogeneous and skilled workers receive a higher premium. The production functions are neo-classical types with constant returns to scale technology, diminishing marginal productivity for factor inputs and operate in perfectly competitive markets. The input coefficients are functions of factor prices and the symbols used here follow depictions in Jones' (1971) specific factor model.

The model uses the following symbols:

$\bar{w}_S$	Formal skilled wage
w	Informal flexible wage
r_j	Return to capital in sector j
X	Output of formal import-competing sector
Y	Output of formal export sector
(P_j^*)	Exogenous price of jth good
I	Output of intermediate good (informal)
Z	Output of non-traded good (informal)

$\overline{L}$ Stock of unskilled labour

$\overline{S}$ Stock of skilled labour

$\overline{K}$ Total supply of capital

t Import tariff rate

(a_{ij}, a_{Kj}) Per unit labour and capital use in sector $j = X, Y, I, Z, i = L,$
        S, I

'∧' represents percentage changes for each variable (for example, $\hat{x} = \frac{dx}{x}$) and detailed algebraic derivations of all the results are provided in Appendix 9A.

The competitive price conditions are given by:

$$\overline{w}_S a_{SX} + r a_{KX} = P_X^* (1 + t) \qquad (9.1)$$

$$\overline{w}_S a_{SY} + r a_{KY} + P_I a_{IY} = P_Y^* \qquad (9.2)$$

$$w a_{LI} + r a_{KI} = P_I \qquad (9.3)$$

$$w a_{LZ} = P_Z \qquad (9.4)$$

And, the full employment conditions require:

$$a_{SX} X + a_{SY} Y = \overline{S} \qquad (9.5)$$

$$a_{LI} I + a_{LZ} Z = \overline{L} \qquad (9.6)$$

$$a_{KX} X + a_{KY} Y + a_{KI} I = \overline{K} \qquad (9.7)$$

$$a_{IY} Y = I \qquad (9.8)$$

The determination of four price variables (r, w, P_I, P_Z) and four output variables $(X, Y, I,$ and $Z)$ from the set of eight equations proceeds in the following way. Given the skilled wage and the exogenous price for commodity X, the return to capital is obtained from equation (9.1). Substituting r in equation (9.2) we get the price of the intermediate commodity I, and from (9.3) the unskilled wage is directly obtained. Substituting w in équation (9.4) determines the price of the non-traded informal service, Z. Similarly, for factor markets, we substitute the output level of informal intermediate commodity I from equation (9.8) into equation (9.7). Equations (9.5) and (9.7) then form a pair of simultaneous equations that solve for equilibrium output levels of X and Y, given the endowments of capital K and skilled labour S. Substituting back the equilibrium value of Y in equation (9.8) we determine the equilibrium output of I in the economy. Finally, from equation (9.6) we determine the value of Z, which is the output of the informal service sector.

We are principally interested in observing the impact of a tariff reduction in the formal import-competing sector on the level of output and employment in the two categories of the informal sector under consideration. While detailed algebraic proof is provided in Appendix 9A, let us offer an intuitive explanation of the phenomenon in connection with the following proposition.

PROPOSITION 9.1.   *A reduction in import tariff raises product prices and wages in both the informal sectors. However, the sector producing the intermediate good expands in output and employment, while the one producing non-traded services, contracts*

Proof.   A reduction in the tariff rate lowers the return to capital in sector X alone, since the skilled wage is exogenous and fixed. Consequently, sector X must contract, which suitably captures the experience in most developing and emerging economies where adoption of freer trade policies and removal of tariff and non-tariff barriers have affected the local import-competing (many under public sector control) sectors adversely. Employment levels of both labour and capital in sector X must also shrink under the circumstances and relocation to other sectors becomes necessary. Since skilled labour is used specifically in sectors X and Y, therefore the latter may draw in more skilled workers and its output may grow if the sector is more skill-intensive compared to the former. This is an exemplification of the Rybczynski effect (see, 9A.11 and 9A.12, in Appendix 9A). On the other hand, capital may move to sector Y or sector I, or both. As discussed, sector I's output level is completely dependent on that of sector Y since it is the sole user of the intermediate commodity produced informally. If capital moves into sector Y, the price of the informal intermediate must improve, given the competitive price conditions. However, since by assumption, the intermediate must be used in fixed proportions with any other combination of capital and labour, its output must also increase. The sequence of events follows the derivations in the said appendix.

A rise in the price of I, and a factor-led growth in sector Y both contribute to an increase in the output of the informal commodity. This is a significant result in itself, because it implies that a contraction of the formal import-competing sector leads to an improvement in formal export production and given its connection with the informal sector through the intermediate input, informal production also increases. Once again, empirical analyses for some of the countries do exhibit this pattern in the post-reform phase, where many formal industries have survived and grown by sub-contracting their production to the informal sector. Even within the bastions of labour union dominated public and other formal sectors, one observes growing tendencies towards informal and contractual employment practices, often without access to many facilities previously enjoyed by formal workers.

The contraction of the formal import-competing sector also demonstrates that unskilled wages increase in the process, another impact quite clearly visible in many of the developing economies, including India. In fact, Table 9B.1 (Appendix 9B) shows that for most provinces in India, average wages for workers in the unorganized non-directory manufacturing sector have risen on an annual basis. Notwithstanding such changes, the informal service sector may shrink on account of an expansion in the production of the informal intermediate commodity. This operates through the mobility of unskilled workers away from the service sector and into the intermediate manufacturing sector, although wages increase in both. However, no empirical estimate of this intra-informal sector mobility of resources exists for not incomprehensible reasons.

Generally, one may argue that the impact of reforms on the informal sector in general is welfare inducing in various ways. First, direct improvement in wages has a clear impact on poverty reduction in the informal sector. Second, the flow of workers into an industrial set-up, albeit informal, and away from morally degrading and highly insecure non-traded service sector jobs, such as street side vendors, low-level construction workers or simply domestic help may be treated as not only an expansion of the industrial or service sector base, but also rewarding in terms of increasing the visibility of labour's involvement in the economy.

Similarly, if there is a *ceteris paribus* rise in the price of the export good Y, the price of the intermediate good increases, and as there has been no change in the return to capital, informal wages must go up. This in turn raises the price of the informal service. Clearly, the rise in the price of the intermediate good expands its production and draws labour away from the service sector into the industrial base. Thus:

PROPOSITION 9.2.   *A rise in the price of export good, Y, shall raise the prices of both the intermediate good and the non-traded good. Informal wages must rise, and labour moves to the intermediate sector thus lowering output and employment in the non-traded sector despite a higher price per unit*

Proof. The discussion earlier and derivations in Appendix 9A.

INFORMAL WAGES AND POVERTY IN INDIA

It is best to admit that relating informal wages and poverty to trade liberalization is a more difficult job empirically, than it is theoretically. The empirical structure is highly dependent on the availability and reliability of data on the informal economy. In Chapter 8 we discussed the scope of empirical evidence for India when it comes to relating the growth of informal wages to the major factors that characterize the informal sector. This section once again draws on the same set of results, in particular those relating to the growth of informal wages to the growth of real fixed assets, real value added and real rural wages. We argue that any measure of urban poverty is strongly dependent on the performance of the informal sector in the cities and our main hypothesis is: If exogenous shocks, such as a tariff reduction for formal industrial units leads to a change in the wages of informal workers, then one should expect a decline in the proportion of workers living in poverty using any standard measure of poverty. From a motivational point of view, we venture into the relationship between informal wages and poverty for one major reason. A large part of the urban poor in India work and live under so-called informal sector arrangements and that any improvement in the wages of informal workers may reflect significantly on the incidence of poverty. There is also a reasonable possibility that a significant overlap between the two sets exists. This would not be the case in rural areas, because in comparison to the rural informal sector a larger share of the poor is engaged in agriculture. Thus, we test for the relationship between the urban head count ratio (UHCR) and urban informal wages (NDMEs). Consequently, using the information and the results in Chapter 8 we measure the effects of rising informal wages on the level of poverty for urban locations in India. We conduct an OLS and an unbalanced panel regression for all the rounds of surveys already discussed. It should be noted that there are many other important variables that are potential candidates in the exercise, such as gender-based wages, specific occupational types and so on, which are excluded here mainly to provide an aggregative explanation of the driving relationship, the growth of informal wages in a period dominated by industrial trade liberalization and its effect on the percentage of people in the below poverty line (BPL) category.[2] In a way, therefore, the relationship is exploratory and may be improved upon both from the modelling point of view as also the coverage.

Hence, dwelling on the relationship between changes in informal wages in the different states and union territories in India over the years and the changes in the percentage of people registered under the BPL category in these states we offer an aggregative view. It should also be noted that informal sector data and BPL data are not from the same samples and no common database that enumerates and reports on both, exists.

The exercise is carried out in two stages: First, we regress the current period's BPL percentage on previous periods' annual informal wage growth, where the results of the OLS suggest a negative relationship significant at the 5 per cent level (Table 9B.1, Appendix 9B). Second, we conduct the analysis as a panel of the states and union territories over four rounds of the survey, and it reveals the presence of random effects. It nevertheless matches the OLS results closely. However, as can be seen from Table 9B.2 (Appendix 9B) the coefficient of IWPREV (real informal wage in the previous period) is still negative but now significant at the 1 per cent level. To summarize, therefore, one may state that the effect of an improvement in annual wages in the informal sector has a negative and significant impact on the incidence of urban poverty across states and union territories in India.

LABOUR MARKET REFORMS AND INFORMAL WAGES

This section disregards the skill heterogeneity as developed earlier in the chapter and instead assumes that all workers, whether in the formal or the informal sector, are homogeneous. Thus, once again, we have a two-sector economy producing X and Y with labour and capital. X is produced in the formal sector with workers paid a fixed wage $\bar{w}$, while those in the informal sector receive a market determined wage w. It is assumed that $w < \bar{w}$. Note that, $\bar{w}$ though exogenous in the framework, can be endogenously determined either through the action of an optimizing union (Carruth and Oswald 1981; Dasgupta and Marjit 2006)[3] or through a model of 'effort observability' as developed by Esfahani and Saleh-Isfahani (1989). Agenor and Montiel (1996) make extensive use of this framework in analysing development policies in a macroeconomic context. The fixity of $\bar{w}$ is assumed because the crucial focus of the analysis rests elsewhere as we shall describe and one can treat changes in $\bar{w}$ as changes in effective hiring costs. Thus, lowering of $\bar{w}$ is synonymous with more flexible labour market conditions.

X and Y are both traded goods with prices exogenously determined in the rest-of-the-world as is natural for a small open economy. We discuss the implications of relaxing this assumption later. However, the fixity of prices is an artefact to focus on pure supply side responses. One can provide a more profound justification behind such an assumption.

In a very interesting paper, Foster and Rosenzweig (2004) argue that whenever there has been a productivity increase in Indian agriculture, the consequent higher rural wages have discouraged rural industrialization. Thus, the supply side effect could not be compensated by greater demand for local goods through the increased income effect. Therefore, the importance of the supply side effect must not be ignored even if there might be some demand side repercussions.

In our model, the production functions exhibit CRS and diminishing returns and the markets are competitive. Capital is imperfectly mobile between the formal and informal sectors. Absolute immobility of capital at one end gives us the specific-factor model while perfect mobility yields a 2 × 2 HOS framework. These are two special cases in our model.

Competitive price conditions imply:

$$\bar{w}a_{LX} + ra_{KX} = P_X(1+t) \tag{9.9}$$

$$wa_{LY} + Ra_{KY} = P_Y \tag{9.10}$$

a_{ij} s are input–output coefficients derived by factor price ratios, 't' denotes a measure of 'protection'/artificial subsidy/protective regulation which protects the market and effectively increases the price. Workers try to find jobs in the high wage sector. The unsuccessful ones are absorbed in the informal sector.

$$a_{LX}X + a_{LY}Y = \bar{L} \tag{9.11}$$

Full employment of capital implies:

$$K_X + K_Y = \bar{K} \tag{9.12}$$

$$a_{KX}X = K_X \tag{9.13}$$

$$a_{KY}Y = K_Y \tag{9.14}$$

However, K_x and K_y once allocated act as imperfect substitutes. In other words, there is a mobility cost.

$$\frac{K_X}{K_Y} = f\left(\frac{r}{R}\right), f' > 0 \tag{9.15}$$

One can show that, $\hat{K}_X - \hat{K}_Y = \mu(\hat{r} - \hat{R})$ $\tag{9.15a}$

where, '∧' denotes proportional change and $\mu \in [0, \infty]$ denotes the mobility elasticity with $\mu = 0$, it is a standard specific factor model. With $\mu \to \infty$, we have perfect mobility of capital.

Equations (9.11), (9.12), (9.13) and (9.14) can be combined as:

$$\frac{a_{LX}}{a_{KX}}\left(\bar{K} - K_Y\right) + \frac{a_{LY}}{a_{KY}}.K_Y = \bar{L} \tag{9.16}$$

Given $P_X(1 + t)$ and $\bar{w}$, (9.9) determines r. Hence, $\dfrac{a_{LX}}{a_{LY}}$ gets determined. Then (9.2), (9.7) and (9.8) determine w, R and K_y.

In this framework, product market reforms imply a decline in t and labour market reforms are synonymous with a decline in $\bar{w}$.

From equations (9.1) and (9.2) it is perfectly possible to pre-empt the isolated implications of product market and labour market reforms in the economy. We nevertheless derive a general condition in Appendix 9C in order to emphasize the potential impact of a simultaneous occurrence of both, which also leads to Proposition 9.3. Intuitively, product market reforms only, that is, a decline in t, with full mobility of capital should indicate a decline in the sectoral rates of return to capital and hence an improvement in the wages received by workers in the informal sector. On the other hand, labour market reforms, where the workers in the formal sector now suffer due to a fall in the negotiated wage, would lead to drawing in capital from the other sector given the initial differential in the rates and subsequently lower the returns to informal workers as well. The argument may be summarized as Claim 9.1.

CLAIM 9.1.

a. *Perfect mobility of capital implies that labour market reforms hurt informal workers while product market reforms are beneficial for them.*

b. *Immobility of capital implies exactly the opposite of (a)*

When both product market reforms and labour market reforms are undertaken simultaneously the implications are countervailing and therefore an improvement in informal wages is only conditionally feasible. And yet, there is a possible case that both can lead to a beneficial impact on informal wages (see Appendix 9A for proof).

PROPOSITION 9.3. $\exists \mu, \mu \in \left(\dfrac{A_1}{B_1 C}, \dfrac{A_1}{B_2 C} \right)$ *such that both types of reforms undertaken simultaneously will improve w*

Proof. A fall in both t and $\bar{w}$ increases informal wage under 'some' capital mobility if and only if the income-share of labour used in the production of commodity X is positive and less than 1. Since this is always true except for the special case where X is produced by labour only, which is not relevant here, there always exists a possibility of wage gain for informal workers (detailed proof in Appendix 9C).

Proposition 9.3 implies that although the success of both types of reforms depends on the extent of capital movement and is in a way conflicting in nature, there are certain degrees of capital mobility as defined in the above range, when the positive impact of tariff reduction outweighs the negative impact of labour market reforms. This is not a trivial result since this is tantamount to identifying the critical degree, or at least the critical zone of capital mobility, that can ensure an increase in informal wages despite the presence of labour market reforms. This zone may certainly be treated as important information when considering capital mobility as a policy variable when improving the conditions of poor informal workers is the target.

Aggressive Labour

An aggressive labour force may negotiate higher formal wages compared to a more submissive labour force. Another way of characterizing labour aggressiveness should be that no matter whether it is the formal or the informal sector, a region is said to be more aggressive if perceived labour costs are higher than in another region with the same $(\bar{w}, w)$. This is justified by the observation that it might be more expensive to maintain the same level of productivity in two regions. A relatively aggressive workforce might imply a bad work culture and loss of actual time of work. Even though for the organized workforce this may not get reflected in the nationally negotiated wage rates, it will be reflected in the local informal wage rates. We capture this effect by a factor $\alpha > 1$ attached to the labour coefficient in competitive price conditions. What we show next is that the Besley and Burgess (2004) proposition is an outcome of our general equilibrium framework.

Once we use the wider interpretation of the phenomenon of labour aggression, the competitive price conditions change to:

$$\bar{w}\alpha a_{LX} + r a_{KX} = P_X(1+t) \tag{9.17}$$

$$w\alpha a_{LY} + r a_{KY} = P_Y \tag{9.18}$$

with, $\alpha > 1$ implying a more aggressive labour force.
Differentiating we get:

$$\hat{w}\theta_{LY} = -\theta_{KY}\hat{r} - \theta_{LY}\hat{\alpha}$$

$$= -\theta_{KY}\left(\frac{\hat{T} - \theta_{LX}\hat{\alpha}}{\theta_{KX}}\right) - \theta_{LY}\hat{\alpha}$$

$$= -\frac{\theta_{KY}}{\theta_{KY}}\hat{T} + \hat{\alpha}\left[\frac{\theta_{KY}\theta_{LX}}{\theta_{KX}} - \theta_{LY}\right] \tag{9.19}$$

Note that even if we do not bring in policy reforms into the picture, greater value of α will reduce informal wages if X is relatively capital intensive, which we suppose is a reasonable assumption. More aggressive labour will affect informal workers because the effect of a unit cost increase will be felt more on a sector which uses more labour per unit. For the same reason the positive effect of trade reforms on w, a drop in T, will be dampened.

* * *

What we have discussed so far, with the help of two closely-related models and supporting evidence, is that essentially the level of informal activity is generally increasing in India with some very recent downturns (as observed from the last round of NSSO data). This chapter not only documented some of these tendencies, but also offered a theoretical explanation of how the informal sector through its linkages to formal manufacturing or independently as a non-traded service sector is expected to respond to trade related reforms. For India, it is observed empirically that wage and employment growth in the urban informal sector, which typically includes the non-directory manufacturing sector, is positive and considerable. The growth in informal wages is capable of reducing the incidence of urban poverty. Although the relationship is sought out from disparate data sources, the overwhelming presence of informal workers and the glaring existence of urban poverty cannot be completely un-correlated. A substantive improvement in these results may require large-scale primary surveys on the urban informal sector and the poverty status of the respondents to arrive at a more meaningful relationship.

This chapter also showed that product market and labour market reforms should have different impacts on informal wages, which we hold as the benchmark for poor people's income in a developing country. The role of capital mobility becomes quite crucial in this context. While a more flexible capital movement between the formal and informal segments helps in improving informal wages in the context of product market reforms, the same may hurt informal workers when hiring (or firing) costs go down in the formal sector. This implies that labour-friendly states will have relatively high informal wages when capital does not move a lot. Therefore, if capital does not move around much, labour-friendly states will protect labour unions and hurt informal workers. Movement of capital can itself be a time dependent phenomenon. In the absence of reported mobility patterns we used growth in fixed assets in the informal sector as a proxy for formal–informal mobility of capital and the supplementary empirical analysis suggests that capital formation in the informal sector pushes up informal wages and the increase in wages had a significant negative impact on urban poverty between 1989 and 2000.

NOTES

1. Chaudhuri (2003) provides examples of how wages are negotiated between employers and labour unions in the presence of an informal sector. The second model in this chapter also solves explicitly for wage negotiations.

2. The authenticity of the BPL list is far from acceptable due to strong political incentives attached to such enlistment in a fragmented society such as India, and we intend to use other measures of poverty and further evidence on informal labour mobility across sectors, in future.

3. See Appendix 9C for a brief derivation on endogenous wage formation in the presence of labour unions in the formal sector.

APPENDIX 9A

A reduction in the tariff rate and the consequent equations of change are given below. Two generic derivations are given below and the rest follows the same procedure.

$$\frac{d\bar{w}_S}{\bar{w}_S}\frac{a_{SX}\bar{w}_S}{P_X^*(1+t)} + \frac{da_{SX}}{a_{SX}}\frac{a_{SX}\bar{w}_S}{P_X^*(1+t)} + \frac{dr}{r}\frac{a_{KX}r}{P_X^*(1+t)} + \frac{da_{kX}}{a_{KX}}\frac{a_{kX}\bar{w}_S}{P_X^*(1+t)}$$

$$= \frac{dP_X^*}{P_X^*(1+t)}P_X^*(1+t) + \frac{dt}{t}\frac{t}{P_X^*(1+t)}P_X^*$$

Since $\bar{w}_S$ and P_X^* do not change, and using the envelope condition

$$\left[\frac{da_{SX}}{a_{SX}}\frac{a_{SX}\bar{w}_S}{P_X^*(1+t)} + \frac{da_{kX}}{a_{KX}}\frac{a_{kX}\bar{w}_S}{P_X^*(1+t)} = 0\right]$$ the above expression yields:

$$\theta_{KX}\hat{r} = \alpha\hat{t}, \text{ where, } \alpha = t/(1+t) \tag{9A.1}$$

where, $\theta_{KX} = \dfrac{a_{KX}r}{P_X^*(1+t)}$, the income share of capital in sector X, and more generally, all θ_{ij}'s are income shares of factor i in the price of commodity j.

Thus, $\hat{r} = \dfrac{\alpha\hat{t}}{\theta_{KX}} < 0, \text{ as, } \hat{t} < 0$

Now using equation (9.2),

$$\hat{P}_1 = -\frac{\theta_{KY}}{\theta_{IY}}\frac{\alpha\hat{t}}{\theta_{KX}} > 0, \text{ as, } \hat{t} < 0 \tag{9A.2}$$

Deriving equation (9.3) and substituting the above information yields:

$$\hat{w} = -\frac{\alpha\hat{t}}{\theta_{KX}}\frac{\theta_{KY}}{\theta_{LI}}\left(1+\frac{1}{\theta_{IY}}\right) > 0, \text{ as, } \hat{t} < 0 \tag{9A.3}$$

Finally, from equation (9.4),

$$\theta_{LZ}\hat{w} = \hat{P}_Z, \text{ such that, } \hat{P}_Z = \alpha\hat{t}\frac{\theta_{LZ}}{\theta_{KX}}\frac{\theta_{KY}}{\theta_{LI}}\left(1+\frac{1}{\theta_{IY}}\right) > 0 \tag{9A.4}$$

The above implies $(\hat{w} - \hat{r}) > 0$

Similarly, equation (9.5) may be derived in the following way:

$$\frac{dX}{X}\frac{a_{SX}X}{S} + \frac{da_{SX}}{a_{SX}}\frac{a_{SX}X}{S} + \frac{dY}{Y}\frac{a_{SX}Y}{S} + \frac{da_{SY}}{a_{SY}}\frac{a_{SX}Y}{S} = \frac{d\overline{S}}{\overline{S}}$$

Such that,

$$\lambda_{SX}\hat{X} + \lambda_{SY}\hat{Y} = -\lambda_{SX}\hat{a}_{SX} - \lambda_{SY}\hat{a}_{SY} \tag{9A.5}$$

where, $\lambda_{SX} = \dfrac{a_{SX}X}{S}$, the skill endowment does not change and more generally, all λ_{ij}'s represent ith factor's physical contribution to the production of commodity j. Using factor price changes and the degree of substitution between factors, equation (9A.5) yields:

$$\lambda_{SX}\hat{X} + \lambda_{SY}\hat{Y} = -\left[\lambda_{SX}\theta_{KX}\sigma_X + \lambda_{SY}\theta_{KY}\sigma_Y\right]\hat{r} \tag{9A.6}$$

Again from equation (9.7), assuming that the informal intermediate input is used in fixed proportions without any substitution with capital or labour, we get:

$$\lambda_{KX}\hat{X} + \lambda_{KY}\hat{Y} = -\lambda_{KX}\hat{a}_{KX} - \lambda_{KY}\hat{a}_{KY} - \lambda_{KI}\left(\hat{a}_{KI} + \hat{I}\right) \tag{9A.7}$$

However, from equation (9.8), $\lambda_{IY}\left(\hat{a}_{IY} + \hat{Y}\right) = \hat{I}$

Since I is used in fixed proportions in the production of Y, thus, $\hat{a}_{IY} = 0$ and the above relationship becomes,

$$\lambda_{IY}\hat{Y} = \hat{I} \tag{9A.8}$$

Substituting (9A.8) in (9A.7), we get,

$$\lambda_{KX}\hat{X} + \lambda_{KY}\hat{Y} = -\lambda_{KX}\hat{a}_{KX} - \lambda_{KY}\hat{a}_{KY} - \lambda_{KI}\lambda_{IY}\hat{Y}$$

that is, $\lambda_{KX}\hat{X} + \left(\lambda_{KY} + \lambda_{KI}\lambda_{IY}\right)\hat{Y} = \left[\lambda_{KX}\theta_{SX}\sigma_X + \lambda_{KY}\theta_{SY}\sigma_Y\right]\hat{r}$

$$\tag{9A.9}$$

These two equations solve for $\hat{X}$ and $\hat{Y}$ simultaneously.
Denote $\tilde{\lambda}_{KY} = \left(\lambda_{KY} + \lambda_{KI}\lambda_{IY}\right)$ i.e., direct and indirect (via production of I) use of capital in the production of Y.

Thus, $\begin{bmatrix} \lambda_{SX} & \lambda_{SY} \\ \lambda_{KX} & \tilde{\lambda}_{KY} \end{bmatrix}\begin{bmatrix} \hat{X} \\ \hat{Y} \end{bmatrix} = \begin{bmatrix} -(\lambda_{SX}\theta_{KX}\sigma_X + \lambda_{SY}\theta_{KY}\sigma_Y)\hat{r} \\ \lambda_{KX}\theta_{SX}\sigma_X + \lambda_{KY}\theta_{SY}\sigma_Y)\hat{r} \end{bmatrix}$ (9A.10)

Using Cramer's rule on equation (9A.10),

$$\hat{X} =$$

$$\frac{-\tilde{\lambda}_{KY}\left(\lambda_{SX}\theta_{KX}\sigma_X + \lambda_{SY}\theta_{KY}\sigma_Y\right)\hat{r} - \lambda_{SY}\left(\lambda_{KX}\theta_{SX}\sigma_X + \lambda_{KY}\theta_{SY}\sigma_Y\right)\hat{r}}{\left(\lambda_{SX}\tilde{\lambda}_{KY} - \lambda_{KX}\lambda_{SY}\right)}$$

or, $\hat{X} = -\hat{r}$

$$\frac{\left(\tilde{\lambda}_{KY}\lambda_{SX}\theta_{KX} + \lambda_{SY}\lambda_{KX}\theta_{SX}\right)\sigma_X + \left(\tilde{\lambda}_{KY}\lambda_{SY}\theta_{KY} + \lambda_{SY}\lambda_{KY}\theta_{SY}\right)\sigma_Y}{\left(\lambda_{SX}\tilde{\lambda}_{KY} - \lambda_{KX}\lambda_{SY}\right)}$$

$$\text{(9A.11)}$$

Denote, $\Delta = (\lambda_{SX}\tilde{\lambda}_{KY} - \lambda_{KX}\lambda_{SY}) < 0$, which implies that sector X is more capital intensive compared to sector Y. Consequently, $\hat{X} < 0$, *as*, $\hat{r} < 0$ *and* $\Delta < 0$.

Conversely, $\hat{Y} =$

$$\frac{\lambda_{SX}\left(\lambda_{KX}\theta_{SX}\sigma_X + \lambda_{KY}\theta_{SY}\sigma_Y\right)\hat{r} + \lambda_{KX}\left(\lambda_{SX}\theta_{KX}\sigma_X + \lambda_{SY}\theta_{KY}\sigma_Y\right)\hat{r}}{\left(\lambda_{SX}\tilde{\lambda}_{KY} - \lambda_{KX}\lambda_{SY}\right)} > 0$$

that is $\hat{Y} = \lambda_{SX}\hat{r}\dfrac{\left[\lambda_{KX}\sigma_X + \lambda_{KY}\left(1 - \theta_{IY}\right)\sigma_Y\right]}{\left(\lambda_{SX}\tilde{\lambda}_{KY} - \lambda_{KX}\lambda_{SY}\right)} > 0$ (9A.12)

Equation (9.8) then yields: $\hat{I} = \lambda_{IY}\hat{Y}$

or, $\hat{I} = \lambda_{IY}\lambda_{SX}\dfrac{\alpha\hat{t}}{\theta_{KX}}\dfrac{\left[\lambda_{KX}\sigma_X + \lambda_{KY}(1 - \theta_{IY})\sigma_Y\right]}{(\lambda_{SX}\tilde{\lambda}_{KY} - \lambda_{KX}\lambda_{SY})} > 0$

and finally from equation (9.6),

$$\hat{Z} > 0, \text{ iff, } \lambda_{IY}\lambda_{SX}\left[\lambda_{KX}\sigma_X + \lambda_{KY}\left(1 - \theta_{IY}\right)\sigma_Y\right] >$$

$$\sigma_1\left(\frac{\tilde{\theta}_{KY}}{\theta_{IY}} + \theta_{KY}\right), \text{ where } \tilde{\theta}_{KY} = \left(\theta_{KY} + \theta_{KI}\theta_{IY}\right)$$

QED.

Proof of Proposition 9.2 follows similarly.

APPENDIX 9B

Table 9B.1   Regressing Current Period's BPL Percentage on Previous Year's Annual Growth of Informal Wage

Dependent Variable: BPLPER
Methodology: OLS

Exp. Variables	Coeff.	t-ratio	R^2	AIC	Log - Likelihood
IWPREV	(–) 0.236	(–) 2.57*	0.13	7.883	(–) 183.24
CONSTANT	27.85	14.53*			

Note: BPLPER = BPL percentage
    IWPREV = Previous year's growth rate of informal wage
Source: Own calculations.

Table 9B.2   Unbalanced Panel Regression of Current Period's BPL Percentage on Previous Year's Annual Growth of Informal Wage

Dependent Variable: BPLPER
Model: Random Effects Model

Exp. Variables	Coeff.	t-ratio
IWPREV	(–) 0.229	(–) 5.17*
CONSTANT	27.12	11.98*

Diagnostics tests for the model:

Random Effects Model: $v(i,t) = e(i,t) + u(i)$
Fixed vs. Random Effects (Hausman) = .01
(1 df, prob value = .940154)
(High (low) values of H favour FEM (REM).)

Sum of Squares	.6723
R-squared	.1248

Source: Own calculations.
Note: BPLPER = BPL percentage
    IWPREV = Previous year's growth rate of informal wage

APPENDIX 9C

Endogenous Determination of $\overline{w}$

The labour union is concerned only with the wage setting in the formal sector, i.e., sector X, given the sectoral stock of capital (we will derive two variations—one with the sector-specific capital and the other with fully mobile capital).

The union's utility function is given by:

$$U = U(\overline{w}, L_X(\overline{w})) \qquad (9C.1)$$

where,
$$L_X = a_{LX} X = \frac{a_{LX}}{a_{KX}} \bar{K}_X = \phi(\frac{\bar{w}}{r}) \bar{K}_X$$

$$= \phi\left(\frac{\bar{w}}{f(P_X, \bar{w})}\right) \bar{K}_X \tag{9C.2}$$

since from competitive price conditions in equation (9.11), r is determined by $(P_X, \bar{w})$.

Now, given $\bar{K}_X$, it is easy to show from (9B.2) that $\frac{\delta L_X}{\delta \bar{w}} < 0$, as $\phi' < 0$.

From (9C.1),

$$\frac{\delta U}{\delta \bar{w}} = 0 \Rightarrow \frac{\delta U}{\delta \bar{w}} + \frac{\delta U}{\delta L_X} \frac{\delta L_X}{\delta \bar{w}} = 0 \tag{9C.3}$$

Let us assume sufficient restrictions on U, such that, $\frac{\delta^2 U}{\delta \bar{w}^2} < 0$. From (9C.3), consider an equilibrium value of formal wage solving the relation: $\bar{w}^*$

We have now set the framework for capturing the labour market reforms. Consider a slight modification of equations (9C.1) and (9C.2), as follows:

$$U = U(\bar{w}\gamma, L_X(\bar{w}\gamma)) \tag{9C.1.1}$$

and
$$L_X = \phi\left(\frac{\bar{w}\gamma}{f(P_X, \gamma\bar{w})}\right) \bar{K}_X \tag{9C.2.1}$$

where, $\gamma > 1 \Rightarrow$ *Pro–labor regulations*
$\gamma < 1 \Rightarrow$ *Anti–Labor regulations*

It also implies that any rise in γ would be a move towards pro–labour regulations and vice versa. Given $(\gamma, \bar{K}_X, P_X)$ and with some restrictions on the functions, $U(.)$, $\phi(.)$ and $f(.)$ we can derive:

$$\bar{w}^* = \phi(\gamma, \bar{K}_X, P_X) \tag{9C.4}$$

We reinstate this optimal value of $\bar{w}^*$ in equation (9C.1.1) and differentiate totally with respect to γ, such that the relationship between the union-determined wage rate and the labour market reform turns out to be negative, that is, $\frac{d\bar{w}^*}{d\gamma} < 0$.

Thus, any percentage change in the formal wage as determined by union bargaining can be explicitly written as a linear combination of the percentage change in the arguments:

$$\hat{\bar{w}}^* = -\alpha_1 \hat{\gamma} + \alpha_2 \hat{P}_X + \alpha_3 \hat{\bar{K}}_X, \qquad \alpha_i > 0, i = 1, 2, 3 \qquad (9C.5)$$

Now using equations (9.11) and (9.12), we can re-write the equations of change (with fixed commodity prices) as:

$$\hat{\bar{w}}\theta_{LX} + \hat{r}\theta_{KX} = -\hat{\gamma}\theta_{LX} \qquad (9C.6)$$

and

$$\hat{w}\theta_{LY} + \hat{R}\theta_{KY} = 0 \qquad (9C.7)$$

Using (9C.6) and (9C.7), $(-\alpha_1 + 1)\hat{\gamma}\theta_{LX} + \hat{r}\theta_{KX} = 0$

Here, as long as, $(-\alpha_1 + 1) > 0$, a rise in $\hat{\gamma}$ will lead to a fall in $\hat{r}$, and the rest of the results hold. In other words, a move towards pro–poor labour regulations would unambiguously reduce the return to capital accruing to that sector. The result would be indifferent even if capital were fully mobile between the two sectors earning the same returns in both the places. The added implication would have been a rise in unorganized wages as well due to pro–labour market reforms. In fact, we have argued in the main text that places where reforms are labour-friendly in nature, the informal sector can register an increase in wages with palpable impact on the level of poverty, provided capital is relatively free to move.

General Condition for Claim 9.1

We are interested in the impact of a decline in t and $\bar{w}$ on w, the informal wage. We have to solve for $\hat{w}$ as a function of $\hat{\bar{w}}$ and $(1 + \hat{t}) = \hat{T}$. We follow Jones (1971) and Marjit and Kar (2007) closely to derive the following, by differentiating equations (9.18) and using (9.17a).

$$-\lambda_{LX}\frac{\sigma_X}{\sigma_{KX}}(\hat{\bar{w}} - \hat{T}) - \mu\lambda_{KX}\left(\lambda_{LY} - \lambda_{LX}\frac{\lambda_{KY}}{\lambda_{KX}}\right)(\hat{r} - \hat{R}) \qquad (9C.8)$$

where, λ s are allocation shares of labour and capital in each sector, σ s are elasticity of factor substitution and θ s are the cost-shares. Substituting for $\hat{r}, \hat{R}$ etc. by differentiating competitive price equations we get:

$$\hat{w} = \hat{T}\frac{[-A_1 + \mu B_1 C]}{-D_1 - \mu D_2 C} + \hat{\bar{w}}\frac{[A_1 - \mu B_2 C]}{-D_1 - \mu D_2 C} \qquad (9C.9)$$

where,

$$A_1 = \frac{\lambda_{LX}\sigma_X}{\theta_{KX}}, \; B_1 = \frac{\lambda_{KX}}{\theta_{KX}}, \; B_2 = \frac{\lambda_{KX}\theta_{LX}}{\theta_{KX}}, \; C = \lambda_{LY}\frac{\lambda_{LY}\lambda_{KY}}{\lambda_{KY}}$$

$$D_1 = \frac{\lambda_{LY}\sigma_Y}{\theta_{KY}}, \; D_2 = \lambda_{KY}\frac{\theta_{LY}}{\theta_{KY}}$$

(9C.9) helps us in framing Claim 9.1.

Proof of Claim 9.1. (a): When $\mu \to \alpha$, from (9C.9)

$$\hat{w} = \hat{T}.\frac{B_1}{-D_2} + \hat{\underset{\sim}{w}}\frac{B_2}{D_2}$$

Therefore, $\hat{w} > 0$ if $\hat{T} < 0$ and $\hat{w} < 0$ if $\hat{\underset{\sim}{w}} < 0$

Proof of 9.1 (b). When $\mu \to 0$, from (9C.9)

$$\hat{w} = \hat{T}.\frac{A}{D_1} + \hat{\underset{\sim}{w}}.\frac{A_1}{-D_1}$$

Therefore, $\hat{w} < 0$ if $\hat{T} < 0$ and $\hat{w} > 0$ if $\hat{\underset{\sim}{w}} < 0$. QED

Proof of Proposition 9.3.
From (9C.9)

$$\hat{w} = \frac{\hat{T}(A_1 - \mu B_1 C)}{D_1 + \mu D_2 C} + \hat{\underset{\sim}{w}}\frac{(\mu B_2 C - A_1)}{D_1 + \mu D_2 C} \qquad (9C.10)$$

It is easy to check that:

$$\frac{\hat{w}}{\hat{T}} < 0 \text{ if } A_1 < \mu B_1 C \text{ and } \frac{\hat{w}}{\hat{\underset{\sim}{w}}} < 0 \text{ if } \mu B_2 C < A_1$$

Therefore, for both types of reforms to have a positive impact on w one must have:

$$\frac{A_1}{B_2 C} > \frac{A_1}{B_1 C} \text{ Or, } \frac{1}{B_2} > \frac{1}{B_1}$$

Or, $B_2 < B_1$ which always holds as $0 < \theta_{LX} < 1$.

10 Reforms and Productivity in the Informal Sector

In the previous chapters we have mostly offered aggregative and theoretical views on the functioning of an informal sector in the context of a developing country. However, we did hint that a few studies based on contemporary primary surveys as well as secondary data would complement the wide-ranging issues that we have tried to analyse so far. To this end, this chapter deals with specific micro-econometric characteristics reflecting on some aspects of formal–informal relations. Similar in spirit to Chapter 8, certain observations in this chapter are also derived from primary surveys conducted in the states of West Bengal, Maharashtra, and Gujarat. This chapter tries to provide answers to some distinct questions:

1. Whether productivity in the informal sector is lower than it is in the formal sector and what are the constraints in raising productivity in the former?
2. What are the channels through which productivity changes take effect?
3. Is productivity change in the informal sector capable of explaining the wage-employment movements significantly?

On the basis of these questions the next section offers a theoretical perspective on productivity in the context of markets characterized by both formal/organized and informal/unorganized activities. The propositions discussed in this section provide the building block for subsequent empirical investigations. The relationship between formal and informal sector productivity and wages constitutes the key issue and rigorous derivations are worked out in the respective appendices to aid the narrative in the main text.

The government of India adopted the policy of large-scale industrialization led by the public sector and kept protective room for village and small-scale industries in the early plan periods immediately following its independence in 1947. However, since the early 1980s the entire industrialization strategy came under strong criticism for a host of reasons and was held responsible for the slow pace of industrial growth and economic development in the country. Consequently, India gradually set out along the path of economic reforms from the early 1980s and pursued these systematically by adopting 'the three-way fast lane' strategy of economic liberalization, privatization and globalization epitomized by currency devaluations in 1991. The reforms largely included removal of trade restrictions and licensing policies for industries, withdrawal and/or reduction of subsidies and government assistance to the industrial sector, disinvestments in public sector units, flexible foreign capital inflow and export promotion policies. Despite pervasive effects and subsequent discussions of these measures, their impact on formal–informal interaction is scarce in literature.

Some of the theoretical conjectures developed in the next section are subsequently verified with available information on unorganized enterprises in India using NSSO data. The section that follows discusses the general methodology that we adopt for determining productivity dynamics in the informal sector. The purpose of the empirical section is not only to reflect on our brief theoretical conclusions but also to generate various interesting results on productivity dynamics in the formal/informal sectors across states in India. Interestingly, this coincides with the time period during which the country embraced phases of deregulations and reforms that facilitate the treatment as a natural experiment (technical details are given in Appendix 10A [the data envelope method], Appendix 10B [productivity changes] and Appendix 10C [productivity gap]).

A THEORETICAL PERSPECTIVE ON PRODUCTIVITY IN THE INFORMAL SECTOR

The existence of an informal or unorganized sector is widely believed to be a consequence of regulatory controls practised by developing countries. In particular, rigid labour laws reflected in significant retrenchment costs, various taxes imposed on registered enterprises and the possibility of escaping such regulations all lead to the emergence of an extra-legal sector. Hernando de Soto's popular book, *The Mystery of Capital*, provides many examples of such activities. It is natural that in the presence of labour market regulations, firms may hire less productive informal workers at lower wages along with the more productive organized workers. But this may not be the only outcome. It is quite possible that informal workers are as productive as formal workers and if there was no monitoring or fear of regulations no unit would hire workers in the formal sector. Yet, there can be an internal solution because firms will anticipate some auditing or monitoring hazards, thus restricting their informal transactions. This is analysed in Marjit et al. (2007c) and Marjit and Maiti (2007).

Intrinsic differences in labour productivity are difficult to measure since a lot depends on complementary factors. If capital is shy of moving into the informal segment, then informal labour's productivity will remain low. The theoretical papers mentioned earlier bring out certain features of the productivity-wage relationship in the informal sector. In Appendix 10B and 10C, we provide two short technical notes dealing with some results in this context.

1. Productivity of informal workers will be clearly related to informal wages as informal wages are mostly market determined and the labour supply curve may not be infinitely elastic. This is also guided by the fact that poor workers must find jobs to survive (Marjit and Kar 2007).

2. Capital should play some role in determining the level of labour productivity. Very strong trade unions/high effective hiring costs in the organized sector may have a mixed effect on informal wages depending on capital mobility (Marjit and Maiti 2006).

3. More productive formal sector workers again should have a mixed effect on informal wages and productivity (Marjit and Kar 2007).

4. Even if informal workers do have similar productivity and work at lower wages, firms may still prefer working with formal labour (Marjit et al. 2007c; Marjit and Maiti 2007).

5. Informal wages and formal productivity are positively correlated.

A few of these assertions are cross-checked with Indian data. In particular we look at the relationship between wages and productivity in the formal/informal sector, the nature of productivity growth in these segments and the role of capital.

DATABASE AND METHODOLOGY

The Data

The database for a study of the informal sector is very poor in India. The lone source of information on the informal manufacturing sector is the large-scale survey report documented by NSSO, government of India, which has been issued every five years since 1978–9. While most of the countries use the term 'informal sector',[1] India defines it as the 'unorganized sector'.[2] The Annual Survey of Industries (ASI), government of India, compiles detailed information on formal manufacturing at the disaggregate level across regions regularly. An enterprise falls under the unorganized segment not because of illegal or underground activities, but because it is not covered by regular accounts, i.e. non-ASI. However, we do not make a strict distinction between the informal and unorganized sector.

One of the major problems of the manufacturing dataset are the frequent definitional changes of industrial classification. A stark definitional change of the National Industrial Classification (NIC) took place in 1997, which was a departure from NIC 1987 in many respects. However, at the 2-digit level we are able to re-classify those codes to make it into a comparable one at the broad industry division. Since some of the repairing manufacturing codes have now been shifted to the service sector under the new definition, we exclude this group for the industrial analysis. For each time point, the industries are clubbed together into 12 industries. According to the new definition, code 01405 representing cotton ginning, clearing and baling is clubbed with code 17–18 under the textile industry (Table 10A.1).

As per unorganized manufacturing, enterprises are further disaggregated into three categories—OAMEs, NDMEs, and DMEs. OAMEs do not hire any labour while NDMEs and DMEs hire up to five workers and more than five workers on fairly regular basis respectively. Till date, NSSO has published five reports on unorganized manufacturing from 1978–89 to 2000–1, but the first three reports do not cover all the information covered in the most recent one. Also note that details of the last round of the NSS survey 2006–7 are not available as yet.[3]

Methodology

We consider five major variables for the present study—number of enterprises, number of workers, gross value added, fixed capital, and wage rates. Real annual gross value added (GVA) of a particular industry has been computed after deflating it by appropriate manufacturing price indices. We have also argued in Chapter 8 that informal sectors do not report fixed capital and instead 'fixed assets' are taken as a proxy for fixed capital. As there are no hired workers in OAMEs, annual emoluments are available for hired workers only from NDMEs and DMEs. The annual emolument per hired worker (by deflating the same with the consumer price index for industrial workers, CPIIW) is represented as wage for the respective sector. It should be noted that no information on wages is available for DMEs for any of the states in India prior to 1989–90.

There are several parametric and non-parametric methods that can be used for measuring productivity growth. Because of greater heterogeneity among informal enterprises, as also between formal and informal producers, we rely on the data envelope method (DEA), a non-parametric method, for a comparative study on productivity growth. The technique involves the use of linear programming methods to construct a non-parametric piece-wise surface (or frontier) so as to be able to calculate the efficiency scores relative to this surface. The change in the efficiency score from one period to another is simply the total factor productivity growth. Now, the sources of the productivity growth could further be decomposed to technological changes and efficient allocation of resources. The constant returns-to-scale is still assumed leading to TFPG = EFFCH*TECHCH (we apply this empirically in the next section), where, TFPG is total factor productivity growth, EFFCH is efficiency changes and TECHCH is technological changes. When the production technology exhibits constant returns to scale the CRS distance function is indeed a measure of the technical efficiency of a firm. Thus, the first factor in the decomposition shows the change in technical efficiency between two periods and can be characterized as a 'catch up' factor (that is, EFFCH). The second factor is a measure of the shift in the production frontier evaluated at two different input bundles. Being the geometric mean of the two, the second factor is a measure of the autonomous shift in the production frontier and represents technical change (TECHCH). Therefore, TFPG is the product of EFFCH and TECHCH (see Appendix 10C for details).

INFORMAL EMPLOYMENT, WAGES, AND PRODUCTIVITY

Size of the Informal Sector

Table 10A.2 displays some simple statistics in favour of the deepening of informal employment in countries like India (for 2000–1). The share of labour hired under informal arrangements was not only high for agro-allied industries like wood, food, beverages and tobacco, paper, and leather but also reported high incidence (about 80 per cent) in non-agro industries like metal products and machinery and equipment. However, the share of informal employment was lower in basic metal works, transport, rubber and petroleum industries for 2000–1 (Table 10A.3). The share of informal employment also varied significantly across states in India—from 72.80 per cent in Punjab to 92.95 per cent in Bihar during the same period (Table 10A.2). In general, almost 86 per cent of all the units were OAMEs. In other words this signifies large representation of home-based units employing two-third of the total workforce in the unorganized segment. The presence of DMEs is still quite negligible (Tables 10A.4 and 10A.5). Moreover, the informal sector contributed 25.5 per cent of the total industrial value addition in 2000–1 and over the post-reform decade this share is on the rise. The state-specific share of industrial value addition contributed by the informal sector as a whole varied from 13.7 per cent in Haryana to 50.9 per cent in West Bengal during 2000–1.

Sector-wise Productivity Differences

Not surprisingly, an informal production unit is much smaller compared to formal units in terms of the number of hired workers, assets, and value addition. On an average, the gross value addition of a formal unit is at least 400 times more than that of an informal enterprise in India as visible from the data on informal manufacturing in 2000–1. However, labour productivity measured in terms of gross value addition per worker shows near stagnant or, if at all, a meagre rise for formal units compared to a discernible upward trend for informal units across most of the states in post-reform India. We test the statistical significance of this productivity difference and identify some of the sources of productivity growth in these sectors for the said period (Table 10A.6).

Once again, as a continuation of the results in Chapter 8, we begin with a conjecture that capital accumulation in the informal sector should be an important driver of productivity growth. The size of fixed assets in the formal sector is much higher than the informal sector, but both fixed asset per enterprise and fixed asset per worker exhibit a rising trend since 1989–90 in both the sectors (Tables 10A.7 and 10A.8). To examine the productivity difference between sectors, we regress labour productivity (gross valued added per worker) on capital intensity with dummy D_i, where $D_i = 0$ for the informal and $D_i = 1$ for the formal sector. The following (pseudo-panel across states for 2000–1) regression results suggest that formal sector productivity was significantly higher than that of the informal sector (equations 10.1 and 10.2):

$$\text{Fixed Effect: } \ln(GVA/L)_{it} = 4.57^* + 0.48^* \ln(K/L)_{it} + 1.22^* D_p$$

$$(10.1)$$

$$R^2 = 0.97, \rho = 0.37$$

$$\text{Random Effect: } \ln(GVA/L)_{it} = 4.15^* + 0.53^* \ln(K/L)_{it} + 106^* D_p$$

$$(10.2)$$

$$R^2 = 0.97, \rho = 0.16, \text{Hausman} = 0.001$$

To estimate the elasticity of labour productivity with respect to capital intensity for the respective sectors, we conducted separate regressions with a control variable. In these regressions the regional openness index of the states (measured in Marjit et al. 2007) is considered as a control variable. The openness index of a particular state is derived by matching the Indian export and import intensity of industries with the production share of those industries in the respective state. Since region-specific factors (for example, infrastructure, development expenditure, labour laws and policies and socio-political factors) have a direct impact on both factor mobility and industrial production, the openness index could effectively capture these factors.

Therefore, instead of using a series of state-specific factors as control variables, one can use the regional openness index as a proxy. Incorporating this factor in the regression model, we find that the elasticity of labour productivity with respect to capital intensity in the formal sector is significantly higher than that in the informal sector. The elasticity of labour productivity with respect to capital intensity is 0.62 in the formal sector, whereas it is 0.48 in the informal sector (Tables 10A.9 and 10A.10).

Since this method of productivity estimation is partial, it is always better to estimate the total factor productivity both for the formal and informal sectors across states. As discussed in the methodology section, the DEA approach can be applied to estimate total factor productivity and its decomposition. According to this approach, states are the units of observation where gross value addition is the single output while labour and capital are the two inputs. The results of DEA are given in Table 10A.11. It is observed that on an average the total factor productivity (TFPG) in both the formal and informal sectors increased during 1990–2001, while TFPG in the formal sector was much higher than that in the informal sector. It is more interesting that the source of TFPG is technological change (that is, frontier shift) in the formal sector and resource efficiency increases (that is, the caching up effect) in the informal sector. In other words, productivity growth in the formal sector is explained by technological change while it is explained by efficient resource use in its informal counterpart.

What is the explanation for the differences in the sources of productivity growth? We argue that trade and industrial reforms must have imparted a positive impact on capital formation. The removal of trade restrictions helped import of foreign technology for formal producers at a lower cost and export of final goods to the larger export markets at better prices. So, trade reforms eventually helped capital formation in the formal sector. The withdrawal of the licensing system delimited the restriction on capacity utilization and the size of plants and machinery usage under any production unit and this also pushed up the rate of capital formation in the formal sector. As a result, productivity growth in this sector has largely been explained by technological changes. Since the informal production units are small and face severe collateral problems, the rate of capital formation is both slow and negligible in this sector. However, our conjecture is that the largest thrust in productivity in the informal sector has been a result of the linkages that formal firms have increasingly sought in the face of steeper competition. The putting out system as elaborated upon in Chapter 8 may be treated as a convincing case in favour of the noticeable growth in the informal sector. However, one of the major limitations of the TFPG analysis is that labour and capital are only two inputs in the study.

Wages, Productivity, and Sectoral Gaps

As productivity of the informal sector is lower than that of the formal sector, the average real wage rate of hired informal workers is expected to be lower than that of the formal sector and this is exemplified across all the states in India (Table 10A.12). Surprisingly, the average real wage rate for formal workers registers a declining trend in most of the states while that of the informal sector registers a sharp rising trend during 1995–2001 (Table 10A.12). To find out the relationship between wages and productivity, we ran both correlation and panel regressions. While the correlation coefficient between formal wages and formal labour productivity declined between 1989–90 and 2000–1, the correlation coefficients between informal wages and informal productivity as well as that between informal wages and formal productivity rose steadily (Table 10A.13).

On the other hand, the regression coefficient of formal wages on formal labour productivity was not statistically significant, but that of informal wages on formal labour productivity was positive and highly significant (Table 10A.14). These results suggest that in a typical developing country, productivity augmenting efforts in the formal sector will be limited by the existence of a wide informal sector where workers can be hired at lower wage rates. In fact, Table 10A.15 offers a characterization of the typical problems faced by informal units and the types of assistance received from various sources. Not surprisingly, most of these units belonging to OAME/DME/NDME categories never received any assistance in the form of loans, subsidies, and so on (Table 10A.16). The expansion of informal wages must push cost-cutting efforts in the formal sector and this essentially improves labour productivity in the formal sector as well (A technical note in Appendix 10B offers some analytically tractable results).

Looking at the stagnant or declining real formal wages vis-à-vis rising informal wages, it is natural to measure movements in the formal–informal wage gap during the post-reform decade in India. We estimate the beta-coefficient of the trend factor, which reveals a converging pattern between these sectors and is given by:

$$\frac{1}{T} \ln(w_{it} / w_{i0}) = \alpha - (e^{-\beta} - 1) \ln w_{io} + \gamma X_{it} + u_{it} \quad (10.3)$$

We estimated equation (10.3) and found the following results:
Fixed effect model:

$$\frac{1}{T} \ln(w_{it} / w_{i0}) = 0.07 - 0.14 \ln w_{io} + 0.001 X_{it}, R^2 = 0.48, \rho = 0.80$$

Random effect model:

$$\frac{1}{T} \ln(w_{it} / w_{i0}) = 0.04 - 0.13 \ln w_{io} + 0.001 X_{it}, R^2 = 0.58, \rho = 0.56,$$

$$\text{Hausman} = 0.13$$

The Hausman test statistic suggests that the random effect model is not rejected. The rate of convergence in the formal–informal wage gap is 3.10 per cent per annum.

Using Appendix 10C we allow for labour productivity augmenting expenditure F only in the formal sector. It is possible that such a venture will be difficult to set up in an extra-legal segment. Also, as we shall see even if the firm can potentially promote such initiatives in the informal segment it might not be optimal for it to do so. This productivity gap and the choice of locating production in any of the two sectors is also testimony to the fact that the formal sector outsources to the informal sector primarily through the vertical linkage between the two sectors (Chapter 4). The working out in Appendix 10C therefore complements the analysis of the decision problem often encountered by potential producers in locating their production units—with a special emphasis on the impact of productivity enhancement in the formal sector on such choices.

* * *

The present chapter discussed the complex relationship between economic reform and productivity in the informal sector. It is difficult to find out an exact match of theoretical conjectures in terms of the empirical evidence. Yet in accordance with the specified objectives of the study we were able to show that:

1. Informal wages and productivity are closely related and the nature of productivity growth in the informal sector is a bit different from that in the formal sector. Moreover, informal wages and formal sector productivity are linked in an interesting way. A theoretical set-up is suggested in the Appendix in this context. An interesting idea is that the more affluent informal sector forces the formal sector to look for productivity augmenting strategies. We showed that although the level of productivity is higher in the formal sector, productivity growth has been higher in the informal segment in the post-reform period.

2. Wages and productivity are naturally linked to capital. We were able to shed some light on the role of capital in determining wages and productivity in the informal sector. Capital mobility plays an important role. However, productivity response to capital is more in the formal than in the informal sector (also see the technical note in the Appendix where we show how capital movement determines productivity growth spill-over from the formal to the informal sector).

NOTES

1. The *organized sector* comprises of enterprises for which statistics are available regularly from budget documents or reports, annual reports in the case of the public sector and Annual Survey of Industries (ASI) in case of registered manufacturing. On the other hand, the *unorganized sector* refers to those enterprises whose activities or collection of data is not regulated under any legal provision and/or which do not maintain any regular accounts. Non-availability of regular information has been the main criteria for treating the sector as unorganized. This definition helps to demarcate the organized from the unorganized. In other words, the enterprises covered under ASI do not fall under the purview of the unorganized sector (55th NSS Round, Report No. 456/55/2.0/1: 2).

2. Here, all unincorporated proprietary and partnership enterprises have been defined as informal sector enterprises. In the unorganized sector, in addition to the unincorporated proprietary or partnership enterprises, enterprises run by cooperative societies, trusts, private, and public limited companies (non-ASI) are also covered. The informal sector can, therefore, be considered as a sub-set of the unorganized sector (55th NSS Round, Report No. 456/55/2.0/1: 2).

3. When this book went to press, the NSSO 2006–7 report was not available. However, we believe that we have adequate record of outcomes till 2004–5 to substantiate our claims.

APPENDIX 10A

Tables

Table 10A.1   Re-grouping Industry Codes according to
NIC 1987 and 1998 Classifications

Industry	1987 Code	1998 code
Food, beverages, and tobacco	20–22	15–16
Textiles	23–26	01405, 17–18
Wood	27	20
Paper	28	21–22
Leather	29	19
Chemical	30	24
Rubber plastics and petroleum	31	23,25
Non-metal	32	26
Basic-metals	33	27
Metal products	34	28
Machinary and equipment	35–36	29–33,36
Transport	37–38	34–35

Source: Summary Statistics, ASI (1997, 1998) and NSS report 56th Round.

Table 10A.2   Share of Workers in Unorganized Manufacturing Sector
by States (% of total state level manufacturing workers)

	Without DME			With DME		
	1989–90	1994–5	2000–1	1989–90	1994–5	2000–1
Andhra Pradesh	79.77	71.90	79.15	82.07	74.14	81.20
Assam	72.71	85.66	83.66	75.21	86.00	84.36
Bihar	87.52	90.05	92.67	88.20	90.58	92.95
Gujarat	64.90	65.55	63.41	75.19	76.05	72.88
Haryana	65.37	53.59	60.12	69.77	60.21	65.90
Himachal Pradesh	87.88	76.67	81.84	88.73	78.31	83.87
Karnataka	81.86	79.20	81.44	85.61	84.03	84.98
Kerala	82.00	63.87	75.86	86.33	69.83	80.28
Madhya Pradesh	80.44	79.83	87.23	82.30	81.13	88.28
Maharashtra	68.16	62.96	71.94	74.10	72.00	78.43
Orissa	95.04	95.36	95.57	95.20	95.45	95.69
Punjab	61.17	55.97	66.47	65.83	62.55	72.80
Rajasthan	85.49	80.12	85.37	86.76	81.20	86.72
Tamil Nadu	77.68	69.45	73.89	81.83	75.79	78.82
Uttar Pradesh	87.37	89.71	91.31	89.18	91.03	92.89
West Bengal	90.74	87.02	91.87	91.41	88.28	92.79
Delhi	72.56	74.00	85.80	85.11	85.74	91.81
All India	82.40	66.91	83.52	84.83	70.91	85.80

Source: ASI and NSSO (respective years); Directory Manufacturing Enterprises.

Table 10A.3 Share of GVA and Workers in the Informal Sector by Industry

	Share of Workers in Informal Sector (%)					Share of GVA in Informal Sector (%)				
	1978–9	1984–5	1989–90	1994–5	2000–1	1978–9	1984–5	1989–90	1994–5	2000–1
Food, beverages, and tobacco	72.23	87.02	85.29	82.32	82.73	41.76	52.18	41.99	33.67	43.09
Textiles	77.98	89.56	83.96	81.50	77.72	33.93	53.48	37.81	28.33	46.35
Wood	94.75	97.01	97.60	97.01	95.28	44.37	71.76	51.36	66.99	93.57
Paper	71.97	68.60	84.55	69.26	80.29	65.34	69.85	66.37	50.14	22.67
Leather	64.54	81.63	80.93	85.09	71.27	70.12	68.72	70.75	51.05	40.50
Chemical	56.93	54.80	38.85	18.37	35.07	8.67	10.92	4.78	4.44	2.95
Rubber plastics and petroleum	76.64	83.58	92.35	89.53	46.87	3.96	5.65	11.45	4.28	10.38
Non-metal	25.53	25.67	20.56	21.59	85.12	33.68	33.42	31.23	28.56	31.82
Basic metals	55.96	60.91	66.22	67.20	15.82	3.66	5.14	4.51	2.30	3.24
Metal products	49.99	59.56	75.96	74.31	81.24	45.38	58.47	49.57	45.32	41.61
Machinary and equipment	25.66	33.58	52.89	49.78	83.53	8.07	10.34	12.66	9.93	25.51
Transport	65.69	71.51	81.75	82.85	23.49	17.61	31.33	32.61	29.67	6.35
All	71.25	82.81	81.46	78.37	78.42	27.07	37.33	29.87	21.71	28.07

Source: ASI and NSSO.
Note: Re-estimated according to NIC definition 1998.

Table 10A.4   Unorganized Manufacturing by Types of Enterprises

Year	Share of Enterprises in (%)			Absolute Number of Enterprises			
	OAME	NDME	DME	OAME	NDME	DME	Total
1978–9	95.68		4.32	7,187,173		324,197	7,511,370
1984–5	86.77	10.67	2.56	15,356,726	1,889,176	452,509	17,698,411
1989–90	86.93	9.56	3.72	12,709,320	1,398,056	543,409	14,620,785
1994–5	84.59	10.40	5.01	10,710,987	1,316,757	634,004	12,661,748
2000–1	86.19	10.05	3.76	14,670,000	1,710,000	640,000	17,020,000

Source: NSS report (various rounds).

Table 10A.5   Workers in Unorganized Manufacturing
by Types of Enterprises

Year	Share of Enterprises in (%)			Absolute Number of Enterprises			
	OAME	NDME	DME	OAME	NDME	DME	Total
1978–9	77.78		22.22	12,984,221		3,709,557	16,693,778
1984–5	74.15	12.62	13.23	25,418,255	4,327,124	4,535,870	34,281,249
1989–90	69.38	13.40	17.22	22,789,981	4,402,547	5,656,635	32,849,163
1994–5	68.11	13.69	18.19	20,512,449	4,124,179	5,478,046	30,114,674
2000–1	67.58	14.99	17.42	25,060,000	5,560,000	6,460,000	37,080,000

Source: NSS report (various rounds).

Table 10A.6 Real GVA per Worker by States (in Rs 100,000)

State	Formal			Informal without DME			Informal with DME		
	1989–90	1994–5	2000–1	1989–90	1994–5	2000–1	1989–90	1994–5	2000–1
Andhra Pradesh	55,859	93,600	99,091	4,288	5,334	7,273	4,394	5,841	8,154
Assam	121,584	102,492	118,578	6,462	5,649	9,960	7,532	5,912	11,194
Bihar	154,334	174,546	221,411	7,425	5,843	8,136	7,813	5,976	8,637
Gujarat	117,194	229,594	283,751	19,301	12,906	16,638	15,132	15,544	19,125
Haryana	109,689	150,910	223,213	8,374	15,522	15,858	14,170	20,137	18,314
Himachal Pradesh	115,405	188,139	354,982	12,191	7,159	11,362	13,403	7,682	14,487
Karnataka	120,800	173,724	194,272	5,330	6,596	8,816	5,646	7,067	9,840
Kerala	106,577	78,337	108,657	5,740	7,969	11,124	6,511	8,595	12,983
Madhya Pradesh	147,232	217,470	277,599	5,271	6,373	6,420	5,985	9,264	7,271
Maharashtra	185,831	268,129	315,094	9,277	11,941	13,557	15,004	16,451	17,494
Orissa	170,424	158,313	212,283	2,273	2,325	3,482	2,556	2,467	3,758
Punjab	113,433	116,937	129,110	12,319	14,850	16,994	14,172	16,885	20,432
Rajasthan	103,813	196,273	251,614	6,882	10,339	12,536	8,152	11,115	13,940
Tamil Nadu	106,940	135,241	149,697	5,029	8,118	9,263	6,516	11,038	11,958
Uttar Pradesh	116,773	192,203	214,509	5,491	6,485	7,498	6,340	7,588	8,860
West Bengal	67,296	98,239	106,662	4,890	5,491	7,078	5,511	6,285	8,542
Delhi	105,609	222,398	191,485	23,237	18,695	26,960	11,544	20,412	29,247
All India	117,200	84,775	198,646	3,948	6,951	8,927	5,394	8,792	11,075

Source: ASI and NSSO (respective years).

Table 10A.7   Real Fixed Assets per Enterprise by States (Rs)

State	Formal			Informal without DME			Informal with DME		
	1989–90	1994–5	2000–1	1989–90	1994–5	2000–1	1989–90	1994–5	2000–1
Andhra Pradesh	6,737,426	13,628,606	12,828,948	7,153	10,070	19,073	NA	10,433	23,621
Assam	8,747,398	11,604,739	26,428,740	9,545	8,181	11,392	NA	8,141	12,960
Bihar	27,343,846	36,655,000	39,336,617	14,161	10,407	15,611	NA	9,899	16,739
Gujarat	12,455,562	21,040,161	34,961,584	33,955	39,400	61,114	NA	64,018	88,207
Haryana	14,211,286	17,171,870	21,477,713	25,923	38,572	85,142	NA	9,300	116,138
Himachal Pradesh	49,515,313	54,427,435	45,903,881	35,812	16,491	34,512	NA	10,045	50,454
Karnataka	10,005,869	14,785,496	25,667,300	9,440	13,488	21,929	NA	20,321	31,917
Kerala	9,537,991	9,141,109	9,612,778	10,462	15,874	32,901	NA	8,267	48,350
Madhya Pradesh	35,444,595	46,791,189	31,438,982	11,032	14,502	19,586	NA	13,624	23,913
Maharashtra	17,339,473	22,167,655	24,906,624	21,228	39,463	53,213	NA	78,891	85,447
Orissa	50,968,757	63,402,305	47,072,000	4,405	3,842	7,381	NA	4,634	8,340
Punjab	11,699,694	15,147,740	8,131,834	32,877	13,820	71,867	NA	16,978	113,637
Rajasthan	18,781,142	22,539,896	18,277,211	20,362	13,952	39,015	NA	12,587	46,254
Tamil Nadu	9,710,269	13,425,883	12,415,718	10,421	8,747	33,725	NA	18,449	53,222
Uttar Pradesh	17,019,438	27,718,705	24,135,866	13,433	9,083	24,308	NA	11,217	33,410
West Bengal	19,464,024	34,923,640	19,355,927	5,833	6,782	12,120	NA	6,223	16,717
Delhi	2,383,993	8,063,169	4,323,406	95,998	93,271	241,282	NA	199,058	317,632
All India	14,126,454	20,474,363	20,739,871	12,839	13,392	28,260	NA	28,921	40,759

Source: ASI and NSSO (respective years).

Table 10A.8 Real Fixed Assets per Worker by States (Rs)

State	Formal			Informal without DME			Informal with DME		
	1989–90	1994–5	2000–1	1989–90	1994–5	2000–1	1989–90	1994–5	2000–1
Andhra Pradesh	154,316	254,548	235,606	4,089	5,243	10,281	NA	5,970	11,501
Assam	136,693	173,320	410,118	5,648	4,117	6,631	NA	4,207	7,234
Bihar	335,559	499,934	650,584	8,588	5,792	8,409	NA	5,765	8,711
Gujarat	243,629	443,014	889,661	15,867	20,156	31,311	NA	19,859	32,146
Haryana	244,875	276,643	439,167	14,449	20,403	47,884	NA	23,929	53,407
Himachal Pradesh	397,096	495,145	781,297	21,898	11,947	24,676	NA	12,016	31,980
Karnataka	186,539	260,346	500,914	5,622	7,611	13,696	NA	8,345	16,247
Kerala	152,507	132,450	177,392	6,236	8,572	19,292	NA	9,606	22,985
Madhya Pradesh	428,826	609,608	549,945	6,469	7,544	10,809	NA	8,173	12,185
Maharashtra	300,772	417,278	564,624	10,982	18,932	29,033	NA	28,445	35,614
Orissa	590,072	761,587	790,651	1,916	1,751	3,372	NA	2,073	3,729
Punjab	227,945	295,733	208,539	18,341	7,764	41,778	NA	9,223	51,973
Rajasthan	292,077	503,268	532,182	11,076	7,862	23,225	NA	8,521	25,159
Tamil Nadu	178,805	273,528	276,399	5,403	4,509	18,619	NA	6,906	23,618
Uttar Pradesh	265,324	481,226	582,058	7,130	4,318	12,499	NA	4,587	14,334
West Bengal	181,678	335,965	258,653	2,912	3,227	6,353	NA	3,820	7,894
Delhi	80,089	246,953	184,040	32,763	35,139	87,316	NA	35,996	79,392
All India	240,626	185,054	441,981	6,828	6,739	15,043	NA	16,592	18,964

Source: ASI and NSSO (respective years).

Table 10A.9   Panel Regression for Formal Labour Productivity (Infapl)

Variables	Fixed Effect Model	Random Effect Model
Const.	4.11*	3.96*
Lnfk	0.61*	0.62*
Openindx	0.001	0.001
R-Square	0.66	0.66
Rho	0.53	0.49
Hausman		0.97

Note: fapl = GVA per workers in the formal sector, fk = capital–labour ratio in the formal sector, i = states, t = period (1989–90, 1994–5, 2000–1), and * = significant at 5 per cent level.

Table 10A.10   Panel Regression for Informal Labour Productivity (lniapl)

Variables	Fixed Effect Model	Random Effect Model
Const.	6.17*	4.57*
Lnik	0.30*	0.48*
Openindx	0.001	0.001
R-Square	0.70	0.70
Rho	0.64	0.29
Hausman		0.001

Note: iapl = GVA per worker in the informal sector, ik = capital–labour ratio in the informal sector, i = states, t = period (1989–90, 1994–5, 2000–1), and * = significant at 5 per cent level.

Table 10A.11   TFPG of Formal and Informal Sector in India by States, 1990–2001

Firm	Formal Sector			Informal Sector		
	effch	techch	tfpch	effch	techch	Tfpch
Andhra Pradesh	6.3	6.9	13.6	−2.0	−1.2	−3.2
Assam	−31.8	5.8	−27.9	10.8	1.5	12.4
Bihar	−10.2	26.8	13.8	8.4	0.1	8.5
Gujarat	6.1	27.1	34.9	0.0	−15.5	−15.5
Haryana	10.8	14.3	26.6	30.5	−10.9	16.2
Himachal Pradesh	26.9	31	66.3	14.1	−14.5	−2.5
Karnataka	−11.2	12.7	0.1	5.0	0.9	6.0
Kerala	−14.6	7.4	−8.3	11.4	1.3	12.9
Madhya Pradesh	6.3	30.6	38.7	−30.4	0.7	−29.9
Maharashtra	0	21.1	21.1	12.5	−10.0	1.3
Orissa	−19.2	37.9	11.3	−1.3	−5.4	−6.7
Punjab	−4.6	14.1	8.8	21.4	−5.0	15.3
Rajasthan	20.6	23.4	48.7	32.7	−2.1	29.9
Tamil Nadu	−5.4	8.2	2.3	3.4	2.5	6.0
Uttar Pradesh	−0.1	24.7	24.6	6.5	1.6	8.2
West Bengal	2.3	9.2	11.8	−13.9	−4.6	−17.9
Delhi	0	0.1	0.1	0.0	−3.9	−3.9
All India	−2.1	17.3	14.8	5.3	−4.0	1.2

Note: EFFCH: Efficiency changes, TECHCH: Technical changes and TFPCH: Total factor productivity change; TFPG = EFFCH*TECHCH, where output; GVA and Inputs are workers and FA. EFFCH: Catching up effect, TECHCH: Frontier shift, TFPG: Total factor productivity growth.

Table 10A.12 Real Annual Wage per Worker by States

State	Formal			Informal not under DME			Informal under DME		
	1989–90	1994–5	2000–1	1989–90	1994–5	2000–1	1989–90	1994–5	2000–1
Andhra Pradesh	15612	18577	16637	2535	7441	7037	NA	6151	7317
Assam	12661	15490	15836	3308	5324	7181	NA	2185	18326
Bihar	40594	45614	47838	3607	5293	7974	NA	3868	9843
Gujarat	23478	23610	25715	6852	10739	12663	NA	13761	13873
Haryana	27319	28486	27215	4460	9175	11028	NA	11600	12579
Himachal Pradesh	21033	23167	21607	4912	6748	12009	NA	6143	15603
Karnataka	28979	30313	25620	4446	6342	8392	NA	4179	7409
Kerala	22728	20257	20249	2958	7530	9718	NA	7013	10083
Madhya Pradesh	28356	30283	31362	4038	7966	8249	NA	5326	7594
Maharashtra	42005	43694	37943	5233	10974	12695	NA	9334	13619
Orissa	26777	27338	33683	3087	5781	6592	NA	5485	6619
Punjab	23226	28693	20596	2958	8026	11274	NA	8408	12763
Rajasthan	26315	29136	24311	6978	8008	12177	NA	8429	12583
Tamil Nadu	24483	24200	20796	3151	6812	9945	NA	10083	12240
Uttar Pradesh	27234	29734	21663	3250	6036	8405	NA	6292	8323
West Bengal	31611	32042	32650	5283	6828	8358	NA	6253	9004
Delhi	25393	4172	14672	1618	11139	14783	NA	12042	16197
All India	27787	28820	25977	3710	7684	10064	NA	7302	10743

Source: ASI and NSSO (respective years).

Table 10A.13 Correlation between Informal Wages and Productivity across States

Year	Correlation Coefficient between Formal Wage and Formal Labour Productivity	Correlation Coefficient between Informal Wage and Informal Labour Productivity	Correlation Coefficient between Informal Wage and Formal Labour Productivity
1989–90	0.56	0.57	0.17
1994–5	0.55	0.76	0.49
2000–1	0.38	0.84	0.55

Table 10A.14 Determinants of Formal Wage, Informal Wage, and Formal Productivity

	lnw_f		lnw_i		$lnapl_f$	
	Fixed Effect	Random Effect	Fixed Effect	Random Effect	Fixed Effect	Random Effect
Const	9.98**	9.54**	6.19**	6.04**	6.38**	8.42**
ln apl_f	0.02	0.05				
ln apl_i			0.32**	0.34**		
ln w_i					0.62*	0.39*
R^2	0.19	0.19	0.27	0.27	0.07	0.08
ρ	0.89	0.86	0.84	0.78	0.67	0.55
Hausman		−28.23		−1.14		0.08

Note: w_f: formal wage, w_i: absolute informal wage, apl_f: formal average labour productivity, apl_i: informal average labour productivity, * = significant at 5 per cent level, ** = significant at 1 per cent level.

Table 10A.15   Percentage Share of Manufacturing Enterprises by Problems Faced in the Unorganized Sector

	Common Problems Faced			
	OAME	NDME	DME	ALL
No specific problem	26.5	20.1	16.9	26.0
Non-availability of electricity	14.0	9.7	8.8	13.6
Power cuts	11.4	31.3	32.7	12.9
Shortage of capital	49.6	54.5	52.7	50.0
Non-availability of raw materials	18.1	12.4	17.2	17.8
Marketing of the product	21.0	20.8	31.2	21.2
Other problems	33.5	36.9	45.1	33.9
Other than common problems				
Lack of infrastructure facilities	8.0	5.5	3.3	7.7
Local problems	20.6	12.9	10.1	19.9
Harassment	4.7	0.5	1.5	4.4
Competition from larger unit	22.2	31.5	27.8	22.9
Non-availability of labour	0.6	3.1	10.9	1.1
Labour problems	2.0	5.4	14.4	2.5
Fuel not available or very costly	4.8	0.7	6.3	4.6
Non-recovery of service charges/credit	17.5	20.0	8.2	17.4
Others	18.9	20.2	17.3	18.9

Source: NSS, 56th Round, 2000–1.
Note: OAME—Own Account Manufacturing Enterprises (no hired labour), NDME—Non-Directory Manufacturing Enterprises (maximum 5 hired workers), and DME—Directory Manufacturing Enterprise (employ more than 5 hired workers).

Table 10A.16   Percentage of Unorganized Enterprises Receiving Assistance by Types

	Unorganized Sector (2000–1)			
Types of Assistance	OAME	NDME	DME	All
1. Loan	2.1	10.0	19.8	2.9
2. Subsidy	0.6	1.4	2.6	0.6
3. Machinery/equipment	0.1	0.8	0.5	1.0
4. Training	0.3	0.4	2.3	0.4
5. Marketing	0.4	0.4	2.0	0.5
6. Procurement of raw materials	0.4	0.6	2.0	0.4
7. Others	0.2	0.3	1.6	0.3
8. Not receiving any assistance	96.0	87.9	77.8	95.2

Source: NSS 56th Round, 2000–1.

Malmquist Indices of Total Factor Productivity

The analytical method of productivity growth by the DEA method is borrowed from Ray (2004). For the general multi-output, multi-input case, the Malmquist productivity index for (x^0, y^0) and (x^1, y^1) as the base is:

$$M(x^1, y^1; x^0, y^0) = \frac{D^c(x^1, y^1)}{D^c(x^0, y^0)} \tag{10A.1}$$

Suppose that the two input–output bundles relate to the same firm but from two different time periods, period 0 and period 1. In that case the Malmquist index in (10A.1) shows how the total factor productivity of the firm has changed from period 0 to period 1. Typically, there will be technical changes over time. In that case, there would be two different production technologies and, correspondingly, two different distance functions for the two different time periods. Suppose, $D^c_t(x, y)$ is the CRS distance function evaluated at the input–output bundle *(x, y)* in period *t (t=1, 2)*. We would then have two alternative measures of the Malmquist productivity index:

$$M(x^1, y^1; x^0, y^0) = \frac{D^c_0(x^1, y^1)}{D^c_0(x^0, y^0)} \tag{10A.2}$$

And,

$$M(x^1, y^1; x^0, y^0) = \frac{D^c_1(x^1, y^1)}{D^c_1(x^0, y^0)} \tag{10A.3}$$

Except for the trivial case of one output and one input, the two alternative measures will be different. The standard practice in literature is to take a geometric mean of the two measures. Thus:

$$M(x^1, y^1; x^0, y^0) = \left[\frac{D^c_0(x^1, y^1)}{D^c_0(x^0, y^0)} \cdot \frac{D^c_1(x^1, y^1)}{D^c_1(x^0, y^0)} \right]^{\frac{1}{2}} \tag{10A.4}$$

Färe, Grosskopf, Lindgren, and Roos (FGLR) (1992) decomposed this Malmquist productivity index as:

$$M(x^1, y^1; x^0, y^0) = \left[\frac{D^c_1(x^1, y^1)}{D^c_0(x^0, y^0)} \right] \left[\frac{D^c_1(x^0, y^0)}{D^c_0(x^0, y^0)} \cdot \frac{D^c_1(x^1, y^1)}{D^c_0(x^1, y^1)} \right]^{\frac{1}{2}} \tag{10A.5}$$

or, TFPG=EFFCH*TECHCH (used in our calculations).

Thus, the first factor in the FGLR decomposition shows the change in technical efficiency between the two periods and can be characterized as a 'catch up' factor (that is, EFFCH). Each of the two ratios inside the square brackets in the second factor is a measure of the shift in the production frontier evaluated at the two different input bundles. Being the geometric mean of the two, the second factor is a measure of the autonomous shift in the production frontier and represents technical change (TECHCH). TFPG is the product of EFFCH and TECHCH.

Suppose that we have the input–output data for N states observed over different time periods. Let $y^t_j = (y^t_{1j}, y^t_{2j}, ..., y^t_{mj})$ be the output bundle of jth state and $x^t_j = (x^t_{1j}, x^t_{2j}, ..., x^t_{nj})$ be input bundle of firm f in jth state for $(j = 1,2,...,N)$ in period t. As explained before, the free disposal convex hull of the input–output vectors observed in that period correspondingly, the *pseudo* production possibility set (T^t_c) showing globally constant returns is the free disposal conical hull of these points. In principle, one can evaluate the distance function at a specific input–output bundle (x, y) with reference to any arbitrary production possibility set. We may describe the distance function as the *same-period distance function*, if one uses (T^t_c) to evaluate the distance function at an input–output combination observed in period t. On the other hand, if the distance function based on the technology from one period is evaluated at an input–output bundle from another period, it can be described as a *cross-period distance function*. As noted before, the (Shephard) distance function is the same as the Farrell measure of technical efficiency and therefore it is obtained directly from the optimal solution of the CCR DEA (Charnes, Cooper and Rhodes, 1978, Data Envelopment Analysis) problem. In particular, the *same period (CRS)* distance function is:

$$D^t(x^t_k, y^t_k) = \frac{1}{\phi^*_k} \qquad (10A.6)$$

where $\phi^*_k = \max \phi$

$$\text{s.t.} \sum_{j=1}^{N} \lambda_j y^t_j \geq \phi y^t_k$$

$$\sum_{j=1}^{N} \lambda_j x^t_j \leq y^t_k$$

$$\lambda_j \geq 0, j = 1, 2, ..., N \qquad (10A.7)$$

APPENDIX 10B

Derivations in Chapter 5, section 5.2 and Appendix 5A are repeated in the beginning. Using the same definitions as before, we derive changes in the level of productivity. Therefore, assuming two commodities X and Y and replicating equations (5.1) to (5.9), we focus on the factor productivity change in each sector.

Let us define factor productivity in sector X, as: $a_{LX} = a_{LX}\left(\dfrac{\bar{w}}{r_X}, t\right)$

where, t is the productivity parameter (Jones, 1971, 2003) that helps to improve labour productivity and essentially, an improvement in the labour productivity in sector X implies a drop in a_{LX}. In other words, a rise in t implies that the amount of L required to produce one unit of X at a given $\dfrac{\bar{w}}{r_X}$ shall drop.

Following Jones, a change in labour productivity as understood from the full-employment conditions is given by:

$$\lambda_{LY}\hat{Y} + \lambda_{LX}\hat{X} + \lambda_{LY}\hat{a}_{LY} + \lambda_{LX}\hat{a}_{LX} = \alpha\lambda_{LY} \qquad (10B.1)$$

where, $\alpha = b^*_{LY} > 0$.

Fully expanding equation 10B.1 and using the competitive price conditions:

$$\lambda_{LX}[-\sigma_X\theta_{KX}(\hat{\bar{w}} - \hat{r}_X) - \sigma_X\theta_{LX}(\hat{\bar{w}} - \hat{r}_X)] + \lambda_{LY}[-\sigma_Y\theta_{KY}(\hat{w} - \hat{r}_Y) -$$

$$\sigma_Y\theta_{LY}(\hat{w} - \hat{r}_Y)] - \left[\frac{\lambda_{LX}}{f} - \lambda_{LY}\right]\hat{K}_Y = \alpha\lambda_{LY} \qquad (10B.2)$$

In the formal sector, $\hat{\bar{w}} = 0 = \hat{r}_X$, since $\hat{P}_X = 0$

From equation (10B.2), however, an improvement in labour productivity (in sector Y) implies,

$$\hat{w}\theta_{LY} + \hat{r}_Y\theta_{KY} = \hat{P}_Y + \theta_{LY}\alpha, \quad \alpha, \text{ as defined above.}$$

Such that, $\hat{r}_Y = \dfrac{\theta_{LY}\alpha}{\theta_{KY}} - \hat{w}\dfrac{\theta_{LY}}{\theta_{KY}}$

Substituting these in (10B.2), we get:

$$-\lambda_{LY}\sigma_Y\left(\hat{w} - \frac{\theta_{LY}\alpha}{\theta_{KY}} + \hat{w}\frac{\theta_{LY}}{\theta_{KY}}\right) - \left(\frac{\theta_{LY}\alpha}{\theta_{KY}} - \hat{w}\frac{\theta_{LY}}{\theta_{KY}}\right)$$

$$\left[\frac{\lambda_{LX}}{f} - \lambda_{LY}\right]\varepsilon\lambda_{KX} = \alpha\lambda_{LY} \qquad (10B.3)$$

We assume throughout that sector X is more capital-intensive than sector Y, such that,

$$\Delta_1 = \left[\frac{\lambda_{LX}}{f} - \lambda_{LY}\right] < 0 \tag{10B.4}$$

From (10B.4), therefore:

$$-\hat{w}\left[\frac{\lambda_{LY}}{\theta_{KY}}\sigma_Y - \varepsilon\frac{\theta_{LY}}{\theta_{KY}}\lambda_{KX}\left[\frac{\lambda_{LX}}{f} - \lambda_{LY}\right]\right] =$$

$$\alpha\lambda_{LY} - \lambda_{LY}\frac{\theta_{LY}}{\theta_{KY}}\sigma_Y\alpha + \varepsilon\frac{\theta_{LY}}{\theta_{KY}}\lambda_{KX}\left[\frac{\lambda_{LX}}{f} - \lambda_{LY}\right]\alpha$$

which solves for $\hat{w}$, as:

$$-\Omega\hat{w} = \alpha\lambda_{LY} - \lambda_{LY}\frac{\theta_{LY}}{\theta_{KY}}\sigma_Y\alpha + \varepsilon\frac{\theta_{LY}}{\theta_{KY}}\lambda_{KX}\Delta_1\alpha$$

where,

$$\Omega = \left(\frac{\lambda_{LY}}{\theta_{KY}}\sigma_Y - \varepsilon\frac{\theta_{LY}}{\theta_{KY}}\lambda_{KX}\Delta_1\right) > 0$$

Thus, $\hat{w} < 0$, iff, $\left(\alpha\lambda_{LY} - \lambda_{LY}\frac{\theta_{LY}}{\theta_{KY}}\sigma_Y\alpha + \varepsilon\frac{\theta_{LY}}{\theta_{KY}}\lambda_{KX}\Delta_1\alpha\right) > 0$

$$\tag{10B.5}$$

Or,

$$\hat{w} < 0, \; iff, \; \frac{\theta_{LY}}{\theta_{KY}} < \frac{1}{\sigma_Y + \varepsilon\dfrac{\lambda_{KX}}{\lambda_{LY}}\Delta_1} \tag{10B.6}$$

In case of zero capital mobility, $\varepsilon = 0$, and $\hat{w} < 0$, iff, $\dfrac{\theta_{LY}}{\theta_{KY}} < \dfrac{1}{\sigma_Y}$

With full capital mobility, $\varepsilon \to \infty$ and the above condition is violated. Therefore, with full capital mobility between the formal and informal sectors, the reverse condition as in (10B.6) holds, and the informal wages must increase, that is, $\hat{w} > 0$, when the productivity of labour in the informal sector increases. It can similarly be extended to capture changes in labour productivity in the formal sector. A more recent work on this topic is by Beladi et al. (2010).

APPENDIX 10C

The basic story of the model is similar to the one analysed in Marjit et al. (2007c). A firm produces a good X. X can be produced by using organized or formal sector workers who earn a pre-determined negotiated wage rate w_1 and/or by accessing informal units which employ labour at a wage rate $w_2 < w_1$. In the absence of any noticeable productivity gap, the firm will be inclined to hire only informal workers albeit there are other costs associated with this. In fact, hiring workers under informal arrangements in industrial set-ups is hardly deemed legal anywhere. Therefore, firms might face potential regulatory problems. One can model the auditing/monitoring/bribery issues explicitly and generate a marginal cost function for outsourcing X_2 of X to the informal sector. This has been derived in Marjit et al. (2007c) using the following structure:

$$\text{MC for } X_2 = w_2 c(X_2), c' > 0, c'' > 0 \qquad (10C.1)$$

Basic intuition is that larger the size of the informal segment, greater is the potential threat of inviting regulators. We allow for labour productivity augmenting expenditure F only in the formal sector. It is possible that such a venture will be difficult to set up in an extra-legal segment. Also, as we shall see briefly, that even if the firm can potentially promote such initiatives in the informal segment, it might not be optimal for the firm to do so if w_2 is really low. If $R(X_1 + X_2)$ is the standard revenue function facing the firm, its optimization problem looks as:

$$\underset{X_1, X_2, F}{\text{Max}} \quad \pi = R(X_1 + X_2) - w_1 \alpha(F) X_1 - w_2 c(X_2) - Z(F)$$

$$(10C.2)$$

To produce one unit of $X(X_1)$ in the formal sector $\alpha(F)$ units of labour is required. $Z(F)$ is a kind of R&D cost. $\alpha(F)$ captures the cost-cutting effort of the formal sector producer and we coin it as R&D activities. We assume that a decision on F is taken first and then on X_1 and X_2. The following curvature restrictions are assumed:

$$R' > 0, R'' < 0, \alpha' < 0, \alpha'' > 0, Z' > 0, Z'' > 0, c' > 0, c'' > 0$$
$$c''' = 0, X = X_1 + X_2$$

From (10C.2) the first order conditions are:

$$R' = w_1 \alpha(F) \qquad (10C.3)$$

$$R' = w_2 c'(w_2) \qquad (10C.4)$$

$$-w_1 \alpha' X_1 = Z' \qquad (10C.5)$$

While solving for (X_1, X_2), F is taken as given. Then we internalize that in equation (10C.5) and we determine optimal F.

From (10C.3) and (10C.4):

$$w_1\alpha(F) = w_2 c'(X_2) \qquad (10C.6)$$

Let $\tilde{X}_2 = c'^{-1}((w_1\alpha(F))/w_2) = f((w_1\alpha(F)/w_2)) \qquad (10C.7)$

Check that for $X_2 < \tilde{X}_2$, the firm will not employ any formal worker as $w_1\alpha(F) > w_2 c'(X_2)$. If $X > X_2$, $X - \tilde{X}_2$ must be produced in the formal sector as $w_1\alpha(F) < w_2 c'(X_2)$ for $X > X_2$. We assume that the size of the market is large enough to accommodate both in-house production as well as outsourcing. Technically this implies a $\overline{X}$ such that:

$$R'(\overline{X}) = w_1\alpha(F) \qquad (10C.8)$$

with $\overline{X} > \tilde{X}$.

This also implies that if the market size is not large enough, only informal workers will be hired. Therefore, the firm will outsource $\tilde{X} = X_2$ units to the informal sector and produce $(\overline{X} - \tilde{X})$ in-house. Note that these solutions are derived for a given value of F. We are following a backward induction method by which $\overline{X}$ and $\tilde{X}$ are solved as functions of F, and then $(\overline{X} - \tilde{X}) = X_1$ is substituted in (10C.8) to solve for F.

Since $\alpha(F)$ denotes the inverse of labour productivity in the formal sector, our task is to check how F responds to changes in w_2—the informal wage rate. Re-writing and assuming F^* is the optional R&D to start with we have:

Therefore,
$$\frac{dF^*}{dw_2} = \frac{w_1\alpha' \dfrac{d(\overline{X} - \tilde{X})}{dw_2}}{\Delta} \qquad (10C.9)$$

where, $\Delta < 0$ (by the second order condition guaranteeing the optimality of F^*)

Now
$$R'(\overline{X}) = w_1\alpha(F) \qquad (10C.10)$$

Given
$$R'' < 0, \overline{X} = \phi(w_1\alpha(F)) \qquad (10C.11)$$

with
$$\phi' < 0.$$

Similarly
$$\tilde{X}_2 = f\left(\frac{w_1\alpha(F)}{w_2}\right), f' > 0 \qquad (10C.12)$$

Therefore,
$$\frac{d(\overline{X} - \tilde{X}_2)}{dw_2} = f' \frac{w_1\alpha(F)}{w_2^2} > 0 \qquad (10C.13)$$

Hence, from (10C.9)

$$\frac{dF^*}{dw_2} > 0 \text{ as } \alpha' < 0, \Delta < 0 \text{ and } \frac{d(\bar{X} - \tilde{X})}{dw_2} > 0$$

Therefore, the change in labour productivity in the formal sector is given by:

$$\frac{d\left(\frac{1}{\alpha(F)}\right)}{dw_2} = \frac{1}{\alpha^2} \alpha'(F^*) \frac{dF^*}{dw_2} > 0 \qquad \text{QED}$$

A higher w_2 induces greater production in the formal sector increasing the marginal benefit from R&D. F increases and $\alpha(F)$ drops making labour more productive in this sector.

11 Two Case Studies on the Informal Economy

This chapter is devoted to two case studies on informal activities in India. The purpose of this chapter is to elicit further issues and evidence that is not apparent from an aggregative analysis at the country level. In particular, we use the case studies to discuss situations where international trade policies and their effects on domestic factor prices turn out to be of critical importance for the existence of informal activities. This chapter incorporates studies on Mumbai (Maharashtra) and Surat (Gujarat).[1] What we intend to show is that the recent transformation of the slums in Dharavi in Mumbai through massive real estate development is counter-productive to a flourishing informal segment of leather products, though the general state of the unorganized leather industry has worsened somewhat over the recent years. In contrast, the paper work industry in Surat is benefiting from the spoils of globalization. Thus the exorbitant profit level in the real estate business may easily displace an informal segment despite possibilities that it earns more profits than units under the formal sector. So the study on Dharavi undoubtedly offers a very special case with wide implications in economics. The detailed case studies reflect on some ground level realities which go beyond what secondary data can capture. These are largely socio-economic case studies covering different types of informal manufacturing activities.

CASE STUDY A: LEATHER PRODUCTS INDUSTRY OF DHARAVI

As you walk into one of the dingy tenements in Dharavi, Mumbai's largest slum, a 50-year-old silhouette of Joseph Stalin hangs forlorn on a wall. This picture in the offices of Dharavi Bachao Andolan, a local non-government organization, is a mute testament to the days when a thriving communist movement prospered in this sprawling settlement. Then, poverty, desperation, and crime brewed a steady supply of anger, crime, and political protest here. Today, the communists have lost the influence that they once had and Dharavi's tin huts and concrete hovels hum with commercial activity. Ramshackle corrugated tin, plywood, plastic, *pukka* bricks, sheets of asbestos, sweat, toil, people and garbage make Dharavi, just like piles of earth, sand, clay and other materials make ant hills. Dharavi, and many other slums like it, are nothing but human ant colonies built by legions of urban poor. They are places, which are at the same time sombre, moving, joyful and interesting. Push and pull factors bring people from villages here everyday in search for something better. They settle here much to the neglect of our apathetic eyes. But under the squalor can be seen a 'great spirit' and ingenuity. Most people refer to Dharavi as 'Asia's largest slum' but we would prefer to call it the 'heart of Mumbai'.

The business laws of the country are not applicable in Dharavi. How can they be applicable to a place that for all legal reasons does not exist? Dharavi is beyond the traditional Indian *babudom* (bureaucracy) of red tape, licenses, duties, municipal permissions, paper work, and taxes. Dharavi is, therefore, in a sense a 'Free Economic Zone'. *The Economist* in an article suggested that 'Dharavi, one of Asia's largest slums, covering 220 hectares (530 acres) near the airport, has some 100,000 people producing goods worth over $500 million a year.' Other figures suggest twice that amount. The real figure is anybody's guess but this just confirms one thing that Dharavi is less a slum and more an unorganized unregulated industrial estate, a showcase of Indian entrepreneurship. Dharavi houses an army of workers, many of whom work long hours in 10 feet by 12 feet rooms, churning out garments, purses, bags and briefcases for suppliers spread across the globe. The businesses flourishing here are as diverse as the colourful saris fluttering on the washing lines atop the slum's huts, and they have brought entrepreneurs' dreams to fruition.

Walking in one of the shopping districts of an Italian city we came across a leather boutique with the most unusual sign outside its door. The sign read, 'Genuine 100% Italian Leather Not Made in India'. This is just an anecdotal introduction for the 2 billion dollar Indian leather industry, which employs over 2 million people. If you ask any knowledgeable shopper in Mumbai, where you can find the cheapest and best quality leather products, the answer invariably will not be the Oberoi Arcade but Dharavi. If you have ever driven down the Mahim–Sion Link Road we are sure you would have noticed the gleaming leather showrooms on either side of the road with names like Quality, Step-In, and Ideal Leather. In their confines you can buy jackets, wallets, bags, belts and a variety of other leather products. These products are mostly export rejects or surplus products, produced by the leather manufacturers of Dharavi.

Dharavi was also one of the top places manufacturing ladies handbags. These bags were made of beautiful soft skin of sheep Napa, which was procured from Chennai, particularly from Vaniyambadi. There was this beautiful bonding of two geographical places—Dharavi and Vaniyambadi. They were inter-dependent on each other.

There is, however, a snake in this sweatshop Eden. Dharavi's businesses and entrepreneurs may soon have to exit the slum, thanks to the city's grandiose redevelopment plan. The leather industry is one of the first to make exit plans.

Since Dharavi's redevelopment plan has no place for disorganized and polluting industrial activities, most leather exporting associations in the area are shifting the Rs 300 crore (1 crore = 10 million) industry to Bhiwandi, which lies on the fringes of the city's suburbs. Even the ageing communists in the slum, who for long carried the flag of the leather workers, sorrowfully agree that the leather manufacturing industry should indeed move out of the area. But the big question is: Is the shifting of such a big unorganized industry possible? Are the workers mentally prepared to shift? If we try to find this out from the leather handbags industry then the answer is a big 'No'. In fact this industry has almost vanished as of today.

Buyers from Europe and the US have scant regard for the disorganized work that goes on in Dharavi. The leather units located in the slum are small job work centres, which are as good as sweatshops. Multinational clients want to source products from centres where leather production and manufacturing processes are integrated. They also want small artisans and tanneries to be linked to one single production unit. Dharavi's industries are too disorganized for this, as the slum is full of small artisans who run their own businesses.

Another problem for the people lies in sourcing skin from tanneries and abattoirs. If the skin is not cured properly, the finished product will not have the right properties. International buyers sometimes reject Dharavi's products as they have a tendency of not being consistent in quality. International leather agents demand to work with only those exporters who can offer quality products on a large scale through mechanized production.

To add to Dharavi's woes is the depleting ranks of Chamars, a caste traditionally known to make quality handcrafted leather products. This community used to run tanneries and cottage leather industries. Now, immigrants from the northern parts of the country have joined this trade. 'Although the new class of labour is quick in sewing leather goods, they need to be trained, unlike the Chamars who are born into the industry,' says Chandu Bhoite, owner of Sai Leather Crafts, and one of the last members of the community who have stayed on.

Leather associations believe that Mumbai has lost its prowess in the leather business to cities such as Kolkata, Chennai and Kanpur. One of the major reasons for the shift in prosperity to other locations was the proximity of abattoirs and tanneries to production centres. Dharavi's entrepreneurs bemoan the lack of foresight on the part of the government. A part of Dharavi could have been developed into a leather park; leather products could have been manufactured in Bhiwandi and sold in this leather park.

But it is not just redevelopment plans that are responsible for the problems of Dharavi's leather industry. Another problem is that much of the work has little official status and lacks professionalism. There is no paper work for the goods that are shipped out of the slum. Production techniques and designs could be stolen right off the shop floor in Dharavi. They feared that these processes could be replicated elsewhere, making it easier for pirated brand names to capture market shares. A final factor pushing most entrepreneurs, linked to corporate sector, out of Dharavi is access to credit. The name Dharavi is associated with a slum, and some banks turn down loan applications because of this bias.

But the biggest factor responsible for the death knell of the leather handbag industry is the moving away of the *karigars* (skilled craftsmen) from Dharavi. This mostly happened after the communal riots of 1993. The karigars (Chamars or low-caste Hindus) belonged to the Marathi (Hindu) community and were very skilled in making handbags. The population ratio of Dharavi before the riots was 70 per cent Hindus and 30 per cent Muslims. It has reversed since the riots.

The redevelopment plan divides Dharavi into five sectors, out of a total area of 175 acres. Eighty per cent of these new tenements will be residential complexes. Currently, 95 per cent of the slum's businesses are on municipal land, and most of the tenants have further sub-let their space to other businesses. A majority of Dharavi's industries do not have the requisite property deeds and rent agreements. However, since it is right in the heart of Mumbai, most small entrepreneurs are reluctant to move out, especially with rising property rates. The rates are as high as Rs 7,500–10,000 per sq. ft (US$ 150–250 per sq. ft), and nobody wants to pay such high prices after redevelopment.

Role of the Export Market

Ironically, no one complains about any shortage of international orders. Currently, the factories churning out leather goods for export work 24 hours a day, seven days a week, since the number of international buyers has shot up. But with redevelopment, small businesses will no longer be able to afford the high rents.

Mumbai accounts for 17 per cent of the leather goods exports, according to the data provided by the Council for Leather Exports. With increasing orders from China and the US, the industry has become highly capital intensive. Entrepreneurs need to invest in expensive machinery, which could easily cost Rs 50 lakh (1 lakh = 100,000) per unit.

How Labour was Affected

The labour involved in making leather handbags suffered due to various reasons, some of which include:

1. The supply of good leather was not properly organized. It was bought from Vaniyambadi (Chennai) and often encountered delays. This in turn delayed export shipments. At times it resulted in cancellation of orders during the manufacturing stages. Exporters had to bear the losses since the leather processed and designed for specific export requirements was deemed useless and it would have been difficult for them to find local markets for these. The longer the waiting time for finding a market, the greater is the possibility that the product quality will go down. In other words, the entire risk was borne by the producer–labour.

2. The labour was working on daily wages, as it was not an organized sector. Most of them worked from their homes using homesteads as makeshift factories. Doubtless, such jobs do not come with securities and tenures.

3. The workers in this industry were jobless for the four monsoon months. During monsoon the leather grows fungus and the industry as a whole is on standstill. During this period of involuntary unemployment the workers usually migrate back to their native places and get involved in farming or doing odd jobs.

4. Skilled craftsmen in this industry have practised this profession through generations till the present time when the younger members are averse to staying amidst uncertainty and poverty. Once again, as we shall notice with regard to the paper and tea industries in India, the unavailability of skilled craftsmen has reached critical limits so much so that firms and gardens might have to be abandoned completely. In a related study on the conditions of tea garden workers in the northern, north-eastern, and southern states in India, we came across cases where (particularly in the south) growing outside opportunities in industrial (textiles and information technology) sectors have attracted the present generation of labour away from their traditional occupation in the tea gardens. In fact, the tea gardens have to compete with these outside opportunities to retain workers and at the same time remain competitive locally and globally. The transition in the condition of informal workers has assumed many dimensions over the past decade since the inception of economic reforms in India; we have tried to account for some of these.

Coming back to the leather industry, workers are better qualified and hence prefer to work elsewhere. The disparity and skill-biased income gaps are large enough and ever more visible with strong presence of media and other sources of information. A skilled worker on an average earns between Rs 3000 (US$75) per month, whereas a literate person and those in the lower strata of the job market can easily earn in excess of Rs 5000 (US$ 150) per month with perhaps no monsoon employment. Although the major impediments regarding schooling, health, basic amenities, income and related uncertainties continue to plague the system, the bottom lines are clear. The workers are now perfectly focussed and informed about the returns from various occupations they are exposed to.

5. With substantial economic restructuring in the country, business opportunities increased all around and the choice of location was driven by many more factors than pure comparative advantage in production. Consequently, workers who were anyway footloose could now easily relocate to various other places. Larger markets in other million plus cities and growing purchasing power in up and coming townships shifted the leather bag industry to places like Delhi, Kolkata, Chennai, and Kanpur.

Role of Technology and the Future

Asia's largest slum Dharavi is set to leverage its own potential to bring about a sea change in its fortune and in turn enrich its standard of living.

Three leading institutes have joined hands with the Slum Rehabilitation Authority (SRA) of Mumbai to change the face of Dharavi in five years by developing and promoting its own resources—the slum's three thriving cottage industries of leather, garments and pottery. Leading retail chains have already started showing interest.

The institutes, Ahmadabad-based National Institute of Design (NID), Central Leather Research Institute (CLRI), Chennai and the Footwear Design and Development Institute (FDDI), Delhi, have come up with a three-step proposal to provide sustainable economic development to Dharavi's dwellers.

Beginning with leather, the institutes have an elaborate plan—from studies to map skills and analysis to gauge gaps in technology and design in creating an international market for leather products through a 'Dharavi Leather Gram'.

'We chose the leather industry as there are as many as 567 leather units in Dharavi and it will be easier to make a beginning by working in an area they are used to. It can be a test case for our work on garment and pottery,' says NID executive director Darlie O'Koshy.

HOW GLOBALIZATION HAS AFFECTED INFORMAL LABOUR/ TRADERS/ENTREPRENEURS: REMODELLING DHARAVI THE AMERICAN WAY!

Dharavi is not 'outside' Mumbai. It is in the heart of it, just across the Bandra-Karla Complex (BKC, a fast developing commercial centre that has surged atop Nariman Point, the current downtown of Mumbai) close to the Mumbai domestic and international airports. Dharavi is not a 'shantytown'; it is a unique, vibrant and thriving cottage industry complex, the only one of its kind in the world where all the raw material is produced and the processes (lining cloth, sewing needles and thread, colours and dyes, pigments, skinning, tanning, cutting, and tailoring) of the final product (leather bags, fancy lady's purses) are carried out at the same location and the value added is very high. Families have been engaged in this industry for generations. The very nature of the process of making fine leather goods requires large tracts of open land for the activity. This is in fact the kind of self-sufficient, self-sustaining 'village' community that Mahatma Gandhi dreamt of and wrote about in his books on the path that India should take for its development.

At this juncture, let us look at some numbers. The entire land of 535 acres will be available for free to the developers. Normally, in the suburbs of Mumbai, the floor space index (FSI) permissible is 1. However, this being treated as a slum redevelopment scheme, the FSI permissible would be 4.5 (Development Control Regulations-DCR-for Mumbai 1991). This means that in this 535 acres of land, after deducting the statutory open space of 15 per cent, the total floor area that could be built on will be 4.5 times the balance land (approximately 455 acres), that is, 2,047.50 acres. For reallocating 100,000 families in 225 square feet carpet area (approximately 330 sq. ft built up area) apartments, the total floor area required would be around 757.50 acres. This would leave a balance of 1,290 acres for 'free sale' by the developer.

Construction of 100,000 apartments for the existing residents at a carpet area of 225 sq. ft each will not cost more than Rs 250,000 per apartment (based on the cost of resettlement in the World Bank aided MUTP II project recently completed). The total cost of reallocation will therefore be Rs 2,500 million or US$ 56.8 million (current exchange rate of INR 44 = 1 US$).

Total land (inclusive of roads, open spaces, and amenities) required for 100,000 apartments in 20 storey buildings according to the standards permitted by SRA will be about 126.50 acres leaving the balance 408.50 acres to be used by the developer for construction of 'free sale' apartments. At the current price (based on recent sale of land by the Mumbai Metropolitan Region Development Authority-MMRDA) of around Rs 28,000 per sq. metre of FSI, the FSI available for sale on the balance land (1,290 acres) would fetch approximately Rs 14,448 million, or US$ 328.36 million. Deducting the cost of 100,000 flats (US$ 56.80 million) there would be a clear profit of Rs 11,948 million or US$ 271.56 million, a return of 478 per cent on the investment.

What is 'unique' about this plan is its Machiavellian attempt to deprive 100,000 families of their traditional livelihood and home-cum-work places so that the land so conveniently located across the BKC can 'host' commercial urban development that can ride piggy back on the infrastructure already created in BKC at the cost of the public exchequer and benefit the developers.

It seems that the redevelopment plan of Dhravai—as it is fairly common in developing countries, fuelling huge debates all around—might happen without adequate compensations offered to those living in the area for decades. We have already discussed issues with property rights and passive tolerance on the part of the government incapable of developing rural areas of the country, as one of the major factors behind the establishment of slums and primitive informal businesses. The real estate boom epitomizes the apathy of these residents with little or no legal rights and the bargaining power that comes with it. Some of these issues are presently finding voices in forums such as Bill Clinton Foundation, albeit it might take ages before the rather complex problems facing such workers are sorted out.

Would it not be simpler and justified to give land tenure to the existing residents of Dharavi so that they can themselves redevelop the area and upgrade its physical environment through self-help efforts by registering ownership to their pieces of land and avail institutional finance? In the larger development debate, a question like this is quite difficult to answer. The trade-off between land and occupation, real estate and export growth, displacement and destitution, political forces and the like would automatically make this issue much more than what can be handled. While we do not try to disentangle any complexity on the issue presently, in future we would like to approach this through interactions between trade policies and development issues.

CASE STUDY B: THE PAPER PRODUCTS INDUSTRY

India has come a long way in the paper industry starting from handmade paper widely used in the Mughal period to the ancient use of leaves and copper or lead sheet plates over traceable history. During Alexander's invasion around 325 BC, there are references to *sindosi*, a material somewhere between cloth and linen and closely resembling the process of paper-making. Paper documents are largely available from Muslim sources in India since about the 12th century AD. It is observed that wood pulp was used for making paper and now due to environmental safety requirements translated into economic considerations, a substitute has been found in 'bagasse'. Bagasse is a residue of sugarcane—after the cane is crushed for extracting juice the remaining vegetation is called bagasse.

India is one of the largest growers of sugarcane and hence there is an abundance of bagasse. Earlier this was wasted but it is now being used in paper mills, replacing wooden pulp and in turn saving trees. This is an important change in view of the growing demand for paper and paper-based products that has skyrocketed since the advent of photocopying and printing machines even in this era of computers.

Note that manufacturing of 'notebooks', an important ingredient in the schooling system for a large country like India was essentially a cottage industry. Since this demands considerable manual labour, employment levels were high. As in most other industries, labour was cheap and most of it was hired on a contractual basis. The demand for notebooks was, however, seasonal. School sessions in India usually start in May/June every year (although sessions are readjusted to and from December–January from time to time) and the units were the busiest during January to June. Production of notebooks faces seasonal fluctuations. Earlier, when demand was low, production was reduced to 10 per cent of full capacity and the workers had to be temporarily laid off until demand peaked in the following school season.

In the early 1990s a huge transformation in this industry took place:

1. Local demand increased as literacy rates picked up.
2. The export market opened up for notebooks made in India along with other forms of pads and writing copies.
3. Organized group-based private tuition in India supplemented school teaching in an unprecedented manner and that created additional demand for copies.

But somehow the gap between demand and supply increased as local units still in the small-scale sector could not match the increased demand. Moreover, it was a labour intensive job, so increased demand meant adding more to the labour force. Units were still using the old types of ruling machines called the *dhage wali* machines to print lines on notebooks. The rate of production was slow as machines were hand operated and the final quality of the product was not up to international standards.

Incidentally, it was during this period that buyers from Europe and the US started looking for other sources of supply beyond China and Indonesia (the biggest suppliers of paper products). They found India an interesting destination with a skilled, hard-working manpower and qualified English speaking clerical staff. Indian business units were easier to interact with as compared to those in China. Trial orders for paper products like notebooks, writing pads, and drawing books started flowing into India and buyers soon realized that India could be a good alternative source if a few changes and modifications were made in the set-up.

Further, foreign buyers found India to be a good alternative to China because Indian manufacturers accepted small orders, whereas Chinese manufacturers wanted huge orders to feed their big capacities. For example, China required at least four containers of orders for one item to make it economically viable for them to produce the product, whereas Indian manufacturers could give ten items in one container. This meant that foreign buyers were not required to keep huge stocks in their warehouses (even after adjusting for transport costs) and enjoyed greater flexibility with finances and commitments. Note that Indian products were slightly more expensive than their Chinese counterparts mainly owing to scale disadvantages. While China was using atomized machines, India was still using manual labour.

Nevertheless, interactions between the exporters and the buyers increased and at the same time due to immense lobbying by manufacturers, government policies on import of machinery were relaxed. This turned out to be a very big step for the paper industry in India. Newer and more advanced machines were imported and units started getting bigger. Production capacity increased and the quality of notebooks improved vastly. The final quality of the products was now up to international standards. Still, Indian notebooks catered to the lower and middle classes of the world market and were sold mostly in Pound Stores and Dollar Stores in Europe and the US.

It is believed, however, that with the progress made over the last decade Indian paper products will start catering to the higher end of the industry. Huge manufacturing units with large capital involvements are in the process of being set up with the sole aim of making top quality, expensive notebooks, particularly with the input advantage that they enjoy through large supplies of bagasse.

Labour in the Paper Industry

The industry was down or just about managing before the 1990s. For the workers it was a hand-to-mouth existence. The labour was of a 'wandering' type, coming mostly from the states of Uttar Pradesh, Bihar, and West Bengal. The wages were low, job security was absent, and, moreover, employment was seasonal. During the off-season, the labour went back to its native places and was possibly engaged in farming exemplifying the well-known seasonal migration of labour *a' la* Harris-Todaro (1970).

As the export market opened up, the slack season for the units and hence the labour force shrunk from six months (July to January) to four months (September to January). Our interviews and close interaction with labour employed in the paper industry reveals that the period of employment increased by at least two to three months annually. Salaries also increased and maintenance of quality was emphasized upon. In effect, the entire industry got a little bit more organized and this offers a strange story compared to what most other industries in India are witnessing—greater informalization within the formal sphere.

In the early 1960s and 1970s, the paper production industry was scattered all over the country and it was a sort of small-scale industry. For the workers, the main job involved ruling (on a hand ruling machine), cutting, sorting and binding. Ruling and cutting of paper was done on machines whereas sorting and binding were purely manual. In the 1990s labour started facing some degree of turmoil and uncertainty as new machines started coming in. The new Linomatic Ruling machine was about ten times more productive than the hand-ruling machine. In other words, one Linomatic machine operated by two people displaced 10 hand-ruling machine operators. So, for a period of time it became tough for these displaced workers. Slowly, however, some of them opted for jobs in other industries while some learned binding jobs and got absorbed in the paper industry albeit in other departments.

Gradually, however, as the industry expanded as a whole, the demand for labour increased, and the industry started drawing more and more labour from earlier sources, especially from the regions of Uttar Pradesh and Bihar. Although the slack season break of approximately four months still remains a handicap, it is expected that the factories will become operational for the full 12 months as the world market expands for Indian made paper products like notebooks. The salaries offered are also as per government requirements of minimum wages per day with working conditions getting better over time.

It is believed that exposure to international trade in paper products and the strong incentive to maintain international standards have been instrumental in the greater formalization within the industry. In fact, the large and steady demand for notebooks, writing pads, drawing books, notepads, and duplicate books from all parts of the world and frequent visits by agencies procuring these items require showcasing sophistication and order within the industry as an important ingredient in the selling process. It is expected that entering into business deals with an unorganized and ill-maintained industrial system would not be preferred by importers who are also conscious of environmental, human rights and several global concerns and protocols. This is something that is also observed in a parallel industry that is of high importance in India—tea. Importers insist on maintaining several regulations, including safety standards, labour laws, ISO quality certificates, use of chemicals, fair trade, and so on, which are clearly beyond what smaller informal units are capable of handling. In fact, we have argued in this volume that informal units survive only by flouting these requirements. However, in this context it should be remembered that there are products where formal units, especially MNCs, regularly use environmentally hazardous factor inputs bypassing legal strictures. But that leads to a whole new dimension where legal institutions and their interactions with powerful formal units become critical. While this is beyond the scope of this book, one must be careful about whether the drive towards greater formalization in such industries is necessarily a win-win solution for all.

In brief, therefore, the two case studies described demonstrate that: (i) a relatively productive and possibly dynamic informal sector may not sustain the onslaught of the real estate boom in major cities in India. Such displacement is a natural consequence of liberalization and inter-sector capital mobility driven by return differentials, and (ii) increase in demand in global markets can transform informal manufacturing into more formal units both in terms of scale and adherence to rules and regulations.

NOTES

1. Different versions of these case studies by Marjit and Kar have earlier been published in CUTS (2007) and India Macroeconomics Annual (2009).

12 The Road Ahead

The informal sector as a subject of study under development economics, labour economics, public economics, or any combination of these with applications in theory and empirics is simply too big to be captured as snapshots and folded within the space of a single book. To reiterate what we said at the beginning—at the point where this debate about some workers trapped between the urban and the rural segments evolved, there was little anticipation that the sector could become the centre of attention within a few decades in many countries. Once thought of as a precipitate of formal activities, the informal sector gradually expanded in as many forms as imaginable in a complex economy. Yet, we believe, it received less than its due emphasis in appropriate contexts essentially because it predominantly remained a feature of underdevelopment. Strictly governed political, economic, and social environments in the developed countries presently offer little space for proliferation of informal activities to the extent that one witnesses in the entire developing world. The recent recessionary pressure, however, might bring back elements of informality in the daily lives of the residents of developed countries. The conditions of employment, as well as consumption and production choices, do reflect increasing reliance on greater flexibility. In general, however, the extent of informal activities is still quite low as compared to that in poorer nations. In this book we have argued that these are not necessarily outcomes of polar choices specific to country types, but polar outcomes of the same choice problem facing rational, selfish, or altruistic individuals and institutions globally. In a wider sense, this makes the case for the informal sector to move beyond the limits framed by the so-called developing country characteristics. But the fact remains that the domain of extra-legal activities, which supports the economic lives of the poor is far more visible and transparent in the developing world as compared to that in developed countries. We have already analysed the political compulsions for promoting the informal sector in developing countries.

Further, waves of globalization and related maze of actions are smearing the boundaries of formality and informality. A large number of country studies document that the distinction once prominent and important in view of rules and norms has made room for the dual existence of formal and informal activities even under the same roof. While the examples of dual economies that we are so familiar with abound, this new duality in terms of production organization should easily be the more dominant form. For example, in Chapter 4 we elaborated that activities like outsourcing and even off-shoring are not limited to the jurisdiction of formal activities only, and that firms are readily exploring avenues to bend earlier norms for remaining competitive. At the same time, it is presently a global phenomenon that participation in labour unions is waning, so much so that the well-known bastions of organized power have accepted employment arrangements that run parallel to their announced policies. Public institutions apparently epitomize this practice by hiring workers at contractual agreements that cover little more than the regular salary. This is significantly prevalent in large and rapidly developing countries like China, India, Brazil, and South Africa. However, it cannot be driven exclusively by demand side effects alone. The steady flow into such employment arrangements is guided by several non-formal practices in many societies that previous generations were not exposed to. The advent of new technologies and several allied changes, such as lower emphasis on social norms, widespread feeling of individualism, smaller family structures, and strong women's participation in the labour force that were mainly Western in nature are currently hallmarks of any urban society.

In the emerging equilibrium one then expects to see significant participation in non-formal jobs, like many countries with high growth in the service sector are currently experiencing. Further, in developing countries the agricultural sector has been practising technologically dual forms of cultivation, particularly since the Green Revolution. The upstream and downstream linkages to agriculture and allied activities have large informal bases. We have provided some examples in this context from our primary survey experiences in rural West Bengal and from the leather products industry in Mumbai and the paper products industry in Surat (Chapter 11). In a related context we have earlier discussed in Chapter 3 that better prospects in agriculture does not necessarily translate into improvements in rural and informal wages. In other full-employment models that we developed, intensive rural–urban mobility of unskilled workers leads to equality of these wages. What we have argued is quite distinct from the erstwhile first generation models along the line of Harris and Todaro where rural migrants were expected to wait for formal jobs to open up. An increase in population pressure and shrinking common resources should alter such conditions. This yields a more stable space for the informal sector where wages are market driven. Given free mobility of labour between agriculture and the urban informal sector, the wage floor is set by that prevalent in the agricultural sector. Even casual empiricism in developing countries shows a clear parity in real wages. The outward mobility from the agricultural sector is then largely influenced by the presence of disguised or at times open unemployment in that sector. Under such specifications, we developed a model to establish that an increase in the prices of agricultural products raises rural/informal wages if and only if capital is relatively immobile between the formal and informal sectors in the very short run. As capital becomes fully mobile in the long run, the wage impact vanishes and improvements in the agricultural sector do not benefit labour.

The interaction between formal and informal activities creates a large number of issues that need careful attention. So, we devoted Chapters 4 to 7 towards understanding the nature of these interactions. These and other studies that we have referred to in appropriate contexts explore avenues through which shifts in the formal sector affect the informal sector. Capital mobility between sectors, in many of these models, plays the most crucial role in understanding this relationship. For example, if the formal sector contracts then it is expected that many workers would be rendered jobless. As long durations of unemployment are a difficult proposition for workers in most poor countries with no social security benefits or unemployment insurance, the informal sector serves as a safety net. It would, however, lower the market clearing wage rate in informal units and make everybody worse-off. The same would also happen if the informal sector absorbs workers from the unemployed pool. Surprisingly, however, the data for some countries shows little or no support for wage cuts despite expansion of informal activities. We provided a plausible explanation about why such an outcome is feasible in a general equilibrium analysis. Unlike in the model where agricultural prospects play important roles, we established that capital mobility can, in fact, help informal workers. Consider a situation after rural–urban migration has taken place and that a large urban informal sector has emerged. Under the circumstances, contraction of urban formal sectors leads to unemployment. We argued that typical industrial workers do not have the choice to remain unemployed for long, particularly when unemployment benefits do not exist. If they join the informal workforce for the same trade that they were practising previously, informal wages are expected to fall. Contrary to expectations, empirical facts show that the wages rise instead. We offered rigorous theoretical exercises to show that if capital also moves (and at a proportionately higher rate) along with labour to the informal sector, the capital–labour ratio rises and informal wages go up as a productivity shock. It is possible to extend this analysis further by considering risk aversions among workers and capitalists and re-investigating the conditions.

In terms of policy propositions, this carries substantial importance when a social planner considers reallocating resources for Pareto efficient outcomes. In the presence of dual labour markets and production organizations, externalities—both positive and negative—are common. The presence of externalities usually leads to sub-optimal choices, which in turn may be able to explain the formation and presence of large informal economies. The political economy variables, as discussed in Chapter 2, might become instrumental for some of these optimizing decisions. The level of governance or tax rates are then the most important guidelines for choice of activity and choice of locations. Informal activities influence many other decisions at individual and household levels, including choice of housing. Migration within a state and within a country is also influenced by the existence of informal activities. More generally, regional mobility of factors of production in disparate but democratic countries like India can thus be explained in terms of these characteristics. For example, low levels of governance and consequently a large informal sector with low tax rates might eventually drive away those who would not mind a higher tax rate if the rule of law is preserved with regard to economic and social activities in other places.

In Chapter 6 we dealt with international trade in goods that are produced in three different sectors representing the entire economy, namely, the formal manufacturing sector, the informal manufacturing sector, and the agricultural sector. While it is commonly known that informal commodities and services are mainly located in the so-called non-traded sector of an economy, handicrafts and other ethnic goods, including processed food items and garments are regularly traded in the rest of the world. The large migrant communities living abroad are steady sources of demand for such commodities. Here again, the coexistence of informal production and formal logistic or marketing firms is quite common. Thus, direct trade related shocks are expected to affect the informal sector both directly and indirectly. This is more prominent when the formal sector maintains vertical production links with the informal sector. A number of studies take up this issue for discussion and Chapter 6 dealt with one early contribution where we explored three possible avenues through which international trade affects the economy-wide welfare level in the presence of traded informal commodities. For example, when the formal sector faces a tariff cut, and if the initial wage gap between the formal and informal sectors is not high (or the reduction in employment in the formal sector is not substantial), then general welfare improves. Conversely, if there is trade liberalization directly for the informal traded commodities, then also one expects welfare gain if the cross-substitution effect between formal and informal goods is not large. Further, expansion in agricultural exports raises the price of food items and may improve welfare if the country is a net exporter of food items when such expansion draws labour away from informal activities.

Note that these models use competitive market structures and full-employment of factor inputs. We subsequently relaxed assumptions on full-employment and allowed open unemployment for re-evaluating the impact of international trade on informal wages and employment levels. Chapter 7 offers a variety of such formal–informal combinations where we consider commodities being produced in both the formal and informal sectors. The extended Heckscher-Ohlin models that accommodate these features show that inter-sector comparison of factor intensity rankings for the same product is crucial for understanding the wage implications of trade policy or pure terms of trade movements.

Chapters 8 to 11 include some exploratory evidence on informal activities in India. These also discuss effects of productivity changes in formal and informal industries. As already elaborated upon, the empirical models are not exact tests of theoretical propositions but should be treated as statistical observations consistent with our theoretical conjectures. These are based on limited secondary data sources available for India. We have emphasized in more than one place that the issue of capital mobility is important for measuring wage implications in the informal sector. Chapter 8 provides an aggregative view on how positive change in informal wages over the last two decades is explained by factors, such as accumulation of fixed assets and growth of value added. Subsequently, DEA was used to capture the implications of productivity changes on informal wages. These exercises undoubtedly lend more credence to the case of the informal sector as compared to sporadic case studies with small samples, as has been dominant in developing countries. However, the very definition of the informal sector makes the task of monitoring and record-keeping quite complex and this may explain the paucity of data on informal production, employment, and earnings. Primary surveys, however carefully and extensively conducted, cannot capture the aggregate picture for a large country like India.

We did not go into the depth of enforcement issues related to regulations and imposition of labour standards in a typical poor developing economy. Demand for formalizing the informal is an issue many are concerned with. Ironically, formal regulations often function like a tax burden leading to closure of many units, retrenchment of workers, loss of entrepreneurship accentuating the number of the poor, and so on. Enforcement of labour regulations increases opportunities for those who can get jobs in the formal sector, without necessarily curbing informal activities. If economies are incapable of creating sufficient formal jobs under such regulations, a large mass remains as *the outsiders*.

We have argued and demonstrated that expanding markets induce firms to become formal. Export prospects lead to mandatory use of letters of credit, forcing firms to record their activities and pay higher wages to the more productive workers. Stricter enforcement can be easily bypassed if there are sufficient incentives against complying with such regulations. The informal sector, on the other hand, provides flexibility to entrepreneurs for running businesses profitably. If such incentives are not there, entrepreneurs will be forced to become workers and entrepreneurial talent will be wasted. In terms of innovation and allied changes that the newer technologies are increasingly fostering, lack of entrepreneurship entails cost to social welfare.

The outside option facing potential entrants into the informal sector is also of critical importance in understanding the extent to which informality vis-à-vis stringent regulations is desirable. It has been documented in global studies, like those conducted by the World Bank, that countries of the South provide little or no socially designed benefits to the unemployed although most have some mandatory policies. The large share of informal workers not benefited by such social protection creates complex issues within an economy. We have made no effort to understand the role of unemployment insurance or unemployment benefits on production organization between the formal and informal sectors. In addition, the nature of informal employment is such that it is neither formally recorded nor deemed as unemployment. Once again, this makes the problem interesting and complex at the same time. In terms of policy, this carries immense potential for future research as much as some of the other topics we could highlight here.

Finally, various other aspects of formal–informal relationships are currently being explored. These involve issues dealing with compliance and regulations, informality and income distribution, growth of the informal sector, implications for environmental conditions, and so on. Recent studies by Mandal and Marjit (2010), Marjit (2010), and Marjit et al. (2008) address some of these topics. However, a lot more research is warranted for comprehending how formal institutional support may be extended to informal enterprises for inclusive development. This remains an interesting and challenging agenda for future research.

Bibliography

Agenor, P. R. 1996. 'The Labour Market and Economic Adjustment', IMF Staff Papers, 32: 261–335.

Agenor, P. 2006. 'External Shocks and Urban Poor', Mimeo, University of Manchester.

Agenor, P. R. and J. Aizenman. 1999. 'Macroeconomic Adjustment with Segmented Labour Markets', *Journal of Development Economics*, 58 (2): 277–96.

Agenor, P. R. and P. Montiel. 1996. *Development Macroeconomics*. New Jersey: Princeton University Press.

Alchian, A. and H. Demsetz. 1972. 'Production, Information Costs, and Economic Organization', *American Economic Review*, LXII (5): 777–95.

Annual Survey of Industries (various issues). Central Statistical Organization, Ministry of Statistics and Programme Implementation, Government of India.

Attanasio, O., P. K. Goldberg, and N. Pavcnik. 2004. 'Trade Reforms and Wage Inequality in Colombia', *Journal of Development Economics*, 74 (2): 331–66.

Banerjee, D. 1994. 'Institutional Constraint on Rural Development: An Exploratory Study of Silk Weaving in West Bengal', Occasional Paper. Kolkata: Centre for Studies in Social Sciences.

Banerjee, A., P. Gertler, and M. Ghatak. 2002. 'Empowerment and Efficiency: The Economics of a Tenancy Reform', *Journal of Political Economy*, 110 (2): 239–80.

Barro, Robert and David Gordon. 1983. 'A Positive Theory of Monetary Policy in a Natural Rate Model', *Journal of Political Economy*, 91 (4): 589–610.

Basu, K. 1984. *The Less Developed Economy—A Critique of Contemporary Theory.* Delhi: Oxford University Press.

Basu, K. 1997. *Analytical Development Economics: The Less Developed Economy Revisited.* Cambridge, MA: MIT Press.

Bautista M. R., H. Lofgren, and M. Thomas. 1998. 'Does Trade Liberalisation Enhance Income Growth and Equity in Zimbabwe? The Role of Complementary Policies', TMD Discussion Paper No. 32. Washington DC: Trade and Macroeconomics Division, International Food Policy Research Institute.

Beladi, H. and S. Marjit. 1996. 'An Analysis of Rural-Urban Migration and Protection', *Canadian Journal of Economics*, 29 (4): 930–40.

Beladi, H., L. De la Vina, and S. Marjit. 2010. 'Labor Saving Technological Progress with Segmented Labor Markets', *Review of Development Economics.*

Besley, T. and R. Burgess. 2004. 'Can Labour Regulation Hinder Economic Performance? Evidence from India', *Quarterly Journal of Economics*, 19 (1): 91–134.

Bowles, S. 1999. 'Globalization and Poverty', Paper presented at the World Bank Summer Workshop on Poverty (July).

Bulow, J. and L. Summers. 1986. 'A Theory of Dual Labour Markets with Applications to Industrial Policy, Discrimination and Keynesian Unemployment', *Journal of Labor Economics*, 4 (3): 376–414.

Carneiro, Fransisco G., and J. S. Arbache. 2003. 'The Impacts of Trade on the Brazilian Labor Market: A CGE Model Approach', *World Development*, 31 (9): 1581–595.

Carruth, A. and A. J. Oswald. 1981. 'The Determination of Union and Non-union Wage Rates', *European Economic Review*, 16 (2/3): 285–302.

Caves, R, J. Frankel, and R. Jones. 1997. *World Trade and Payments*, (Ninth Edition). New York: Harper Collins.

Chao, C. C. and Eden Yu. 1995. 'International Capital Mobility, Urban Unemployment and Welfare', *Southern Economic Journal*, 62 (2): 486–92.

Chandra, Vandana and M. Ali Khan. 1993. 'Foreign Investment in the Presence of an Informal Sector', *Economica*, 60 (237): 79–103.

Charnes A, W. W. Cooper, and E. Rhodes. 1978. 'Measuring the Efficiency of Decision Making Units', *European Journal of Operational Research*, 2: 429–44.

Chaudhuri, S. 2003. 'How and How Far to Liberalize a Developing Economy with Informal Sector and Factor Market Distortions', *Journal of International Trade and Economic Development*, 12 (4): 403–28.

Chaudhuri, S. and D. Banerjee. 2007. 'Economic Liberalization, Capital Mobility and Informal Wage in a Small Open Economy: A Theoretical Analysis', *Economic Modelling*, 24 (6): 924–40.

Chaudhuri, S. and U. Mukhopadhyay. 2002. 'Economic Liberalization and Welfare in a Model with an Informal Sector', *The Economics of Transition, The European Bank for Reconstruction and Development*, 10 (1): 143–72.

_____. 2002. 'Removal of Protectionism, Foreign Investment and Welfare in a Model of Informal Sector', *Japan and the World Economy*, 14 (1): 101–16.

_____. 2009. *Revisiting the Informal Sector: A General Equilibrium Approach*. Heidelberg: Springer.

Choi, J. P. and M. Thum. 2004. 'Corruption and the Shadow Economy', Mimeo, Michigan State University and CES-IFO, Munich.

Chong, Alberto and M. Gradstein. 2007. 'Inequality and Informality', *Journal of Public Economics*, 91 (1–2): 159–79.

Coase, R. 1937. 'The Nature of Firm', *Economica*, IV (November): 386–405.

Dabla-Norris, E., M. Gradstein and G. Inchauste. 2008. 'What Causes Firms to Hide Output? The Determinants of Informality', *Journal of Development Economics* 85 (1–2): 1–27.

Dasgupta, Indraneel and S. Marjit. 2006. 'Evasive Reform: Informalisation in a Liberalised Economy with Wage-setting Unions', in B. Guha-Khasnobis and R. Kanbur (eds), *Informal Labour Markets and Development*. New York: Palgrave-MacMillan. Part I, chapter 4:30–50.

Demery, L. and L. Squire. 1996. 'Macroeconomic Adjustment and Poverty in Africa: An Emerging Picture', *World Bank Research Observer*, 11: 39–59.

Dessey, S. and S. Pallage. 2003. 'Taxes, Inequality and the Size of the Informal Sector', *Journal of Development Economics,* 70 (1): 225–33.

De Soto, Hernando. 2000. *The Mystery of Capital*. USA: Basic Books.

De Soto, Hernando. 1989. *The Other Path: The Invisible Revolution in the Third World*. HarperCollins.

Dixit, Avinash. 2004. *Lawlessness and Economics: Alternative Modes of Governance*. New Jersey: Princeton University Press.

Dollar, D. 1992. 'Outward-Oriented Developing Economies Really Do Grow More Rapidly: Evidence from 95 LDCs, 1976–1985', *Economic Development and Cultural Change*, 40 (2): 523–44.

Economist, The. 2005. 'India: Inside the Slums', 29 January.

Esfahani, H. S. and D. Salehi-Isfahani. 1989. 'Effort Observability and Worker Productivity: Toward an Explanation of Economic Dualism', *Economic Journal*, 99 (397): 818–36.

Färe, R., S. Grosskopf, B. Lindgren, and P. Roos. 1992. 'Productivity Changes in Swedish Pharmacies 1980–89: A Nonparametric Malmquist Approach', *Journal of Productivity Analysis,* 3: 85–101.

Fazzari, S. and B. Peterson. 1993. 'Working Capital and Fixed Investment—New Evidence of Financing Constraints', *Rand Journal of Economics*, 24 (3): 328–42.

Feenstra, R. and G. Hanson. 2001. 'Global Production and Rising Inequality: A Survey of Trade and Wages', NBER Working Paper No. 4238.

Fields, G. S. 1990. 'Labour Market Modeling and the Urban Informal Sector: Theory and Evidence', in D. Turnham B. Salomé, and A Schwarz (eds), *The Informal Sector and Evidence Revisited*. Paris: OECD.

Fields, G. S. 1975. 'Rural-Urban Migration, Urban Unemployment and Underemployment and Job Search Activity in LDCs', *Journal of Development Economics*, 2 (2): 165–88.

Fields, G. S. 2005. 'A Welfare Economic Analysis of Labour Market Policies in the Harris-Todaro Model', *Journal of Development Economics*, 76 (1): 127–46.

Foster, Andrew and Mark R. Rosenzweig. 2004. 'Agricultural Productivity Growth, Rural Economic Diversity, and Economic Reforms: India, 1970–2000', *Economic Development and Cultural Change*, 52 (3): 509–42.

Fugazza, Marco and Jean-Francois Jacques. 2004. 'Labour Market Institutions, Taxation and the Underground Economy', *Journal of Public Economics*, 88 (1–2): 395–418.

Funkhouser, Edward. 1994. 'The Urban Informal Sector in Central America: Household Survey Evidence', University of California, Santa Barbara', Working Papers in Economics, pp. 23–94.

Gibson, Bill. 2005. 'The Transition to a Globalized Economy: Poverty, Human Capital and the Informal Sector in a Structuralist CGE model', *Journal of Development Economics*, 78 (1): 60–94.

Goldberg, P. K. and N. Pavcnik. 2003. 'The Response of the Informal Sector to Trade Liberalization', *Journal of Development Economics*, 72 (2): 463–96.

Government of West Bengal. 1975. *Report on the Enquiry into the Existing Working Condition of the Workers of Bell Metal and Bras Metal Industry,* Information and Public Relation Department, Government of West Bengal.

Grinols, E. 1991. 'Urban Unemployment and Foreign Capital', *Economica*, 56: 107–21.

Gruen, F. and W.M. Corden. 1970. 'A Tariff that Worsens Terms of Trade', in I.A. McDougall and R.H. Snape (eds), *Studies in International Economics*. Amsterdam: North Holland, pp. 55–8.

Gupta, M. R. 1993. 'Rural Urban Migration, Informal Sector and Development Policies—A Theoretical Analysis', *Journal of Development Economics*, 41 (1): 137–51.

————. 1997. 'Informal Sector and Informal Capital Markets in a Small Open Less Developed Economy', *Journal of Development Economics*, 52 (2): 409–28.

Gupta, M. R. and S. Chaudhuri. 1997. 'Formal Credit, Corruption and the Informal Credit Market in Agriculture: A Theoretical Analysis', *Economica*, 64: 331–43.

Hanson, Gordon and Ann Harrison. 1999. 'Trade Liberalization and Wage Inequality in Mexico', *Industrial and Labor Relations Review (ILR Review)*, ILR School, Cornell University, 52 (2): 271–88.

Harris-White, Barbara and Anushree Sinha. 2007. *Trade Liberalization and India's Informal Economy.* Oxford: Oxford University Press.

Harris J. and M. Todaro. 1970. 'Migration, Unemployment, and Development: A Two-Sector Analysis', *American Economic Review*, 60 (1): 126–42.

Harrison, Ann E. and Edward Leamer. 1997. 'Labor Markets in Developing Countries: An Agenda for Research', *Journal of Labor Economics*, 15 (3): S1–19.

Harrison, Glenn, Thomas F. Rutherford, and David G. Tarr. 2003. 'Trade Liberalization, Poverty and Efficient Equity', *Journal of Development Economics*, 71 (1): 97–128.

Hasan, R., D. Mitra and B. P. Ural. 2006. 'Trade Liberalisation, Labour Market Institutions and Poverty Reduction: Evidence from Indian States', *India Policy Forum*, 3: 71–122.

Hillman, A. 2003. *Public Finance and Public Policy.* Cambridge: Cambridge University Press.

International Labour Organization. 1972. *Employment, Incomes and Equality: A Strategy for Increasing Productive Employment in Kenya.* Geneva: ILO.

————. 1999. *Key Indicators of the Labour Market.* Geneva: International Labour Office.

————. 2002. *Decent Work and the Informal Economy: Report IV, 90th Session.* Geneva: ILO.

International Labour Organization and Delhi Group. 2007. 'Concepts, Definitions and Sub-classifications', (draft chapter 2). *Manual on Surveys of Informal Employment and Informal Sector.* Geneva: ILO.

Jain, L. 1986. 'A Heritage to Keep the Handicrafts Industry, 1955–85', *Economic and Political Weekly*, XXI (20): 878 and 880–1.

Jones, R. W. 1965. 'The Structure of Simple General Equilibrium Models', *Journal of Political Economy*, 73: 557–72.

————. 1971. 'A Three Facor Model in Theory, Trade, and History', in J. N. Bhagwati Jones, Mundell and Vanek (eds), *Trade, Balance of Payments and Growth 1971. Papers in International Economics in Honor of Charles P. Kindleberger.* Amsterdam: North Holland.

————. 2003. 'Joint Outputs and Real Wage Rates', *International Review of Economics and Finance,* 12 (4): 513–16.

Jones, R. W. and S. Engerman. 1996. 'Trade, Technology, and Wages: A Tale of Two Countries', *American Economic Review*, 86 (2): 35–40.

Jones, R. W. and S. Marjit. 1985. 'A Simple Production Model with Stolper–Samuelson Properties', *International Economic Review*, 26 (3): 565–7.

————. 1992. 'International Trade and Endogenous Production Structure', in W. Neuefeind and R. Reizman (eds), *Economic Theory and International Trade—Essays in Honour of J. Trout Rader.* Heidelberg: Springer.

Kar, S. and S. Marjit. 2001. 'Informal Sector in General Equilibrium: Welfare Effects of Trade Policy Reform', *International Review of Economics and Finance,* 10 (3): 289–300.

————. 2007. 'Mainstreaming International Trade into National Developmental Strategy', Consumer Unity and Trust Society, International (CUTS), Geneva.

———. 2009. 'Urban Informal Sector and Poverty', *International Review of Economics and Finance*, 18 (4): 631–42.

Knight, Frank. 1946.'Immutable Law in Economics: Its Reality and Limitations', *American Economic Review*, 36 (2): 93–111.

Kulsherestha, G. and S. B. Singh. 2001. 'Informal Sector in India: Its Coverage and Contributions', in A. Kundu and N. Sharma (eds), *Informal Sector in India—Perspectives and Policies*. New Delhi: Institute of Human Development, pp. 48–50.

Kumar, N. 2000. 'Economic Reforms and their Macro-economic Impact', *Economic and Political Weekly*, 35 (10): 803–12.

Lewis, W. Arthur. 1954. 'Economic Development with Unlimited Supplies of Labour', *Manchester School of Economic and Social Studies*, 22 (2): 139–91.

Maiti, D. 2004. 'Production Organisation and Dynamics of Rural Industrial Growth: A Study with Special Reference to Some Manufacturing Industries of West Bengal', Unpublished PhD Thesis, Vidyasagar University, Midnapore.

Maiti, D. and S. Marjit. 2008. 'Trade Liberalization, Production Organization and Informal Sector of the Developing Countries', *The Journal of International Trade & Economic Development*, 17 (3): 453–61.

Mandal, Biswajit and S. Marjit. 2010. 'Corruption and Wage Inequality?', *International Review of Economics & Finance*, 19 (1): 166–72.

Marcoullier, D. and Leslie Young. 1995. 'The Black Hole of Graft: The Predatory State and the Informal Economy', *American Economic Review*, 85 (3): 630–46.

Marjit, S. 1987. 'Trade in Intermediates and the Colonial Pattern of Trade', *Economica*, 54: 173–84.

———. 1991. 'Agro based Industry and Rural Urban Migration: The Case of an Urban Employment Subsidy', *Journal of Development Economics*, 35 (2): 393–8.

———. 1998. 'Agricultural Trade, Rural Wage and the Informal Sector', Mimeo, Centre for Studies in Social Sciences, Calcutta.

———. 2003. 'Economic Reform and Informal Wage—A General Equilibrium Analysis', *Journal of Development Economics*, 72 (1): 371–8.

———. 2005. 'Complementarity and International Trade—On Some Recent Developments in Structural General Equilibrium Trade Models', in S. Lahiri and P. Maiti (eds), *Economic Theory in a Changing World*. New Delhi: Oxford University Press.

———. 2010. 'Firm Heterogeneity, Informal Wage and Good Governance', Mimeo, Centre for Studies in Social Sciences, Kolkata.

Marjit, S. and R. Acharyya. 2003. 'International Trade, Wage Inequality and the Developing Economy: A General Equilibrium Approach', Research Monograph. Heidelberg, New York: Physica/Springer Verlag.

Marjit, S. and H. Beladi. 1996. 'Protection and Gainful Effects of Foreign Capital', *Economics Letters*, 53: 311–16.

_____. 1999. 'Complementarity's between Import-competition and Import promotion', *Journal of Economic Theory*, 107 (2): 889–906.

_____. 2002. 'The Stolper Samuelson Theorem in a Wage-differential Framework', *The Japanese Economic Review*, 53 (2): 177–81.

_____. 2008. 'Trade, Employment and the Informal Sector', *Trade and Development Review* 1 (1). Available at http://tdrju.net/index.php/tdr.

Marjit, S., H. Beladi, and Avik Chakraborti. 2004. 'Trade and Wage Inequality in Developing Countries', *Economic Inquiry*, 42 (2): 295–303.

Marjit, S., S. Ghosh and A.K. Biswas. 2007c. 'Informality, Corruption and Trade Reform', *European Journal of Political Economy*, 23 (3): 777–89.

Marjit, S., Amit K. Biswas, and H. Beladi. 2008. 'Minimize Regulations to Regulate—Extending the Lucas Critique', *Economic Modelling*, 25 (4): 623–7.

Marjit, S. and Chowdhury, Prabal Roy. 2004. 'Asymmetric Capacity Costs and Joint-Venture Buy-outs', *Journal of Economic Behaviour and Organisation*, 54 (3): 425–38.

Marjit, S. and S. Kar. 2004. 'Pro-Market Reform and Informal Wage: Theory and the Contemporary Indian Perspective', India Macroeconomics Annual, pp. 130–56.

_____. 2007. 'Urban Informal Sector and Poverty—Effects of Trade Reform and Capital Mobility in India', PEP-MPIA Working Paper No. 2007–09, Canada. Available at www.pep-net.org, last accessed in March 2007.

_____. 2008a. 'Labour Productivity Growth, Informal Wage and Capital Mobility—A General Equilibrium Analysis', in Ravi Kanbur and Jan Svejnar (eds), *Labour Markets and Economic Development*. New York: Routledge, and International Policy Centre, University of Michigan Working Paper No. 54 (2007), pp. 286–98.

_____. 2008b. 'Productivity and Wage in the Informal Sector', in N. Jayaram and R.S. Deshpande (eds), *Footprints of Development and Change Essays in Memory of Professor V.K.R.V. Rao*. New Delhi: AF.

Marjit, S., S. Kar, and R. Acharyya. 2007a. 'Agricultural Prospects and Informal Wage in General Equilibrium', *Economic Modelling*, 24 (3): 380–85.

Marjit, S., S. Kar, and H. Beladi. 2007b. 'Trade Reform and Informal Wage', *Review of Development Economics*, 11 (2): 313–20.

Marjit, S., S. Kar, and D. Maiti. 2009. 'Labour Market Reform and Poverty—The Role of Informal Sector', in Bhaskar Dutta, Tridip Ray, and E. Somanathan (eds), *New and Enduring Themes In Development Economics*. New York: World Scientific, pp. 229–40.

Marjit, S, S. Kar, and P. Sarkar. 2005. 'Capital Mobility and Informal Wage in a Small Economy—Two Examples', *South Asia Economic Journal*, 5 (2): 261–66.

Marjit, S. and D. Maiti. 2006. 'Globalization, Economic Reform and Informal

Labour', in B. Guha-Khasnobis and Ravi Kanbur (eds), *Informal Labour Markets and Development.* New York: Palgrave-MacMillan. Part I, chapter 2, pp. 9–28.

————. 2007. 'Trade Liberalization, Production Organization, and Informal Sector of the Developing Countries', *Journal of International Trade and Economic Development,* 17 (3): 453–61.

————. 2009. 'Informality and Productivity', India Macroeconomics Annual–2009. New Delhi: Sage.

Marjit, S., V. Mukherjee, and M. Kolmar. 2006. 'Poverty, Taxation and Governance', *The Journal of International Trade and Economic Development,* 15 (3):325–33.

Marjit, S. and A. Raychaudhary. 1997. *India's Exports: An Analytical Study.* New Delhi: Oxford University Press.

Marjit, S., Udo Broll, and S. Sengupta. 2001. 'Trade and Wage-gap in Poor Countries: The Role of the Informal Sector', in Amitava Bose, Debraj Ray, and Abhirup Sarkar (eds), *Contemporary Macroeconomics.* New Delhi: Oxford University Press.

Mazumdar, D. 1983. 'Segmented Labour Markets in LDCs', *American Economic Review,* 73 (2): 254–9.

McKenzie, David and Yaye Seynabou Sakho. 2010. 'Does it Pay Firms to Register for Taxes? The Impact of Formality on Firm Profitability', *Journal of Development Economics,* 91(1): 15–24.

Myerson, R. 1999. 'Theoretical Comparison of Electoral Systems: 1998 Schumpeter Lecture', *European Economic Review,* 43(4–6): 671–97.

National Commission for Enterprises in the Unorganised Sector (NCEUS). 2007. *Report on Conditions of Work and Promotion of Livelihoods in the Unorganised Sector.* New Delhi: Government of India.

National Sample Survey. 1989–90, (45th Round), 1993–94 (50th Round), 1994–95 (51st Round), 2000–01 (56th Round), *Survey of Unorganized Manufacturing.* Delhi: Department of Statistics, Government of India, Report No. 456/55/2.0/1.

National Sample Survey Organization. 1999–2000. National Sample Survey (55th Round), *Non-agricultural Enterprises in the Informal Sector in India, 1999–2000—Key Results,* Report No. 456/55/2.0/1, p. 2.

National Sample Survey Organization. 2005–06. National Sample Survey (62nd Round), *Unorganised Manufacturing Sector in India-Employment, Assets and Borrowings,* Report No. 525/62.

Olofin, S. O. and A. O. Folawewo. 2006. 'Skill Requirements, Earnings and Labour Demand in Nigeria's Urban Informal Sector', in Basudeb Guha-Khasnobis and Ravi Kanbur (eds), *Informal Labour Markets and Development.* New York: Palgrave-Macmillan, pp. 180–95.

Peltzman, S. 1976. 'Toward a More General Theory of Regulation', *Journal of Law and Economics,* 19 (2): 211–40.

Persson, T. and G. Tabellini. 2000. *Political Economics: Explaining Economic Policies*. Cambridge, MA: MIT Press.

Ranis, Gustav. 2004. 'Arthur Lewis' Contribution to Development Thinking and Policy', Economic Growth Center, Discussion Paper No. 891, Yale University.

Ranis, Gustav and Frances Stewart. 1999. 'V-Goods and the Role of the Urban Informal Sector in Development', *Economic Development and Cultural Change*, 47 (2): 259–88.

Rauch, James. 1991. 'Modelling the Informal Sector Formally', *Journal of Development Economics*, 35 (1): 33–47.

Ray, S. C. 2004. *Data Envelopment Analysis: Theory and Techniques for Economics and Operations Research*. New York: Cambridge University Press.

Saint-Paul, Gilles. 1996. 'Labor Market Institutions and the Cohesion of the Middle Class', *International Tax and Public Finance*, Springer 3 (3): 385–95.

Samuelson, P. A. 1971. 'On the Trail of Conventional Beliefs about the Transfer Problem', in J. N. Bhagwati, R. A. Mundell, R. W. Jones, and J. Vanek (eds), *Trade, Balance of Payments and Growth: Papers in International Economics in Honor of Charles P. Kindleberger*. Amsterdam: North-Holland, pp. 3–21.

Sarkar, A. 2006. 'Political Economy of West Bengal', *Economic and Political Weekly*, 41 (4): 341–8.

Sarkar, A. 1989. 'A Keynesian Model of North-South Trade', *Journal of Development Economics*, 30 (1): 179–88.

Savard, L. and E. Adjovi. 1997. 'Adjustment, Liberalisation and Welfare, in the Presence of Health and Education Externalities: A CGE applied to Benin', Centre de Recherche en Économie et Finance Appliquées (March), Working Paper 97 - 07, University of Laval, Montreal, Canada.

Sethuraman, S. V. 1997. 'Urban Poverty, and the Informal Sector: A Critical Assessment of Current Strategies'. Available at http://www.ilo.org/public/english/employment/recon/eiip/publ/1998/urbpover.htm, last accessed in April 1998.

Simon, Herbert A. 1991. 'Organization and Markets', *The Journal of Economic Perspectives*, 5(2): 25–44.

Sinha, A. and C. Adam. 2006. 'Trade Reforms and Informalization: Getting behind Jobless Growth in India', in B. Guha-Khasnobis and Ravi Kanbur (eds), *Informal Labour Markets and Development*. New York: Palgrave-MacMillan, pp. 29–49.

Sinha, Anushree. 1999. 'Trade Liberalisation and Informal Households: A Study using a CGE Model for India'. Research Report No. 26, Queen Elizabeth House, University of Oxford, UK.

Singh, Manjit. 1990. *The Political Economy of Unorganized Industries*. New Delhi: Sage Publications, pp. 16–25.

Stallings, B. and W. Peres. 2000. *Growth, Employment and Equity: The Impact of the Economic Reforms in Latin America and the Caribbean, Economic Commission for Latin America and Caribbean.* Washington DC: Brookings Institution Press.

Stark, O. 1982. 'On Modeling the Informal Sector', *World Development,* 10 (5): 413–16.

Stigler, G. 1971. 'The Theory of Economic Regulation', *The Bell Journal of Economics and Management Science,* 2 (1): 3–21.

Straub, Stephane. 2005. 'Informal Sector: The Credit Market Channel', *Journal of Development Economics,* 78 (2): 299–321.

Topalova, Petia. 2005. 'Trade Liberalization, Poverty and Inequality: Evidence from Indian Districts', NBER Working Paper No. 11614.

Tripp, A. M. 1997. *Changing the Rules: The Politics of Liberalization and the Urban Informal Economy in Tanzania.* Berkeley and London: University of California Press.

Turnham, D. 1993. *Employment and Development: A New Review of Evidence.* Paris: Development Centre Studies, OECD.

University Grant Commission (UGC) India. 1996. 'Financial Viability of Informal Sector in Calcutta', Mimeo, Department of Economics, Calcutta University.

Verick, Sher. 2006. *The Impact of Globalization on the Informal Sector in Africa.* Economic and Social Policy Division, United Nations Economic Commission for Africa (ECA), and Institute for the Study of Labor (IZA). Available at http://www.iza.org/conference_files/worldb2006/verick_s872.pdf, last accessed on 27 May 2006.

Webster, L. and P. Fidler. 1996. *The Informal Sector and Microfinance in West Africa.* Washington DC: World Bank Regional and Sectoral Studies.

Williamson, O., M. Wachter and J. Harris. 1975. 'Understanding the Employment Relation: The Analysis of Idiosyncratic Exchange', *The Bell Journal of Economics,* 6 (1): 250–78.

Winters, L.A. 2000. 'Trade, Trade Policy and Poverty: What are the Links?', Discussion Paper No. 2382. London: Centre for Economic Policy Research.

Wuyts, M. 2001. 'Informal Economy, Wage Goods and Accumulation under Structural Adjustment Theoretical Reflections based on the Tanzanian Experience', *Cambridge Journal of Economics,* 25 (3): 417–38.

Xaba, Jantjie, Par Horn, and S. Motala. 2002. 'Informal Sector in Sub-Saharan Africa', Working Paper on the Informal Economy No. 10. Geneva: International Labour Office.

Zagha, Robert. 1998. 'Labour and India's Economic Reforms', *Journal of Policy Reform,* 2 (4): 403–26.

Name Index

Summers, L. 64, 204

Tabellini, G. 22
Thum, M. 19, 24
Topalova, Petia 131, 132
Todaro, M. 1, 193, 198
Tripp, A. M. 134
Turnham, D. 51

Verick, Sher 134

Williamson, O. 110
Winters, L. A. 131
Wuyts, M. 134

Young, L. 19, 23, 48
Yu, Eden 64

Xaba, Jantjie 134

Subject Index